"SAVE MY KID"

"Save My Kid"

How Families of Critically Ill Children Cope,
Hope, and Negotiate an Unequal
Healthcare System

Amanda M. Gengler

NEW YORK UNIVERSITY PRESS

New York

NEW YORK UNIVERSITY PRESS
New York
www.nyupress.org
© 2020 by New York University

References to Internet websites (URLs) were accurate at the time of writing. Neither the author nor New York University Press is responsible for URLs that may have expired or changed since the manuscript was prepared.

Library of Congress Cataloging-in-Publication Data
Names: Gengler, Amanda M., author.
Title: "Save my kid" : how families of critically ill children cope, hope, and negotiate an unequal healthcare system / Amanda M. Gengler.
Description: New York : New York University Press |
Includes bibliographical references and index.
Identifiers: LCCN 2019004712 | ISBN 9781479863938 (cloth) |
ISBN 9781479864621 (paperback)
Subjects: LCSH: Critically ill children—Medical care—United States. | Critically ill children—Family relationships. | Parents of terminally ill children—Psychology. | Catastrophic illness—Social aspects—United States. | Child health services—United States. | Health services accessibility—United States.
Classification: LCC RJ47.7 .G46 2019 | DDC 618.92/0029—dc23
LC record available at https://lccn.loc.gov/2019004712

New York University Press books are printed on acid-free paper, and their binding materials are chosen for strength and durability. We strive to use environmentally responsible suppliers and materials to the greatest extent possible in publishing our books.

Manufactured in the United States of America
10 9 8 7 6 5 4 3 2 1
Also available as an ebook

*For Benjamin, Noah, Brent, Jayden, Shawn, and Deirdre,
and for my father, Dale*

"Hope" is the thing with feathers -
That perches in the soul -
And sings the tune without the words –

And never stops - at all -
And sweetest - in the Gale - is heard -
And sore must be the storm -
That could abash the little Bird
That kept so many warm -

I've heard it in the chillest land -
And on the strangest Sea -
Yet - never - in Extremity,
It asked a crumb - of me.
—Emily Dickinson, "Hope Is a Thing with Feathers"

CONTENTS

Jamilla Finley's daughter, Teyariah, was six years old when she was diagnosed with stage-IV neuroblastoma, an invasive nervous system cancer. "Once the doctors told me it was cancer, I think I fainted," she told me. "I don't even remember what happened from there because my nerves were tore all to pieces."

A black mother of three in her mid-thirties, Jamilla quit her job as a security guard and took a leave of absence from her online MA program in order to transfer Teyariah's care from a regional hospital near their home to Kelly-Reed, an elite private university research hospital several hours away. At Kelly-Reed, Teyariah could undergo stem-cell transplantation and receive monoclonal antibody immunotherapy. Before coming to Kelly-Reed, Jamilla was often disappointed by her interactions with the physicians at the regional hospital where Teyariah was first treated. She felt that she couldn't "talk with them or bond with them," and recalled that they only told her vaguely, "'Oh, the survival rate is 30 percent, we might can make it 60 percent.' I mean, can you tell me something else?" This limited engagement in her daughter's care left Jamilla unnerved, and perhaps more importantly, unmoored.

Kelly-Reed offered Jamilla a stronger, more solid anchor to hold onto, a line to hope for her daughter's recovery. At Kelly-Reed, Teyariah had access to more sophisticated treatments and doctors and nurses who Jamilla believed truly cared about her family. Teyariah's primary physician at Kelly-Reed provided Jamilla with more information that boosted her confidence in her daughter's care. "Dr. Fadian," she recalled, "he was like, 'This is what we can do to make her survival rate more' . . . I mean he actually broke everything down to me [so] that I could understand and I appreciated that."

But obtaining these treatments at Kelly-Reed required them to spend many months in residence. Teyariah's father lost his job as a factory supervisor when his time away from work exceeded the maximum amount protected under the Family and Medical Leave Act (FMLA). This left the Finleys' with income only from his unemployment check, compounding their financial struggles. On top of her fears for Teyariah and the increasing financial strain, Jamilla worried that she wasn't being a good-enough mother to their two-year-old, who was with them at Kelly-Reed, or her fourteen-year-old, who was back home, living with Jamilla's sister and continuing to attend school.

"It's a lot of stress. I haven't had no rest," Jamilla confessed. "I've been going every day since last year, which it's affected my body [too]." Jamilla lived with a continuous pain in her abdomen that her doctor could find no physical explanation for. During particularly acute moments, she explained, "I feel like sometimes I might be passing out."

Jamilla dreaded going to the hospital, anticipating the heartache of witnessing not only her daughter's pain and suffering, but that of the other children she would see there. "I cry. Who wouldn't cry? I cry a lot. I cry in the shower," she told me. But Jamilla worked hard to keep her feelings of fear and despair under control, and most of all, out of the view of her daughter. "I have to keep my composure," she explained with conviction." A child looks at the parent, so if I'm frustrated and I'm upset, she's going to get upset. So what's that going to do to her? It will make her temperature go up, make her worry about not only me—she'll be worried about herself. So I try to stay calm and relaxed. If I need to cry, I step out, and then I come back in." Keeping her emotions in check and maintaining an unwaveringly hopeful presence was serious business for Jamilla. Failing to do so, she believed, might directly harm her daughter's health and wellbeing. The stakes could not be higher.

Jamilla recalled "only one time" when Teyariah herself had openly expressed feelings of hopelessness. Jamilla's anguish was palpable as she recounted her daughter's words: "Mama, I'm so tired. I'm tired of all this. I just want to give up and quit." Jamilla continued: "You don't even know what to tell your own child when she tells you that. . . . She's not but seven years old. That's the only time I've been through that, but I told her, 'You're not going to quit; you've got to keep fighting,' and she said, 'Okay Mama, I'll try.'"

The emotional burden Jamilla carried was immense. But she was determined to remain unflaggingly positive for Teyariah and her entire family. Hope was the fuel that allowed her to do the emotion work required to accomplish this, and to keep moving forward through the myriad tasks involved in shepherding her daughter through the long treatment process. "It's overwhelming," she admitted matter-of-factly. "But you've just got to believe and hold on."

PART I

Families in Crisis

1

Hope Is a Thing with Feathers

Nora Bialy stood at the counter in the middle of the large, brightly lit Ronald McDonald House kitchen washing strawberries, dunking them in melted chocolate, and placing them haphazardly on long sheets of waxed paper to cool.[1] A petite, white, forty-one-year-old mother of four, with short dark hair, dressed comfortably in jeans, sneakers, and a blue floral print cardigan, Nora wanted to get her sixteen-year-old son, Benjamin, to eat as many of them as she could. "He could use the calories," she told me. A former dietician by training, Nora had been keeping a close eye on Ben's nutritional status for some time now.

A white sociology graduate student in my early thirties, I had been volunteering for several months at the Ronald McDonald House, a nonprofit organization that provides temporary housing to families of critically ill children. During that time, I had met and gotten to know a number of families like the Bialys and become increasingly curious about how they navigated the medical mazes involved in caring for a critically ill child. When I began conducting formal research for this project, Nora enthusiastically agreed to be my first interviewee. While she multitasked, Nora matter-of-factly recounted the sequence of events that had brought them to Kelly-Reed, a top-ranked private university research hospital hundreds of miles from their home.

When he was twelve years old, Nora explained, Benjamin started throwing up, having terrible headaches, and occasionally losing his balance. At first they thought he had a bad sinus infection, but after a few weeks of antibiotics, Nora and her husband grew increasingly concerned. Nora's husband, William, a child psychiatrist, "knew it could be something more serious," she told me, "so we actually pushed for [a] neurology consult, before [his providers] were really ready to give us [one]." Her husband called someone he knew and got them in to see a neurologist the very next day. When the neurologist identified pressure behind Benjamin's optic nerve, she sent him immediately for an MRI (magnetic resonance image), which revealed a large mass at the back of his skull—suspected, and later confirmed, to be a medulloblastoma brain tumor.

As soon as the radiologist broke the news, Nora called the answering service for a neurosurgeon she had used in the past for her own spinal surgery. She got him on the phone "within like ten minutes." Though they were not very far away from another highly ranked children's research hospital, Nora's neurosurgeon suggested a pediatric surgeon at a university hospital a bit farther away, because, he told Nora, "for this particular type of childhood cancer, that's where [I] would go." Though the radiologist who read the MRI had arranged for them to be taken to a local teaching hospital by ambulance, Nora had Benjamin transported to the hospital she now deemed "best," and Benjamin was in surgery with the physician her neurosurgeon recommended within twenty-four hours.

Six weeks of radiation and fourteen weeks of chemotherapy following the surgery seemed to have done the trick, successfully shrinking Ben's tumor. William and Nora went over the treatment plans, read medical journal articles, and knew that the treatment Benjamin was receiving was the latest "standard-of-care" protocol. They took comfort in the prestige of the hospital and the physicians delivering Ben's care. "When you're at hospitals like this one, or Kelly-Reed," she assured me, "you're getting cutting-edge treatment. It's right on the tip of—it's the best information available for that point in time."

But a few months later, Ben's tumor came back. "Eighty percent of the kids who get [this type of tumor] do respond 100 percent to the standard treatment," she told me. "And there's 20 percent that don't. Unfortunately he [fell] into that 20 percent." After an autologous stem-cell transplant at this same hospital also failed to stop the tumor from growing, Benjamin's physician suggested that they enroll in an experimental immunotherapy trial at Kelly-Reed. Nora coordinated with friends and neighbors to pitch in to provide childcare and meals for her husband and their other three children while she and Ben were away. Once they arrived at Kelly-Reed, Ben was taken into surgery again to remove as much of the growing tumor as possible. This time, tissue from his tumor would be used to create an individually developed tumor cell vaccine. Once delivered, the vaccine would help teach his immune system to fight and kill the unique cells that comprised his particular tumor.

Nora hoped this would be the medical miracle they had been waiting for.

* * *

Connie and Nicholas Henderson had a different experience obtaining treatment for their critically ill son. A white couple in their mid-forties, the Hendersons repeatedly took four-year-old Elijah to their family physician and local rural county emergency room with severe abdominal pain, but their concerns were minimized and they were sent home. Nicholas, a high school graduate who worked as an asphalt technician when work was available, and Connie, who hadn't finished high school and stayed home with Elijah and their ten-year-old son, Nate, were baffled by the suggestions their local physicians made, which at one point included giving Elijah four adult doses of Miralax in one day. But the Hendersons didn't know what else to do. Connie told me despairingly:

> We tried for nearly a month to get somebody to listen to us, you know? We was telling them that there was something wrong with him, [more] than just the flu and stuff, and it took us nearly a month to finally get somebody to listen to us to do some kind of test on him to find out what was causing a problem. . . . I mean, what can you do when you can't get nobody to listen to you? We've made six trips in three weeks trying to get somebody to listen to us, and wouldn't nobody do anything, until that one doctor said, "Well, I think it's his appendix, we need to have a CT scan done," . . . and they did a CT scan and that's when they found the tumor on his liver. But it took that long just to get somebody to listen to us, you know?

The Hendersons felt completely helpless during this time. When I asked what the doctors at the emergency room told them when they were turned away, Nicholas explained:

> They'd say, "Well, if there was too much wrong, his belly would be real tight"—which it was extended—"and he would be running a real real high fever." But at the same time, they weren't considering I was giving him Tylenol and Motrin around the clock [as they recalled being instructed to do]. But then when we got to [the regional hospital] one of the younger doctors had jumped on us because we was giving him Tylenol and Motrin around the clock. And I told her, I said, "We're just doing

what our doctor told us to do." And, they said, "Well, you ain't supposed to do that, that's bad for the liver," and I'm like, "Well, I'm just doing what I'm supposed to do."

Connie interjected, "What they *told* us to do." (Emphasis hers)

Clearly, the Hendersons felt exasperated by their experiences seeking help for their son. Unfortunately, their experience did not improve as Elijah's treatment unfolded.

After the CT scan identified their son's tumor, the Hendersons were sent to a regional teaching hospital in their area. The doctors there told them that Elijah would need chemotherapy to shrink the tumor before they could operate. Nicholas explained that at the first treatment, "They kind of OD'd him on it, because it burned him up and messed up his heart rate and everything." They had to wait several weeks before trying again with a different chemotherapy, but that drug had no effect at all, and Nicholas worried they might use the original chemotherapy again, harming his son. The doctors told Nicholas they would use a much lower dose this time. Nicholas stumbled over the name of the drug they used, guessing it might be "Duberoxin." Ten-year-old Nate whispered "Doxorubicin," correcting him. The third and fourth sessions were more effective, but still didn't shrink the tumor enough to allow for the operation. Without other options, the regional hospital then arranged for a liver transplant at Kelly-Reed. Just days after the surgery, Elijah, a pale, thin boy, with light eyes and close-cropped hair, was already back at the Ronald McDonald House, proudly showing off his scar and running around the conference room mischievously with his older brother while I interviewed his parents.

At no point along the way did the Hendersons feel confident about the quality of their son's care. Connie believed that "if we could have gotten a doctor to listen to us in the whole month that we tried to get 'em to listen to us, they could have caught this before it got this far." Nicholas shared this suspicion, because "they said this type of cancer, it's fast growing. And I guess it grew that fast, within that thirty days." Their exasperation was only deepened by the fact that the oncologist at the regional hospital told them a simple blood test could have identified the problem much sooner.

Unlike their previous experiences with the medical system, the Hendersons felt positive about their treatment at Kelly-Reed. Still, Nicholas worried about whether he had gotten the best possible care for his son. His anguish was plain as he voiced his uncertainty:

> Before he had his transplant, I guess, like any other parent, you're kind of wondering, "Well, did I make the right decision? Or could I have done something different?" And before he was diagnosed with cancer, I used to see St. Jude's on TV all the time. And I'd sit and watch it, and it'd bring tears to my eyes. And I'd thank God that wasn't my kid. And then, when it was [my kid], that kind of tore me up [Nicholas became choked up]. But I thought about that. Am I making the right decision? Do I take him there [to St. Jude's], or where do I take him? And the doctor back at [the regional hospital] says, "Well, we're contacting everybody," and they said, "Well, Kelly-Reed was the first one to respond." We never really second-guessed the doctors. We're just sort of, kind of, wondering if it was the right decision.

When I asked Nicholas if they tried to learn about the doctors or the hospital, before they arrived, he said, "No, I just sorta, kinda put my faith and trust in God and hoped that He would kinda help guide things the right way, and make everything turn out alright." But it was clear that for the Hendersons, abstract faith didn't offer the same level of confidence and reassurance that the Bialys' medical research, knowledge of institutional prestige hierarchies, and trusted referrals provided them. Nora Bialy felt relatively secure in her hope for her son that night in the kitchen. But Nicholas Henderson was haunted by doubts, even though—paradoxically—his son was doing much better than Nora's was.

Captaining or Entrusting Care

A child's critical illness is, for children and parents alike, what medical sociologist Michael Bury calls a "biographical disruption" that requires parents, close family members, and older children to entirely reconsider how they imagined their lives would unfold.[2] Both the Bialys and the Hendersons wanted to do everything they could to save their children from life-threatening illnesses. But they had very different resources available to them and took a different approach to managing their child's illness as a result. The Bialys regularly adopted an illness management strategy I call *care-captaining*. If we think of navigating a child's life-threatening illness as akin to steering a ship through stormy waters, then care-captaining involves metaphorically taking the helm of the ship and working hard to influence the course the child's treatment will follow.

The Hendersons generally adopted a different approach, which I call *care-entrusting*. This strategy involves turning the helm of the ship over to "the experts"—a child's healthcare providers—whom care-entrusting parents often view as better equipped to steer the most effective course of treatment. Both approaches have pros and cons, and as we will see in the chapters ahead, they are not mutually exclusive. Most parents care-captained and care-entrusted at some point in the illness process, but were often driven toward one strategy or another depending on which approach allowed them to create and maintain as much hope as possible for their child's recovery. Maintaining hope helped families proactively manage the upsetting emotions triggered by a significant threat to their children's lives. How effective parents could be at care-captaining, however, and obtaining the kind of medical advantages it could net them, depended a lot on the resources they could mobilize to support their efforts.

In this book, I examine how families like the Bialys and the Hendersons access highly specialized medical care for children's life-threatening illnesses and how they negotiate their children's care throughout the course of treatment. I asked what families did when their child first became ill or was diagnosed with a life-threatening condition, and what they continued to do as the illness and treatment plan progressed. I asked, and sometimes observed, how they juggled conflicting opinions and made difficult decisions. Ultimately, I came to understand that the intense emotions provoked by a child's critical illness—like the fear, uncertainty, and physical and emotional distress voiced by Jamilla Finley in the prologue to this book—played a potent role in shaping families' choices to care-captain or care-entrust. Access to needed resources of all kinds were crucial, of course, but families' efforts to minimize emotional upset as much as humanly possible also profoundly influenced their decisions, social interactions, and illness management strategies throughout their child's illness.

By analyzing their experiences, I hope to make better sociological sense of the intricate interactional dynamics that can exacerbate inequalities among those negotiating the healthcare system. Teasing out the often-overlooked role that emotional goals play in this process reveals their centrality to the reproduction of inequalities in healthcare broadly. Given this complex interrelationship, reducing inequalities in healthcare would require more than a reallocation of resources designed to help all families obtain greater access to the kind of care available at institutions such as Kelly-Reed. It would require a substantial reallocation of resources *and* a sea change in the emotional cultures surrounding sickness and caregiving in the United States today. Given the degree of inequality in contemporary US healthcare, the need for such change is pressing.

Healthcare Inequality and Cultural Health Capital

The landscape of healthcare in the United States is a steeply hierarchical one. Those with more resources are able to access substantially better care than those with less. This is true even for those seeking help for the most common health problems. Medical researchers at the University of Alabama, for instance, identified outcome disparities for heart attack patients who received care at different types of hospital facilities.[3] Patients treated at major teaching hospitals (such as Kelly-Reed) had improved survival rates in comparison to those treated at minor teaching hospitals (such as the regional hospital that first treated Elijah Henderson). Those treated at nonteaching hospitals had the lowest survival rates.

The quality of care provided for routine chronic conditions varies dramatically as well. Sociologists Karen Lutfey and Jeremy Freese identified significant inequalities between two diabetes clinics, one serving primarily middle-class patients and one serving primarily poor and working-class patients.[4] The first clinic offered greater continuity of care (in which the patient sees the same provider from one visit to the next), more patient education, and tended to prescribe more complex—and more effective—treatment regimens. The clinic serving primarily poor and working-class patients offered little in the way of patient education (even though these patients stood to benefit more from it, as they brought less medical knowledge to the table), kept patients waiting for extended periods of time, and tended to prescribe simpler regimens that were easier to manage, but less effective. The problem was not simply bias on the part of providers, but the resources available to them and their patients. For patients who struggled to hold down multiple jobs, lacked reliable transportation, and juggled ad-hoc childcare arrangements, intricate treatment regimens may indeed have been impractical and without perfect implementation might in fact have harmed their health further. Through these and other avenues, Lutfey and Freese argue, social inequalities breed health disparities between groups.[5] Access to experimental or "cutting-edge" treatments and medications is often even more unequally distributed.[6]

Social scientists and public health scholars have conducted countless studies documenting inequalities like these throughout the US healthcare system. Much of this literature has focused on difference across patient characteristics (such as race, class, gender, and sexual orientation) and physician bias, with less emphasis on what patients and physicians actually do together during the help-seeking and treatment process.[7] This is important because patients and families are increasingly expected to possess "lay expertise" and be active consumers of their healthcare.[8] As a result, researchers have recently begun paying greater attention, along the lines of Lutfey and Freese's work, to how the structural features of the healthcare system combine with the actions of patients and providers to produce health disparities.[9]

In order to bring interactional dynamics like these into clearer view, sociologist Janet Shim developed a theory of cultural health capital, which highlights the sorts of resources that can be advantageous for patients and families as they interact with healthcare providers.[10] Cultural health capital, as Shim conceptualizes it, is a lot like the general cultural capital we often take for granted in everyday life. We all have cultural capital that is potentially valuable in different settings. An ability to recognize and identify a classical symphony like Beethoven's Fifth, or a heavily sampled hip-hop riff like James Brown's "Funky Drummer" might help us prove our musical savvy and solidify cultural group membership in different contexts with different audiences.[11] Not knowing what foie gras is might betray our class origins in an upscale restaurant just as a trendy designer handbag might signal outsider status for a teen transferring from a suburban to a rural high school. Failing to possess the right cultural capital can impede one's access to a job, acceptance among peers, or ability to be taken seriously by teachers, police officers, or loan providers. In a particularly poignant example of the consequences of poorly matched cultural capital, one of the young black men that sociologist Victor Rios observed in his study of youth in an urban community failed to shake his interviewer's hand at the end of a job interview at a chain restaurant.[12] When Rios, who observed from a distance, asked him why, he stated plainly, "Because you're not supposed to shake a white lady's hand." The social norms he had learned in order to keep out of trouble and avoid appearing threatening within the social context of his neighborhood clashed with the norms required to demonstrate professionalism, friendliness, and respect in the workplace. Some forms of cultural capital, then, are linked to power and access to resources, whereas others may be linked primarily to surviving risky environments and interactions.

In the medical arena, similarly taken-for-granted skills and knowledge—such as the ability to accurately read a prescription bottle, use anatomically correct terms to describe symptoms, engage in discussions of complex biological processes, and communicate efficiently with physicians—can improve understanding and trust in healthcare relationships. Shim defines cultural health capital as "the repertoire of cultural skills, verbal and nonverbal competencies, attitudes and behaviors, and interactional styles" that patients bring to interactions and that "can be leveraged in healthcare contexts to effectively engage with medical providers."[13] Building on Pierre Bourdieu's concept of habitus, Shim suggests that people often deploy cultural health capital without even thinking about it.[14] It simply becomes second nature to ask questions succinctly, volunteer information physicians are likely to find important, and avoid delving into unrelated details that healthcare providers may view as irrelevant or unnecessary.[15] In their observations of clinical encounters between patients and providers, Shim and her colleagues, Leslie Dubbin and Jami Chang, found that something as simple as taking notes during a visit could demonstrate a "proactive commitment to health," which in turn led physicians to invest more time in a patient and do more to facilitate referrals or medication refills on their behalf.[16] Elizabeth Gage-Bouchard similarly found that physicians spent more time with parents of pediatric cancer patients who displayed significant cultural health capital and expressed greater affinity for these families.[17]

I began this project with an average level of cultural health capital. I vaguely recalled introductory principles of biology and even had a rudimentary knowledge of pharmaceuticals from a psychopharmacology course I took in college. But I didn't have much experience navigating the medical system beyond going to the doctor for relatively common medical issues and following "doctors' orders." Though I had been volunteering at the Ronald McDonald House associated with Kelly-Reed for several months when I met Benjamin and Nora, Nora was the first parent I formally interviewed for my research on families' help-seeking strategies. I was new to the medical lingo she tossed around and unfamiliar with the logistical details of the treatments she described. As I spoke with Nora and other parents who had considerable cultural health capital and started spending time with these families in medical settings, I began increasing my cultural health capital. Though I had no way of knowing it at the time, this education would turn out to be fortuitous when, six months later, my father was diagnosed with a glioblastoma brain tumor. Had I not met families like the Bialys, I doubt I would have thought to conduct PubMed searches, look for out-of-state clinical trials, or request tests that might offer my father more possibilities for treatment than we would have otherwise known we could pursue.

Cultural health capital was the grease that oiled the wheels of a care-captaining approach to managing illness. Families with more of it were taken more seriously by providers, although attempting to care-captain without much cultural health capital could lead to rocky interactions and frustration for all involved. But cultural health capital was not the whole story. The powerful desire and pervasive cultural mandate to sidestep and minimize uncomfortable emotions and hold onto hope at all costs also strongly influenced families' decisions to care-captain or care-entrust at different moments throughout the treatment process—and shaped physicians' responses to them. Resources were instrumental, but emotions also fueled families down very different help-seeking paths.

Holding Out Hope: The Emotion Work of Managing Illness

Hope was everywhere at the Ronald McDonald House. Despite the grave situation facing many of the families who stayed there while their critically ill children received care at Kelly-Reed, the space itself refuted the possibility that anything bad could ever happen there. A cross between an oversized home and a motel, it had a large communal living room, kitchen, and dining room at its hub, where colorful slogans celebrating hope, courage, and strength were splayed across the walls and tucked in every nook and cranny. The optimism of the space itself was exceeded only by the unflagging positivity of the staff who inhabited it. During one of my early shifts at the front desk, the director at the time told me earnestly that he wanted every family who walked through the door to be "greeted by a smiling face." Months later, a new director crackled with energy and excitement as he smiled broadly and told a community group on a house tour, "We want people to come here and see that this is a *happy* place, *not a sad place.*" The group was there to cook dinner for the families, and were oriented to what sociologist Arlie Hochschild would call the "feeling rules" of the setting right away.[18]

Feeling rules, as Hochschild describes them, are the social expectations for appropriate emotional expression in different social contexts. That one should feel sad at a funeral or joy upon receiving an extravagant gift are "feeling rules"—and such expectations alone can powerfully shape and shift our emotional experiences. When our emotions are out of sync with feeling rules, we often engage in emotion work to bring our feelings back in line with what others expect them to be. In her early research with flight attendants and bill collectors who were forced to produce specific types of emotion on demand as a requirement of their jobs, Hochschild exposed the concerted efforts people undertake to mold their emotions to achieve individual goals and meet social demands. This was an important corrective to psychological theories of the time, which focused primarily on the biological processes involved in emotional experience. Hochschild showed emotions to be far less natural and far more socially influenced than previously understood.

The highly cultivated optimistic atmosphere I encountered at the Ronald McDonald House reflects a particular set of feeling rules around illness in the United States and the high societal value placed on remaining "positive" in the face of significant challenge. Ironically, this expectation is pushed most strongly on those dealing with the greatest misfortune. Journalist Barbara Ehrenreich critiqued the US culture of positivity, which she described as a "longstanding national obsession" in her 2009 book, *Brightsided.*[19] The book was inspired in part by her own illness experience. When Ehrenreich was diagnosed with breast cancer, she was appalled by the "pink sticky sentiment" of what sociologist Gayle Sulik calls "pink ribbon culture." For Ehrenreich, this pervasive emotional culture denied the reality that breast cancer patients might actually suffer or die. She was particularly horrified at the implication that whatever fate had in store for her, she should accept it "while clutching a [pink] teddy [bear] and with a sweet little smile on my face."[20]

Ehrenreich was not alone in this read on breast cancer culture. Sulik found that the women she interviewed experienced "optimism" as a fundamental feeling rule.[21] Meeting this expectation involved "normalizing their experiences, avoiding complaints, and using breast cancer as a catalyst for empowerment," not to mention the intense emotion work required to "conceal feelings of anxiety, depression, concern, and pain."[22] Some of the women in Sulik's study even reported being "kicked out" of online breast cancer support groups for expressing anger or being criticized by doctors for having a negative attitude.

Indeed, there is widespread belief even among physicians that remaining positive and hopeful can bolster one's health.[23] But all this emotion work—the massive effort required to sweep worries under the rug and keep physical suffering to one's self—can be a significant stressor. It can place a heavy strain on everyday social interactions, and cause families to reshape and shrink their social networks.[24] This can be most intense for those at the end of life, as bioethicist David Wendell Moller argues, pointing out that the "American tendency to ignore suffering and death leads to profound isolation for both dying persons and loved ones."[25] The cultural narrative about what it means to have a "productive" response to tragedy—centered on the imperative to transform misfortune of all kinds into an "opportunity" for personal growth—devalues and dismisses fundamental components of the human experience: grief, suffering, and loss.

As I sat at the front desk one night watching a young couple in tears leave for the hospital to visit their extremely premature newborn in the neonatal intensive care unit, I wondered how they felt about being surrounded by a wonderland of glee and triumph. But for other families, this upbeat atmosphere provided the foundation from which to engage in what sociologist Annsi Peräkylä terms "hope work."[26] Although hope work can move in two directions—involving concerted interactional efforts to build it up or tear it down—the staff and the majority of the families who stayed at the Ronald McDonald House were deeply invested in cultivating and holding on to as much hope as possible.

There is some debate, particularly among psychologists, as to whether hope itself is an emotion. Psychologist Richard Lazarus, who argued that hope should be understood both as an emotion and as a coping process, described hope as an "affective blend" in which one feels a mix of negative and positive emotions.[27] To be hopeful is to feel gladness that things may turn out well, while simultaneously retaining at least some degree of anxiety that they may not. We might say that one is most hopeful when the scales are tipped heavily toward the positive feelings, but until the hoped-for outcome is achieved, a hint of fear or anxiety remains. Hope work might thus be envisioned as the interactional efforts we engage in while trying to push ourselves or others up or down on this emotional seesaw.

Anthropologist Cheryl Mattingly similarly conceptualizes hope as a *practice.* Among the African American families of chronically and sometimes terminally ill children Mattingly studied, hope was a "moral call, bound up in views of what it means to live a good life, to be a good person."[28] "Practicing hope" allowed families to enact these moral identities and made nightmare circumstances "habitable." Mattingly found hope in small moments in clinical encounters, such as a doctor's playful exchange with a child, or a small moment of joy during a physical therapy session. Though it might seem to bubble up at times, Mattingly clarifies that hope is "a stance toward reality that requires careful cultivation."[29] For the families in both Mattingly's study and my own, practicing hope could help normalize interactions that might otherwise feel depressing or awkward, given our broader cultural discomfort with expressions of sadness and pain.

The medical side of managing a child's critical illness is also tightly bound up in a practice of hope. As sociologists Alan Petersen and Iain Wilkinson point out, hope "posits a certain relationship between the present and the future, where the present somehow unfolds into the latter, enabling the fulfillment of better lives . . . free of disease, disability, and suffering . . . and is strongly linked to the consumption of medical technologies, particularly therapies that promise to offer cures."[30] Similarly, in an early sociological analysis of hope Henri Desroche imagined hope as a rope flung into the air, hooking onto something not quite visible, just beyond the horizon.[31] Advanced medical technologies, hospital rankings, a physician's prestigious pedigree or publication record, and even minor adjustments in care that might improve a child's baseline condition or level of comfort could become the metaphorical "hooks" the families I studied needed in order to emotionally hoist themselves toward a future in which their child would be well. In tying hope closely to biomedical interventions, care-captaining and care-entrusting could *both* offer families pathways to hope—but how much was dependent upon the extent and nature of families' cultural health capital.

As we saw in the two cases that opened this chapter, the Hendersons, who primarily care-entrusted, struggled to move up the rungs of the healthcare system and access appropriate care for their son before ultimately obtaining care at a "world-renowned" institution. Accessing care at Kelly-Reed more swiftly might have given them a more solid anchor on which to moor their hopes from the beginning of their son's illness. Even after arriving at Kelly-Reed, however, they did not immediately attach the same set of symbolic meanings to this particular hospital that other parents with more cultural health capital could. As a result, they were stuck with lingering uncertainty about their son's care and a melancholic sense that they may not have done enough for him. Care-captaining, in contrast, was often the ultimate path to hopefulness, as it was rooted in the idea that by directly influencing the provision of their child's medical care, families like the Bialys could help bring about the best outcome possible. When coupled with significant cultural health capital, care-captaining could generate concrete medical advantages parents could build their hopes upon and interpret as evidence that hoped-for outcomes would be achieved. But for families without much cultural health capital, care-entrusting—and believing steadfastly that there was nothing more they needed to do but defer to healthcare providers' directives—could usually provide them with more hope than haphazard and ineffective efforts to care-captain could.

As we'll see, even families with extensive medical knowledge and medical networks to draw on could feel the allure of care-entrusting. At times, stepping back and trusting their child's medical team to do what was needed enabled even well-resourced families to maintain more hope and emotional stability than they might have by staying intensively medically involved at all times. Such periods of less frenetic engagement—moments perhaps, even, of relative calm—may offer parents brief opportunities to recharge throughout long and stressful ordeals. Those who could successfully blend and switch between illness management strategies had the broadest and most effective emotion-management toolkit available to them. This reality points to an important and underappreciated avenue through which inequalities are both experienced and reproduced.

Emotions and the Reproduction of Inequality in Family Life

Almost all parents feel anxious about their children's futures. When a child is diagnosed with a life-threatening illness, everyday anxieties take on new, horrifyingly immediate form. Sometimes this anxiety was explicit, as we saw in Nicholas Henderson's open concern that he may not have accessed the best possible care for his son, or Jamilla Finley's unrelenting abdominal pain. Sometimes it was expressed in more subtle ways—as in Nora Bialy's fervent commitment of time and energy to preparing elaborate high-calorie treats she hoped would both nourish and bring pleasure to her thin, ill teen. Modern approaches to parenting encourage parents to pour themselves into their children in the best of times, [32] and the emotional and practical demands of parenthood multiply exponentially during times of crisis.

When sociologist Annette Lareau observed families with elementary-school aged children in her 2003 ethnographic study, she documented dynamics similar to care-captaining and care-entrusting in parents' approaches to childrearing more generally.[33] Middle-class parents, she found, typically adopted an approach she calls "concerted cultivation." By this logic, children need to be carefully and constantly nurtured, stimulated, educated, and encouraged to question the world around them. Parents facilitate this process by getting deeply involved in orchestrating their children's lives. They enroll their children in an array of cultural, academic, and athletic activities, turn everyday conversations into vocabulary lessons, and encourage children to advocate for themselves and converse with adults as equals. This equips middle-class children with a variety of interactional resources that help them to impress teachers and other authority figures, confer advantages on traditional school and college applications, and may curry favor with future professional employers.

Alternatively, working-class parents generally take an approach Lareau calls the "accomplishment of natural growth." This involves giving children self-directed playtime so they can learn from their mistakes, learn to take care of themselves and others, and develop personal responsibility. To facilitate the accomplishment of natural growth, children are given clear directives, expected to perform care-taking responsibilities for themselves and family members, and are taught to obey authority. This approach equips children with important skills that will be of value to them in their adult lives, and may endear them to service-sector and blue-collar employers. However, these skills carry less weight on traditional college applications or with professional employers, thereby inhibiting their opportunities for social mobility in these spheres.

Lareau does not devote significant attention to the emotional dynamics and anxieties about children's and parents' futures that likely drive these diverging approaches to childrearing. But other scholars' work on the increasing sense of fear and insecurity felt by families across the economic spectrum points in that direction. Growing instability in employment has put more pressure and an increasingly heightened focus on the home front.[34] Families—even those with healthy children—express great uncertainty about their children's futures, worrying that their children may not achieve economic success, make healthy choices, or escape what can seem like ever-present dangers in the world around them.[35] In response, families actively "develop mechanisms for coping with the anxiety generated by an insecure world."[36] To cope with fears around everything from sudden infant death syndrome to teen sexuality, parents have adopted new technologies that allow them to closely monitor and surveil children of all ages.[37] Some of the middle- and upper-class families whom sociologist Marianne Cooper interviewed managed worries about their children's economic futures by investing enormously in getting their children into "top schools" that might "open doors" for them. Families in her study who struggled to make ends meet could not go to such elaborate lengths and focused instead on making each day as loving and enjoyable as possible with the goal of teaching their children to interpret a life with "less" as a rich and meaningful one.[38] The homeschooling mothers whom sociologist Jennifer Lois interviewed took over full responsibility for their children's education in large part to cope with the intense emotions around motherhood, to enact the most devoted form of motherhood they could imagine, and to "savor" the fleeting time they had with children while they were still young.[39]

Sociologist Ana Villalobos further reveals the intense emotions pulsing at the heart of childrearing strategies in her study following mothers of children from birth to age three.[40] She found that as the outside world is perceived as ever more dangerous—from kidnappings to super-germs to toxic chemicals in household products—mothers are expected to do more and more to protect their children and keep them both physically and emotionally secure.[41] This could be an impossible task, and one that drove many of the women in her study to an emotional breaking point. In an effort to manage a pervasive sense of insecurity, some mothers kept their children as close as possible through attachment parenting. Others tried to "inoculate" children, or "toughen them up," through exposure to "the real world"—hoping that doing so would make them strong and provide them with the armor they needed to feel and to be safe. At either end of the spectrum, mothers' emotional goals for children and themselves were at the root of the parenting strategies in which they invested. The need to feel they were doing all they could to do right by their child was desperately felt, even if "right" looked very different from one family to the next. Parents who refuse or renegotiate childhood vaccination schedules may be driven by similar beliefs and anxieties. If parents see vaccines as posing even a minor degree of risk to their children, this risk may simply feel too *emotionally* threatening for them to accept.[42]

The urgency of parents' efforts to do right by their children is connected to the fact that, as sociologist Ara Francis puts it, "'normal' children are a central feature of personal life, and parenthood is a foundation upon which much else depends."[43] Francis's research shows that when this basic premise is threatened, families with children who face challenges ranging from autism to substance abuse are thrown entirely off-kilter and become mired in a pervasive struggle she terms "family trouble." Parents often feel stigmatized by their children's problems, and mothers in particular worry that others assume they are to blame for causing them or failing to manage them appropriately.[44] Linda Blum's interviews with mothers of children with "invisible disabilities" (such as Attention-Deficit/Hyperactivity Disorder [ADHD] or Asperger's Syndrome) point directly to the importance of identity work in driving mothers' interventions. Blum found that the women she interviewed did an extraordinary amount of work navigating mazes in both the medical and educational systems not only to access services for their children, but to demonstrate their "goodness" as mothers.

This book brings these logics to bear on a moment of extreme crisis in family life. In my research, emotions ran particularly close to the surface much of the time, as children's lives hung precariously in the balance. The cases examined here show how the efforts of parents of critically ill children to keep their fears at bay and buoy feelings of hopefulness push them toward or away from different illness management strategies— compelling them either to care-captain or care-entrust. These strategies in turn help them obtain medical advantages for their children and/or emotional benefits for themselves, depending on how well the cultural health capital available to them fits with the illness management strategy they employ. As such, parents' emotional goals and strategies for achieving them facilitate inequalities in their illness and healthcare experiences in complicated, sometimes conflicting ways.

Care-captaining has the potential to net children medical advantages—from access to cutting-edge, life-saving treatments they otherwise might miss out on to smaller, more mundane "microadvantages" in everyday comfort—like less interrupted sleep or less time on heavy-side-effect drugs. Taking this approach may also provide an outlet for families with even modest amounts of cultural health capital to burn off anxieties and feel good about the fact that they are "doing something," concretely, to help protect and pave a pathway of hope for their child. But care-captaining involves emotional risks as well, especially for families with little cultural health capital. For those with fewer resources, care-entrusting may be the only reasonable way to maintain a stable sense of hope and to avoid deeply unsettling feelings of inefficacy. In the end, it may be that neither approach to creating or protecting hope is successful enough or possible to sustain at all times; hence, families may switch and blend strategies as a child's illness progresses. What is clear is that the powerful impulse to minimize fear and anxiety and the corresponding commitment to producing and maintaining as much hope for critically ill children's recoveries as possible play a substantial role in shaping families' trajectories through the healthcare system and thus perpetuating inequalities between them. These dynamics deserve close and critical analysis.

Plan of the Book

In the chapters ahead I offer rich snapshots of the illness and treatment experiences families shared with me, pulling back the curtain on the behind-the-scenes work and emotional chutes and ladders involved in caring for a child with a life-threatening illness. In chapter 2, I provide further detail on how I came to and conducted this study and about the families and physicians who participated in this research. Chapter 3 profiles parents whose primary illness management strategy was care-captaining. In describing the process through which the Marins, the Brady-Fischers, and the Rivera-Cruzes accessed and negotiated care at Kelly-Reed and other elite medical centers, I demonstrate the advantages care-captaining could garner families who were able to do so successfully and show how physicians interpreted their efforts. Surprisingly, parents' care-captaining efforts could help physicians feel better as well. I also consider the resources required to successfully engage in this approach.

In chapter 4, I contrast these experiences with those of families who primarily care-entrusted, introducing readers to the Harris-Lacostes, the Shaws, the Khalid-Tahirs, the Donnoly-Santoses, and the Moores. I lay out the very different philosophies these families applied to managing their children's medical care and outline some of the alternative channels through which they advocated for their children. These families missed out on some of the medical advantages care-captaining could produce and, with fewer resources, often struggled to negotiate the logistical demands of caring for a critically ill child. Yet care-entrusting often made more emotional sense for families with little cultural health capital, and as such provided them some important nonmedical benefits.

Chapter 5 delves more deeply into the emotional dynamics just beneath the surface of these approaches by analyzing the cases and moments in which families blended or switched illness management strategies. For families with enough cultural health capital to care-captain at strategic moments, stepping back and care-entrusting at most other times could facilitate a less harried illness experience. This was the case for Deirdre Klein, who often chose to defer to physicians and generally avoided doing her own research after accessing care at Kelly-Reed. Conversely, attempting to care-captain without much cultural health capital could lead to extreme stress and conflict with healthcare providers. This was the case for Tina Morgan, who was constantly exasperated by her lack of control over her daughter's care, and butted heads with providers who did not order tests she requested or take her concerns and desire for involvement more seriously. These cases, along with instances in which other families switched strategies, illuminate the powerful emotional forces driving families' decisions about how to manage their child's illness.

In chapter 6, I analyze the emotional costs and benefits of these strategies in the terrible moments when children's lives were ending. Considering the experiences of two families whose children died at Kelly-Reed, I show how powerful the imperative to hold onto hope—"no matter what"—could be. Hope was so deeply embedded in the fabric of the illness and treatment experience that even the physicians I spoke with struggled to escape its pull—using a transformed version of hope to help parents withdraw care at the end of children's lives. Even when children's lives were lost, the resources parents had available to them, and the freedom with which they could or could not switch between illness management strategies as needed, led to very different experiences of their children's final weeks of life.

In chapter 7, I turn to my own sudden personal immersion into the world of negotiating life-threatening illness. When my father was diagnosed with a terminal brain tumor, the significant advantages of care-captaining and the potential consequences of care-entrusting were brought into even sharper relief. By living an experience somewhat parallel to that of the families I was studying, the emotional dynamics at the root of these illness management strategies crystalized in my own daily life. Having learned from the families I met at the Ronald McDonald House how to care-captain and otherwise "fight" for hope on his behalf, I was able to bring my father closer to life-extending treatments than he would have received had we primarily care-entrusted. For both my father and me, ensuring that we were doing *everything we possibly could* by looking for new anchors for our hopes at every juncture became a language we used to communicate commitment to one another. But the flip side of the tenacity of hope became terribly clear in the final weeks of his life, for which we found ourselves woefully underprepared. I learned intimately that hope can ultimately serve as both a stepping stone and a stumbling block as illness unfolds.

In the concluding chapter, I grapple with the implications of these findings. The quest for hope could save lives when it brought families to the "right" treatment or to a uniquely positioned physician who could best treat a child's particular rare condition. It could garner families and their children smaller, microadvantages throughout the treatment process. And it could help everyone involved express the depth of their care. But its pursuit could also change how families engaged with the social world around them. And if every medical intervention failed and death was imminent, holding out unrelenting hope for recovery could breed additional pain and suffering, turmoil and regret.

This book will likely raise as many questions as it answers. It does not offer simple solutions to the profound challenges families of children (or anyone else) managing life-threatening illnesses confront. But it clearly reveals that much more can and should be done to support families across the socioeconomic spectrum when children become ill and require extensive medical care. We need to facilitate smoother and swifter access to high-quality, cutting-edge care for those without the ability to effectively care-captain as needed. And a more flexible and critical engagement with the rhetoric of hope surrounding life-threatening illness for young and old alike might do much more for the patients and families facing this harrowing circumstance than its desperate and unyielding adoption can achieve. In mapping the terrain these families traveled, my "hope" is to begin a sociologically informed conversation that helps point us in that direction.

2

Studying Families of Critically Ill Children

The recently renovated children's hospital at Kelly-Reed was a sleek, open-concept, futuristic space. Its very architecture suggested that this was a place where advanced technology could save the day. A massive wall of windows overlooked a beautifully landscaped garden and fountain area, and colorful geometric shapes hung suspended mid-air in the cavernous lobby. This vast open waiting area was filled with a variety of contemporary-styled chairs and couches, included a large play area with tabletop toys, and featured a many-foot-long tropical aquarium. A central glass elevator carried families to the floors above, whose wavy corridors were all openly visible from the main level. From each subsequent floor, one could peer over a half-wall and gaze down at the expansive lobby below.

Between the bold primary colors splashed across multiple surfaces and the bustling energy, laughter, and exclamations of children of all ages echoing up to the high ceilings, one might have wondered if one had stepped into a high-tech children's museum rather than a medical center. At its busiest, the whole place teemed with life and activity. Only the occasional child in a wheelchair or mobility stroller hinted that this might be a healthcare setting.

A few floors up, the scene was only slightly different. On most floors, families checked in for outpatient appointments with different clinical specialists (neurology, urology, cardiology, and so on). These smaller waiting areas contained toys, children's books, and sometimes even volunteer-led arts and crafts activities. Once they were ushered through the clinic doors and into the examination rooms, friendly, enthusiastic nurses joked with children and chatted cheerfully with parents. The physicians the families were there to see were generally specialists with highly sought expertise in particular pediatric conditions and held teaching and research appointments in addition to their work in the clinic. But once they entered the room, they, too, were affable, laidback, and surprisingly unhurried during their interactions with the families whom I observed.

One upper floor consisted primarily of patient treatment rooms circling a large shared space in which children camped out for hours at a time while receiving outpatient chemotherapy or other infusions. Here, medicine mixed a bit more openly with the whimsy. Monitors beeped, and most children were connected to one or more medication-delivering device. Children were usually more subdued, and might spend time resting or sleeping, reclined under brightly printed fleece blankets. But each treatment room and the communal area boasted flat-screen televisions and portable video games to keep kids entertained during lengthy, tedious treatments. A long fairy-tale themed mural stretched across the length of the common space, and once or twice a day volunteers or child-life specialists set up games, activities, and art projects—recruiting bored kids to join them with animated pitches.

Children who required hospitalization, or inpatient care, stayed primarily on one floor of the main hospital, to which the children's hospital was directly connected. This floor consisted of several distinct units (including the pediatric intensive care unit, or PICU; the neonatal intensive care unit, or NICU; and the pediatric stem-cell transplant unit, referred to colloquially as "Unit 27"). The hallways leading to these units were similarly boldly painted, covered with more colorful abstract shapes, and displayed framed children's artwork. Across both buildings, these bright, cheerful, child-centered spaces belied the severity of the conditions many of the children who entered them faced.

The cheerfulness of these spaces may have encouraged my own blind optimism. I was extraordinarily naive when I began this project. I somehow imagined that modern medicine had pediatric cancer pretty well under control, and I had little or no familiarity with some of the rare diseases I would soon learn about from the families I met at the Ronald McDonald House. I recognized the possibility that an extremely premature infant might not survive. But I otherwise genuinely did not initially anticipate that the children I was studying might die.

That I could hold such a deep misconception is especially striking given that, unlike other researchers who studied ill and dying children who had never before encountered childhood death,[1] I had—twice. As a teenager, I babysat weekly for a woman whose three-year-old nephew had cancer. I stayed with her children while she went to the hospital to support her sister. I had visited him with the family, and when he died, I attended the wake, babysat during the funeral, and helped them fundraise to support the foundation they set up in his memory. Some years later, I became even more intimately involved in caring for a dying child, when, during my early-twenties, I spent eighteen months living with close friends whose twins were born without the genes required to regulate calcium—a condition incompatible with life. Their daughter Sarah came home from the hospital a few months after her birth with a "do not resuscitate" order, but lived for over three years on home hospice care before she died. Her twin sister, Tess, had died when she was sixteen weeks old. I had been schooled in the emotional crucible of grieving parents and as Sarah's third primary caregiver for a significant portion of her life, had felt a sharp sliver of that grief myself.

Yet the persuasive rhetoric of the Ronald McDonald House and the broader discourse of constantly advancing medical science led me to view my research years later as entirely different and unrelated. I was studying parents' interactions with the healthcare system, their efforts to negotiate medical mazes, and the work involved in obtaining cutting-edge treatments for kids whose lives could be saved. This was something my friends had never had reason to do because Sarah and Tess did not have a condition that could be treated. I had put them in a different category in my mind.

That I could maintain the naiveté with which I began this project despite my own prior encounters with childhood illness and death is a testament to the power of our contemporary medical culture to suggest that almost anything can be treated—and almost anyone can be saved. Major academic medical centers use logos that cross out the word "cancer." Patients whose conditions are successfully treated, especially by newly developed ground-breaking technologies, are profiled on their websites. And beautiful gleaming spaces like the ones described above seem to proclaim that we have vanquished suffering. This is the prism through which many patients and their families approach medicine.

The Setting

My fieldwork at the Ronald McDonald House affiliated with Kelly-Reed began in the fall of 2011. One of 309 houses operating under the Ronald McDonald House Charities umbrella, this chapter was run by a local board of directors and housed anywhere from twenty-five to forty-five families on a given night.[2] Some families stayed for only a few nights; others stayed for weeks or months, particularly those whose children required lengthy chemotherapy and radiation treatments, or stem-cell or traditional organ transplants. A top-ranked private university research hospital, Kelly-Reed drew "guests" from anywhere and everywhere. Some children came from other countries, and their families paid for treatment entirely out of pocket. Other children came from more distant areas of the state and had Medicaid insurance coverage. Families were referred to the Ronald McDonald House by nurse coordinators or hospital social workers at Kelly-Reed or their home hospital/clinic, and a donation of $10–$15 per night was requested, but not required. Basic staples were available in communal refrigerators and cupboards, and families could bring in their own food as well. Each evening a volunteer group (often members of local churches, sororities, or teams of employees from local businesses) came in to prepare a large family-style home-cooked meal for anyone who wished to join in.

As a guest services volunteer, I answered the phone, received and recorded donations, wrote thank you notes, folded letters and stuffed envelopes, gave house tours to families checking in, hunted down extra towels, shampoo, or pillows, and transported families to and from the hospital as needed. Occasionally, I also took families to the airport or the grocery store, or on other various errands. I generally worked three- to six-hour shifts once or twice a week, from the fall of 2011 until the summer of 2013.

The Ronald McDonald House was a bustling place. Short-term families checked in and out, long-term families came and went from the hospital, and children and well siblings raced through the hallways. On the weekends, community groups sometimes came in to prepare brunch for the families, clean, or do activities with the children. November and December were by far the busiest months, as the organization attracted an exceptionally high level of philanthropic attention. The hallways brimmed with boxes of donated toys and household goods. The play-room was transformed into "Santa's workshop," where parents could se-lect and wrap gifts for their children. Other toys were stored to be used as prizes for game nights or in monthly birthday parties held throughout the year. Some community groups visited during the day to sing, play music, or bake cookies.

At other times of the year, the house could be cozier. The large com-munal living room space contained a large-screen TV and an extensive DVD collection, and sometimes one or more families settled in there to relax after dinner. During the colder months, a fire often burned in the large wood fireplace in the center of the room, stoked by the di-rector of maintenance throughout the day and occasionally nurtured along by the evening staff on quiet nights. Some evenings, a middle-aged white woman and her yellow Labrador came to visit. An announcement was made over the intercom, and a few families came down from their rooms to pet Scout, the therapy dog.

These social spaces and activities provided me ample opportunity to get to know families. I quickly became intrigued by the great lengths some families had gone to in order to access care at Kelly-Reed. One of the families I met during my first weeks at the house had traveled from New Zealand to obtain a curative treatment for a fatal immunodefi-ciency disorder pioneered by a physician at Kelly-Reed and, at the time, available at no other hospital in the world. I wondered how families managed the extreme uncertainty involved in navigating a child's life-threatening illness and the stress of making connections, coordinating logistics, and covering the costs of travel and time away from home and work. I met with the director about six weeks after I began volunteering to discuss my research interests and was given permission to interview families who agreed to participate in the case-study component of my research.[3]

Research Methods

In recruiting families, I took a qualitative approach described by soci-ologist Mario Small as "multiple-case selection."[4] In this method, "one case yields a set of findings and a set of questions that inform the next case," giving researchers the flexibility to select cases that offer important comparative leverage. Small suggests that "if the study is conducted properly, the very last case examined will provide very little new or surprising information. The objective is saturation."[5] These principles guided me as I added families to the sample. As the study progressed, I sought to include what sociologist Howie Becker terms "negative cases"—or "disconfirming" cases in which an initial pattern is challenged or complicated—for instance a family with very little cultural health capital who frequently care-captained or a family with reasonable amounts of cultural health capital who nonetheless primarily care-entrusted.[6] I wanted to ensure that my findings would not be limited to a particular type of disease, age group, or regional culture. As a result, I deliberately sought to include families of diverse social backgrounds, whose children (newborn to age eighteen) were diagnosed with a variety of life-threatening conditions.

Of the eighteen case-study families recruited, seven were white, six were black, two were biracial, two were Latinx, and one was South Asian. Three traveled to Kelly-Reed from outside the continental United States (Canada, Puerto Rico, and Argentina). Eleven were married to or partnered with their child's other parent. In two families, parents were divorced or separated but co-parenting. Three parents were single mothers, and two were custodial grandmothers (one single, one married). Nine families had at least one parent with a college degree and at least one parent working in a professional or managerial job. Nine remaining families held hourly wage working-class jobs; had quit working-class jobs to care for ill children; were retired from working-class jobs; or were already unemployed or receiving disability before the child's illness. (See appendix B for a table outlining demographics for each case-study family.)

Eight case-study families (and nine children) had come to Kelly-Reed so that their children could undergo stem-cell transplantation. Stem-cell transplants can be derived from a donor's umbilical cord blood or bone marrow or in some cases, a patient's own cells, which are harvested, modified, and then returned to them (these are known as "autologous transplants"). These are lengthy, high-risk treatments performed only in cases of life-threatening disease. Prior to transplantation, the patient's immune system is destroyed with high doses of chemotherapy (immune ablation) so that it will not attack the new cells when they are administered. Because patients are severely immune-compromised until the new cells have fully engrafted and they develop a "new" immune system, they must remain on a unit (most often referred to simply as "Unit 27") at Kelly-Reed with strict precautions and positive pressure HEPA (high-efficiency particulate air) filtration for several months or more. In the weeks and months following transplant, patients are unable to fight off simple infections, which can become life-threatening if they are exposed before their new immune system is well developed. Patients are also at risk of graft versus host disease (GVHD) if their body attacks the new cells, which can lead to multiple organ failure. Physicians and families negotiate a delicate balancing act between too little and too much immune suppression for weeks on end, working in the context of significant uncertainty and ambiguity to avoid the consequences of erring too far in either direction, resulting either in infection or in GVHD. On Unit 27, children's statuses could fluctuate rapidly and dramatically. Parents' hopes for their children's futures soared as high as ever, given the promises of success—but were also more fragile than ever, given the exceptional vulnerability of their children during this risky process.

Because families "lived" on Unit 27 for an extended period of time, this unit contained its own kitchen, a large playroom, and a family lounge with shared restroom and shower facilities for parents (the private bathrooms attached to each child's room were only to be used by the patient). Specially trained volunteers sometimes played with children in their rooms or in the playroom (in part to offer respite for parents), and group activities and special events were organized for all children on the unit. These varied from complex instructor-led art projects to science demonstrations hosted by staff from a nearby museum. School-aged children received individualized instruction in their rooms from teachers affiliated with the local public school system, and other outside professionals (such as physical therapists) visited the unit to provide services to patients during these long stays.

Because of the high risks of transplantation, the specialized expertise required to manage hard-to-predict outcomes, and the potential involvement of rare diseases, six senior physicians oversaw the care of all the children on Unit 27. Each child was assigned to one of these doctors who served as his or her "primary physician." Primary physicians oversaw pre-transplant work-ups and followed patients most closely at outpatient clinic visits after discharge—potentially for months and years to come. But on a day-to-day basis, inpatient children on Unit 27 (which consisted of sixteen private rooms) were seen by the senior physician on rotation (or "on service") at the hospital. The entire team discussed all families during weekly meetings.

After I had completed data collection with case-study families and concluded my fieldwork at the Ronald McDonald House, I interviewed five of the six physicians on Unit 27, and one other physician, Dr. Oliver, who had pioneered a specialized tissue transplant for children with a particular rare chromosomal deletion syndrome. Dr. Oliver has since trained providers at one medical center in Europe to perform this new procedure and hopes that others will follow. One of my case-study families and an additional family whom I interviewed at a later date came to Kelly-Reed for this particular transplant, and Dr. Oliver was their primary physician.

Three case-study families came to Kelly-Reed to obtain other novel treatments not widely available at the time, including enzyme replacement therapy for a glycogen and lysosomal storage disorder, as well as cancer vaccine immunotherapy. Six of my case-study families had children who underwent surgery to correct congenital defects, had standard organ transplants or cancer treatments, or received primarily life-sustaining intensive care.

After conducting initial extensive interviews with case-study families, I observed thirteen of them during interactions with providers in the hospital, on clinic visits, at physical therapy appointments, during patient education sessions, and/or while undergoing tests or treatments (such as MRIs, spinal taps, or infusions). I did not have the same type or frequency of access to all families. I met some of them late in the treatment process and others when they first arrived at Kelly-Reed. Some were either staying at the Ronald McDonald House for months during my fieldwork or returned on a regular basis, which provided me opportunities to "catch-up" with them frequently and conduct regular informal and formal follow-up interviews about their children's ongoing treatments. But others had shorter stays, were nearing the end of their treatment when I began interviewing, or were just beginning their treatment as my time in the field was ending, so I was not able to observe them in a medical setting.

While equal access and equivalent observations with all families might have been ideal from a methodological perspective, it was impractical given the realities of the setting and the unpredictable, constantly shifting circumstances involved. Ethically, I felt that it was important to approach families at relatively "calm" points in their child's treatment,[7] and I followed families' leads about how involved they were comfortable with me becoming after this point. Some families were happy to have me join them on multiple clinic visits or visit them at the hospital regularly, even when treatment was failing and children were nearing the end of life. Others wanted privacy during more difficult phases of treatment. I became closest with the Marins, the Rivera-Cruzes, and the Harris-Lacostes, and was able to remain in touch and follow up with a number of other families after they returned home as well.

All of the names of children, families, and physicians are pseudonyms, as is "Kelly-Reed." Physicians whom I formally interviewed are assigned full pseudonyms, while physicians to whom parents simply referred or whom I observed during medical visits but did not formally interview are identified by a one-letter pseudonym. Referring to their child's physician simply as, for instance, "Dr. L" was common practice among many families and staff at the Ronald McDonald House.

All formal interviews, which were generally about two hours long and conducted in families' rooms, the conference room, and other common areas at the Ronald McDonald House, or at the hospital,[8] were tape-recorded and transcribed verbatim by myself or a professional transcriptionist. In the latter case, I carefully reviewed and corrected each transcript personally to ensure accuracy and to maintain close proximity to the data.[9] I strove to write as richly detailed field notes as possible following my shifts at the Ronald McDonald House and medical observations with case-study families. All of these data were coded and analyzed throughout the data collection process following an inductive, grounded theory approach.[10] In the years since I originally collected this data, regularly returning to my notes, transcripts, and recordings has allowed me to travel back, in a sense, to those moments. I have spent countless hours during the preparation of this manuscript rereading transcripts and field notes, listening to audio recordings, and otherwise "swimming around" in my data. Returning to them repeatedly throughout the writing process has allowed me to interpret them more clearly in light of the events that followed and the insights I gained throughout the data collection process. Keeping families' voices and experiences front and center—and seared acutely in my mind—helps me to convey them as vividly and faithfully as possible to readers, who may then better evaluate my argument and develop their own interpretations.

Studying Families across Race, Class, and Gender

Although social class differences between families emerged as the strongest influence on their illness management strategies in my data, there is no doubt that other differences between them also shaped their illness and treatment experiences. Among the small set of families I studied, I did not identify substantial differences across race in parents' inclinations to care-captain or care-entrust, but race unquestionably shaped the context in which they chose to do so. For instance, the women Cheryl Mattingly interviewed during her research with African American mothers caring for chronically ill children reported that it could be "dangerous to act 'loud' or [be perceived as] 'go[ing] ghetto'" when advocating on behalf of their child.[11] Some felt the need to hide their own medical expertise and work to "appear compliant even in situations where [they knew] more about [their] child's disease than the professionals and may privately disagree with what the clinician tells [them] to do."[12]

One black mother in Mattingly's study had no choice, on one occasion, but to repeatedly demand a physician be brought in to evaluate and rectify a serious problem with her child's peripherally inserted central catheter, which was indeed found to contain a life-threatening blood clot. After the incident was resolved, she deliberately worked to mend her relationship with the nurses she had argued with by distributing fruit baskets and thank you notes extolling their virtues. White parents in my study also took actions similar to these—passing out Valentine's Day treats or baking cookies for their child's care team to keep in their good graces—but were likely motivated simply by a desire to curry extra favor and attention for their child or by appreciation for the staff who took good care of them. They did not do so in the context of anticipating and seeking to overcome stereotypes about what sort of parents they were likely to be or feel obligated to apologize for their care-captaining efforts.

It is also worth noting that in the one instance I observed of a mother with very little cultural health capital attempting (with little success) to care-captain regularly, this mother was white. The racialized controlling images Mattingly's subjects implicitly pointed to may well have deterred black mothers with little cultural health capital from making many attempts to care-captain.[13] Middle-class mothers of color in my study who had sufficient cultural health capital to draw on (or the resources to develop it) *did* care-captain, however, and were successful in doing so. While it is important to recognize the similarities in many of the dynamics around care-captaining and care-entrusting that crossed racial lines and are highlighted in the chapters ahead, the deeply racialized context in which all healthcare interactions unfold cannot be understated.

Likewise, though gender—combined with race and other social identities—certainly shapes the experience of navigating a child's life-threatening illness, on the whole, care-captaining and care-entrusting looked quite similar for mothers and fathers. As with race, the gender identities of every actor involved constantly influenced the dynamics of patient/family-physician interactions, as I will underscore at times in the pages ahead. And there is no doubt that mothers were consistently held to a different, higher set of expectations than fathers. But unlike others who have studied families with children who have non-life-threatening medical needs, I did not find, generally speaking, that children's critical illnesses "exacerbate[d] [the] gender division of labor and responsibility."[14]

Among two-parent families, in fact, the labor of family caregiving may have shifted toward greater equality. Most often, either both parents were in residence at Kelly-Reed, or fathers stayed home to serve as primary caregivers to the ill child's well siblings. Although I interviewed more mothers than fathers—both because of this common arrangement among families with multiple children and because several families were headed by single mothers or grandmothers—the fathers I interviewed who *were* in residence at Kelly-Reed were as knowledgeable about their children's illnesses and as deeply engaged in care-captaining or care-entrusting as the mothers in these families were. It is possible that the extreme crisis that results from a child's diagnosis with a life-threatening condition jolts families out of more traditional patterns—at least for some families at some moments.

Because my main goal here is to elucidate the illness-management and emotion-management strategies parents adopt, and because fathers and mothers both spoke similarly about these issues, I use generic terms such as "parents" and "families" to reflect the fact that my findings apply to fathers—and, in my observations at the Ronald McDonald House more broadly, step-parents, grandparents, and other relatives who were actively caring for critically ill children—despite the higher number of women/mothers who were interviewed directly. I fully recognize that this more gender-neutral approach is an imperfect solution, but it seemed the most practical one to adopt here.

Lastly, it is important to note the broader context in which the families in this study are situated both globally and historically. Advancing technologies have long shaped the landscape in which parents develop expectations for family life. Before the development of antibiotics, vaccinations, and other public health improvements that have led more families than ever before to expect (all of) their children to survive them, children's deaths were often met with a "mixture of indifference and resignation."[15] It is only this shifting social and technological landscape that has allowed children to take on the "emotionally priceless" position within families that they largely occupy today. In cultural contexts marked by extreme violence or poverty—particularly those in profoundly under-resourced nations—infant and childhood death can be deemed so routine and mundane that, as anthropologist Nancy Scheper-Hughes has shown, parents and community members may seem hardly to grieve at all. In such environments it would be nearly impossible to believe that critically ill children could be expected to recover and thrive.[16] Anthropologist Lisa Stevenson similarly argues that the value placed on life itself is dependent on one's social and cultural context.[17] The presumption that "staying alive" is a goal worth pursuing may be questioned in contexts where there is little to hope for. These realities serve as a reminder that the unspeakable character of childhood death described here reflects structural features of contemporary social life in the United States and other well-resourced nations, which make it possible for parents to invest deeply in their children. It is this particular constellation of conditions that provide the ingredients that are required for a culture of hope around serious childhood illness to flourish.

Using Emotions as Clues in Ethnographic Research

Physicians who have written reflectively about the practice of medicine provide substantial evidence for how their own emotional responses to patients influence their interactions with them. Internal medicine physician and author Danielle Ofri admits that the patients she feels little connection with or empathy for can feel like a chore to work with.[18] Conversely, caring deeply about particular patients can make it more difficult for physicians to have honest conversations about death and dying when needed. Surgeon and author Atul Gawande wrote that early in his career he sometimes avoided such conversations with patients he had a special affinity for, due in part to his own unwillingness to see or admit that they would not recover.[19] With greater experience he came to understand that this was a disservice to his patients, who might have benefited from deciding to stop interventions sooner.

Similarly, I felt immense empathy and respect for the families in my study. In such cases, the challenge for a sociologist is the ability to maintain analytic distance and remain willing and able to recognize and scrutinize even those areas that might not be flattering to our subjects.[20] Throughout this project, I strove to maintain a rigorous analysis of my data by paying close attention to the role emotions played not only in the dynamics of help-seeking, but in the process of research itself. As I proceeded, I followed the advice of sociologists Sherryl Kleinman and Martha Copp, who encourage fieldworkers to remain reflexive about their own emotional experiences from the outset of any ethnographic endeavor.[21]

For instance, though I recognized and strove to avoid the cliché of viewing families persevering through immense hardship as "inspirational," I was in awe of much of what they did and the composure with which they did it. I felt special admiration for Deirdre Klein, a mother who was living with cancer herself while negotiating her son's treatment for leukemia. Deirdre's steady equanimity deeply impressed me. She struck me as someone I wished I could be more like, particularly in her ability to live calmly and gracefully in the face of overwhelming uncertainty. My admiration for her may well have colored my interpretation of her approach to managing illness as an especially effective blend of care-captaining and care-entrusting.

But at the same time, this emotional response was a *clue* that prompted me to dig deeper to better understand what enabled her to maintain such a stable emotional state in spite of the multiple health crises she was juggling. My analysis in chapter 5 of the emotional benefits of "blending" strategies grew in part from an *interrogation* of my own emotional hunches in the field. Sociologists Krista McQueeney and Kristen Lavelle similarly suggest that emotions can serve as a barometer of sorts, pointing the researcher toward areas that are ripe for analysis.[22]

Another set of interactions that pinged my emotional radar were those in which I simply greeted families I knew when I ran into them at the Ronald McDonald House and asked how their children were doing. I was well aware of the tricky emotional dynamics involved, in part because I had already asked case-study families about the emotional drain of providing constant updates to social networks during my initial interviews.[23] Yet I felt no less compelled to ask. Failing to express interest in the wellbeing of someone's child did not seem to be a reasonable alternative. Following Kleinman and Copp's edict that "ignoring . . . uncomfortable feelings amounts to ignoring data," I gave these interactions significant thought.[24] That I often failed to quash the impulse to adopt a hopeful and optimistic tone in making these inquiries helped me to better see just how hard it was to avoid slipping into the knee-jerk positivity that infuses the culture of medicine in the United States. Even though I held an explicit understanding and critique of these dynamics, I never managed to fully extricate myself from them.

My vicarious heartache as I watched children struggle against multiple nurses who held or pinned them down for shots or IVs functioned similarly, encouraging me to pay closer attention to parents' feelings about their children's suffering. The "emotion notes" I typed up during particularly difficult points in my study reveal my early glimpses into the excruciating emotional positions parents found themselves in. After my second visit with a child who had been admitted to the PICU and placed in a medically induced coma while his health deteriorated, I wrote: "I understand now why people who others might look at from the outside and say, 'Let them go'—why that seems insane. He could still come around. He could still be okay. It's at least *possible*." I had begun to document just how powerful the need to hold on to the hope of even slim chances of recovery could be. I was no less caught up in this thinking when I later found myself in the illness driver's seat after my father's diagnosis with a terminal brain tumor. The extraordinary tenacity of hope was not something I established through interviews or observations alone, but was a finding that fully revealed itself through my own and others' repeated emotional experiences.[25]

I was not yet a parent myself when I collected the data for this project and began writing this book. This somewhat more "outsider" position likely allowed me to ask questions and encouraged parents to explain things to me in ways that might otherwise have been taken for granted had we shared this fundamental life status. Now that I have personally experienced the intensely all-consuming love and devotion one can feel for one's child, my standpoint has shifted in analytically useful ways. Of course, intellectually I understood from the outset that the parents I studied felt this way for their children, and I expected to feel the same for my own. Yet even after a long, hard-fought journey of fertility treatments and repeated pregnancy losses, I was stunned by the boundless, inexhaustible love I felt for the tiny little person ultimately placed in my arms—and the ferociousness of my felt need to protect him from every bit of pain, distress, trauma, and fear that I possibly could. I was entirely unprepared for the near obsession I felt to do everything humanly possible to make his world a cocoon of comfort, affection, and security during the first months of his life, as unrealistic and unsustainable as I quickly discovered this to be. As my son has grown from a tiny fragile newborn into a curious and adventurous toddler, I am learning to temper this urge given the reality that life involves pain—bumps and bruises, disappointment, frustrations, loss. But the impulse itself remains surprisingly tenacious.

Experiencing the overwhelming power of these embodied emotions gave me new insight into the unbearable place in which the parents in my study found themselves. And it brought home to me, with even greater force, just how significant the microadvantages families obtained for their children and themselves by care-captaining throughout the treatment process could be. Being able to spare a child a few extra days on a heavy side-effect medication, preventing a bad reaction from a breathing treatment, or even just reducing the number of additional needle sticks a child had to undergo—for parents whose child's pain is *their* pain (magnified), these small advantages can feel like major, vital victories. Moving from the standpoint of nonparent to parent over the course of this research underscores how one's identity as a researcher shapes the research itself.[26] Standing in both positions at different times throughout this study has, I believe, ultimately benefited this work.

Being "Human" in the Field

After the first child I had come to know well died, I reached out to a faculty member in my graduate department who had done research in hospitals to ask how she handled patient deaths. Her advice to me was that in these moments, the best we can do is to simply "be human" with one another. This was a balance I tried to strike throughout the project. I tried to avoid being a nuisance to families, overly intrusive, or "in the way," especially at heightened moments of crisis. This could sometimes require significant compromise between "access to valuable data" (which often requires intrusiveness) and stepping back at moments when privacy—or even just one less body in the room—might be the best thing for the child and family.

I tried to err especially on the side of keeping out of the way when children neared the end of life. Hospital deaths invariably entail a variety of others, many of them strangers, being involved in one of the most intimate moments of our lives.[27] Though I may have been overly cautious, I did not see any reason for me to add to this burden despite the "data" observation of such moments might have provided.

Sometimes, I had clear cues. Charlotte Caldwell left the Ronald McDonald House in a bit of a rush one night because her seventeen-year-old son, Brent, who was recovering from a stem-cell transplant, was developing a serious rash (from GVHD), and they were told he should be readmitted immediately. Though clearly harried, she minimized her alarm and casually estimated they would be back in a few days. A week later, they were still in the hospital. I sent Charlotte an email to see how they were doing and ask if they needed anything. I did not receive a response. Unsure of what might be happening, I did not call or write again. I saw her on Unit 27 the following week while I was in the playroom with another child in my study. Though Charlotte brought me up to date, her exhaustion was plain. I asked if I could help in any way, and she politely thanked me and declined. I sensed that she was distancing herself so that she could focus on Brent without distractions. A few weeks later, Brent died.

Some might have prioritized access and worked harder to stay involved in times like these: knocking on the door, calling to follow up on an unreturned email, or explicitly asking to visit. Persistence is generally rule #1 in fieldwork, when in any setting people's busy schedules—even when they are happy to participate—can pose an obstacle to access. In this case, I chose instead to treat my relationships with families as fragile—to reach out delicately, but to leave the ball in their court in order to avoid imposing or invoking a sense of polite obligation when children's illnesses were following a different trajectory than they expected. My gratitude for the time families had already offered me—and the traces of guilt I felt for taking up precious moments in what were proving to be severely shortened timelines with their children—cemented this choice for me. Other families' interactional cues indicated my presence was helpful and comforting during the final weeks of their children's lives. The time I spent with them and their children at these moments was deeply meaningful, and a responsibility I take very seriously in writing about them in the pages ahead.

Finally, readers may notice that outside of my discussion related to end-of-life issues in chapter 6, I tend to present the extension of children's lives as a positive, even when these lives are filled with significant ongoing challenges or severe physical and cognitive limitations. The question of whether extending the lives of children with debilitating neurological diseases like Tay-Sachs or metachromatic leukodystrophy is the best outcome for children or families is an especially thorny one. It is one that some of the transplant physicians I interviewed grappled with themselves. Some of these physicians chose not to take primary responsibility for such cases because of their concerns about the quality of life children faced afterward, and chose instead to limit their caseload largely to children whom they expected to recover more fully if treatment succeeded.

My affection for families whose children are severely neurologically compromised but living far beyond their anticipated life expectancies has left me unwilling to engage this question here. Four years after Savannah Marin's son, Jacob, had undergone stem-cell transplantation for Tay-Sachs—a fatal degenerative neurological disorder—I asked Savannah during a follow up interview in the summer of 2015 if she had any regrets about transplanting Jacob. Jacob has lived much longer than otherwise expected, but has remained extremely physically and cognitively limited (unable to speak, walk, or sit up on his own), and continued to suffer from seizures. Savannah told me she did worry that they might have "stolen" some quality of life from him by seeking transplant as quickly as possible, before the disease had taken full effect. Though early transplantation is most likely to succeed, Savannah wondered if decreasing the time in which he was able to more fully cognitively engage with the world around him had been the right choice.

But what mattered most to her was that "we still have our child here with us now" and Jacob was, she pointed out, nearing age five (a milestone he has since far surpassed), exceeding his initial two-to-four-year life expectancy. In comparison to children with Tay-Sachs who did not undergo transplantation, Savannah viewed Jacob *not* as "barely holding on," but as looking "*pretty darn good*" (emphasis mine). Savannah still believed there was potential for ongoing research to identify new treatments that might help her son recover more fully in the future, even if this was a long shot. Because I have deep affinity for the Marins, I am happy that they are happy and have chosen not to delve into these complex ethical questions here.

This is the limitation that can accompany the development of close personal relationships with one's subjects. Yet becoming and remaining "close" with several of the families in my study also heightened my felt obligation to "get things right." This likely improved the final research. It also may have influenced my (unavoidable) decisions about what to include and what to leave out. I point to this perennial research challenge here in the interest of allowing readers to judge my findings accordingly, and to reaffirm the insight of critical scholars that all research is shaped by the researcher's relationship to his or her subjects in myriad ways.[28]

More generally, as this project progressed, I felt considerable discomfort that other's tragedies—and later my own father's illness and death—were becoming the raw material with which I would write my dissertation, earn my doctorate, and publish academic articles and this book. I worried, while writing, whether or not I was doing justice to the families who so generously trusted me with their experiences. I remained acutely aware of the risk that their stories could be exploited for treacly sensationalism. I have tried to take care to remain focused in my writings on the analytic or methodological points they illustrate. My hope, of course, is that the final product accomplishes something that others might benefit from—a more balanced approach to one's own or a loved one's illness or simply a familiar reflection and deeper understanding of a parallel experience. I also hope it provides an analytic lens that can be used to illuminate and help address inequalities in the illness experience and the delivery of healthcare and clarify how emotional goals drive medical decision-making in both productive and counterproductive ways. This prospect allows me to make an uneasy peace with this endeavor.

PART II

Unequal Illnesses

3

Care-Captaining

Climbing the Rungs of the US Healthcare System

I mean, if we needed information? We got information.
Nothing happened unless we were sound with what was
going on.
—Todd Marin, father of eighteen-month-old Jacob

When parents with significant cultural health capital were confronted
with a child's life-threatening illness, many took charge and began
care-captaining immediately. By mobilizing medical social networks
and negotiating with insurance companies, they could often quickly
climb to the top of the US healthcare system in order to access specialized expertise and cutting-edge medical technologies. Throughout the
course of their child's illness, these families engaged in vigilant surveillance of their children's medical care, conducted their own research,
comfortably negotiated with the experts who provided their children's
care, and requested tests and treatment modifications they deemed
appropriate.

Families who care-captained throughout their children's illnesses
often made managing their child's medical care their full-time job. Care-
captaining could become all-consuming, to the point that one or more
caregivers had little time for anything other than managing a child's critical illness. Parents who care-captained were primarily middle or upper
class, as care-captaining could require substantial resources—time, the
ability to cover extensive travel costs, access to medical research, and
so on. In this chapter, I will show how care-captaining could produce
tangible medical advantages for children and enhance relationships with
healthcare providers, while demonstrating how this strategy was driven
by powerful, ongoing emotion work that fueled parents through such an
intensive endeavor.

"Hovering like Hawks": Securing Medical Advantages

When Jacob Marin was four months old, his mother, Savannah, noticed an occasional twitch in his left eye. A white, thirty-two-year-old, first-time mom with a bachelor's degree in nursing, Savannah was puzzled, but not alarmed. She casually mentioned it to her pediatrician at Jacob's next well-baby check-up. The pediatrician told her it was "probably nothing," but found it unusual enough to refer her to a pediatric ophthalmologist who saw Jacob about a month later. Savannah reported that after dilating his eyes, this doctor got flustered: "He was kind of shifting his papers, and writing things down, and trying to, like—you could tell something was wrong."

The ophthalmologist didn't tell Savannah what he suspected, but he did ask her if they had any Jewish ancestry (they did not) and commented that he hadn't seen this since "textbooks in school." While the Marins waited to see the specialist he referred them to at a nearby West Coast teaching hospital, Savannah told me that she "kind of googled" [based on those comments], and diseases like Tay-Sachs had come up. Savannah immediately tried to push such possibilities away: "I was like, 'We don't have any of that in our families, Nah. Whatever.' So, I shut down the computer, 'I don't even want to think about this.'" But when the Marins took Jacob to see the specialist a few days later, their fears were confirmed when the doctor became "excited." He wanted to "stick a speculum in [Jacob's] eye, to be able to take pictures [of the cherry-red macula, the hallmark sign of Tay-Sachs], because it's not very common." At that point, Savannah told me: "We're realizing as this guy is like, examining him, and talking to his fellows and everything, that, you know, 'Oh, my gosh, our kid is being turned into a science experiment! Just tell us what we need to know so we can get him out of here!'"

A diagnosis of Tay-Sachs—a rare, fatal, genetic, degenerative neurological disorder—was confirmed through blood tests a few weeks later. Jacob was almost seven months old. The only option for him in their West Coast home state was palliative hospice care. Savannah recalled, "Like, they really were like, 'I'm sorry, your child's going to die before he's three years old.'" Her husband, Todd, a white, thirty-five-year-old contractor with military training in mechanical engineering, recounted with thick sarcasm the diagnosing doctor telling them, "'Go look for clinical trials—you go do your homework and I'll do mine.'" Savannah was appalled as well, adding: "Oh, and he *said* that! He *said*, 'You go do your homework and I'll do mine.' But when we saw him at the next clinic visit, he hadn't done anything. Like, I mean he, ha! Maybe he had printed out another sheet from his database on what Tay-Sachs was, and told us, 'Oh.' He said, 'Looks like he has two to four years to live'" (emphasis hers).

The Marins were unwilling to accept this outcome. They "did their homework" and scoured FDA databases for clinical trials. While the most promising ones—in particular, gene therapy trials—were not yet enrolling human subjects, the Marins kept digging. They contacted the founder of a nonprofit Tay-Sachs research foundation who told them about an experimental cord blood–derived stem-cell transplant at Kelly-Reed, thousands of miles from their home. He put them in touch with a family whose then ten-year-old son had received the transplant for Tay-Sachs. Todd and Savannah became especially hopeful when, during their phone conversation, they heard the boy in the background singing to his grandmother and chiding his sister for blocking the TV. To the Marins, this meant that "he was able to understand something about the environment around him, and have pleasure and displeasure. So we were like, 'That's the minimum we want for Jacob,' like, you know, we want him to have a *life*, and enjoy it" (emphasis theirs).

While they waited for test results that would determine Jacob's particular mutation, or variant of the disease, Savannah flew with Jacob to another university research hospital on the East Coast to be seen by national Tay-Sachs experts. An energetic and enthusiastic mom with an athletic build and long light-brown spiral curls, Savannah, who wore a pendant with Jacob's middle name suspended on a thin gold chain around her neck, gushed as she recalled these experts' rosy appraisal of her son. These doctors were "amazed that he was so interactive with his toys, that he could sit. . . . They were like, 'Wow!'" she told me, gazing lovingly at her son.

This positive assessment reassured Todd and Savannah that if they could get Jacob a few more years of life by going through with the transplant, there might be advances in research that would offer a longer-term solution in the future. So Savannah began negotiating with her insurance company to get the million-dollar treatment approved. After requesting that they contract with Kelly-Reed to do the pre-transplant work-up that the insurance company wanted them to have done within their home hospital system, and then, if accepted, cover the transplant itself, she recalled the case manager exclaiming, "Savannah, you don't know what you're asking!" Savannah told me that she replied adamantly, "I *do* know, *I want you to save my kid*" (emphasis hers). A few weeks later, the insurance company and the hospital signed an agreement: the transplant would be covered. Savannah took an extended leave of absence from her job, and Todd quit his job and filed for unemployment benefits. The Marins put their house up for sale, placed their belongings in storage, and moved from the West to East Coast in the hopes that they had found a way to give their son a rare shot at survival.

* * *

The Marins began care-captaining for Jacob from the moment of his diagnosis. Their efforts involved not only seeking out experimental treatments and fighting their insurance company to pay for the one they deemed best, but monitoring and influencing his care at every step of the treatment process. Before arriving at Kelly-Reed, the Marins read medical journal articles published by the director of the program and by the primary physician to whom Jacob would be assigned. Todd told me that they "definitely looked him up and saw a lot of his writing—he's well published and [has] got a lot of information out there."

Savannah also began seeking supplemental therapies for Jacob within weeks of his diagnosis. She explained her logic for doing so:

> My brain goes to, okay, if he has a neurological disease, that's going to affect the neural connections, let's make *more* neural connections. He's a *baby*. The more we do with him, the more connections he'll have. So then maybe he would have more places that the [metabolic] waste would have to build up, so ... I'm like, "We should be getting him therapy!" Let's make him as strong as possible right now, so he has even *further* to have to deteriorate. *Nobody* at that point was recommending any type of therapies. So I request it. "Hey, can he get PT? And OT?" And, [after learning of an infant swim therapy program at a local hospital] I'm like, "Whoa! Let's do water therapy! And PT, and OT!" And at first everybody's like,

"Well, um, oh, okay, that makes sense," you know. They're like, "Uh, he has *Tay-Sachs.*" Yeah, we know! (Emphasis hers)

Recall that cultural health capital can be thought of as a collection of "cultural skills, verbal and nonverbal competencies, attitudes and behaviors, and interactional styles" that allow patients to engage effectively with healthcare providers.[1] Savannah's background as a nurse equipped her with exceptionally high levels of cultural health capital. Savannah posessed an understanding of what neural connections were and how they developed. This led her to hypothesize that having more of them (as a result of physical and occupational therapies) might slow the progression of a disease that systematically destroys them. She felt comfortable speaking up and requesting therapies that "nobody at that point was recommending," and she had a general idea of how to go about making such requests, and from whom. In the bigger picture of obtaining care for Jacob, Savannah knew what clinical trials were, understood how to search for them, and was able to understand the medical language used in their descriptions. She possessed a basic understanding of the hierarchy of the US healthcare system, knew that some hospitals had more resources than others, and understood that research hospitals might offer new treatment options not yet available in other places. She also knew that in the case of chronic or life-threatening illness, insurance companies often assign caseworkers. Savannah located her caseworker, and parlayed the more general skills associated with cultural capital (in particular, interacting and negotiating with authority figures) into coverage for an otherwise prohibitively expensive experimental medical treatment. Savannah's medical vocabulary, biological and pharmaceutical knowledge, and comfort in interacting with highly regarded authority figures equipped her with the resources needed to intervene regularly in Jacob's care and treatment.

Todd and Savannah—both of whom had entered the military after high school, which led them to meet and eventually marry—also stayed with Jacob every day throughout his six-month hospitalization. They felt strongly that they should be deeply involved in all aspects of his medical care. Todd explained to me, "[The] doctors don't see your kid twenty-four hours a day. If you're able to stay with your kid 24/7 and see how they react to everything, then *you* know" (emphasis his). On the occasions when graft versus host disease (GVHD) took root and caused Jacob's organs to begin failing, he was transferred to the pediatric intensive care unit (PICU) for weeks at a time.[2] During this heightened moment of crisis, the Marins stepped up their surveillance, and traded off twelve-hour shifts from 7 a.m. to 7 p.m., so that one of them would be with Jacob, and awake, both night and day. Savannah told me:

> If there was something funky, Todd would text me, or call me, and be like [gasp] "Oh what's this about," you know? "[What's going on with] his labs, or [what's] this about? This is what they want to change on his meds," and then, if he was like, "I don't think this is right," or whatever, then I could, you know, we would have a conversation about it, so he could advocate for him even when I wasn't there. Because I mean, in the PICU, you know, you have to. Like . . . they are constantly trying to change meds and change schedules on the platelet transfusions, and like, all kinds of stuff.

Being constantly present meant that the Marins remained aware of the minute details of Jacob's treatment (no matter how minor or routine). They could hold providers accountable if they found any of Jacob's care lacking and intervene in, and potentially alter, the care he received. Savannah's perspective on her role in her son's care is clear in the language she uses—Jacob's providers might *try* to change medications or platelet transfusion schedules—but she saw it as her and Todd's role to oversee and approve or disapprove of such changes. Such parental authority and autonomy, particularly among middle- and upper-class parents, are generally assumed and taken for granted. Sociologist Jennifer Reich reminds us that "parents with resources are most able to demand services, more likely to view providers as contributing advice rather than dictating behaviors, and less likely to be reported to state agencies like child protective services."[3] Though expectations of autonomy are more regularly abridged in healthcare settings, the Marins never considered relinquishing this authoritative role in any substantive way.

Holding fast to their sense of parental authority over their child during months of inpatient hospitalization helped them feel that they could protect him from potential medical harm. The Marins told me that by being constantly present they were able to steer Jacob away from medical missteps that would have been made by a provider who wasn't as familiar as they were with Jacob's specific needs and previous reactions. As Todd explained:

> [Jacob's providers] have certain things that they follow too, if they hear something, this is automatically what we do. [But] I already know that Jacob had a negative response to certain things. We had a respiratory therapist come in, for instance, and, "Oh, I heard him doing this, so I'm going to automatically do this." I'm like, "No, you're *not* going to do that, because if you do that, then we're going to have more of a complication, because we've already been through this process before, we already know he doesn't have a good response to this." And if I hadn't done that, and I hadn't been there, it would've just been done. And then we could've had more of a negative thing. (Emphasis his)

Here, Todd was able to spare Jacob discomfort and potential physical setback, and feel efficacious as a parent by directly improving his child's care and quality of life—if only at one particular moment during a long and grueling process.

Todd and Savannah's continuous presence at Jacob's side also allowed them to tailor their interventions to different providers, develop credibility with them, and better weigh the advice of different physicians. Todd explained that because of their close observations, "we knew the intricacies about different doctors too. We knew which doctors were going to be really reserved and really cautious. We knew which ones were going to be more likely to do certain things. So you kind of learned a couple things about the doctors that we were seeing." The Marins used this information to make their efforts to influence Jacob's care more effective.

Vigilant surveillance, then, could be parlayed into influence. Over time, the Marins identified nurses whom they could enlist in their efforts to negotiate with doctors about Jacob's care. As Todd said of these nurses,

> We looked forward to them being on because we knew we didn't have to stress as much or watch every little thing that happened and make sure every, you know, everything was being followed the way it needs to be followed. . . . They just follow their regimen, the way it was supposed to

be, and then they followed instructions. [If] Savannah decided that, you know, Jacob wasn't going to be wearing diapers today, and he was just going to have it a certain way? She would go to report that and they would just do it, they'd just follow through with it . . . and a lot of the nurses would go on the rounds and talk to the doctors and then they would come to us and we would all have a conversation, but if we made it known to these nurses, you know, what we were trying to accomplish that day, they would go in and try to work on our behalf, and then when they came back, you know, we all can compromise, but we could—we could count on them to go and voice whatever our concerns were, and it would get taken care of, where [otherwise] that was not always the case.

The Marins were not pushy or entitled people in general—the sort who might send back a meal because it was not to their liking. They were friendly, laidback, and easygoing overall. But they understood Jacob's care to be a *negotiation* between themselves and their child's doctors, a negotiation in which they should get equal, if not greater, say. Even if they ultimately had to "compromise," Jacob's physicians may need to "compromise" too. Because of their high levels of cultural health capital and middle-class privilege more broadly, they had the credibility to be taken seriously by their child's healthcare team.

The most significant arena of negotiation was around Jacob's medications. Todd and Savannah wanted him to be taken off of damaging medications, like steroids, as quickly as possible. Savannah told me:

I can't tell you how many times we've asked about a medication, and they've, you know, changed it sooner than they would have, or later, or whatever. . . . If you don't ask, then they're just going to keep on going on their schedule, and if [on Unit 27] there's five docs involved and everybody has their own opinion, one doc might have taken that medication off three days ago, the doc that's on right now might not have even seen it on the list. He saw it, but it didn't register. And then the doc next week might be like, "Oh no, he needs to have twice as much!"

Given these differences in opinion across doctors, the Marins used their own judgment to determine what was best and then worked to push providers in the direction they wanted them to go. Savannah explained:

We were like, "Okay, when can we take this off, or when can we take that off?" Like with his steroid wean, we wanted him off steroids as soon as possible, because we know, "Oh, that could have . . . contributed to the bleed in his gut, let's get him off." And of course it contributes to like fluid retention, and high blood pressure and all those other bad things. And immune suppression, and you know, like a lot of things. But then they had to put him back on when he had other surgeries and stuff, so it's like, "Okay then, let's hurry up and get him back off again." And his body, like the last time we took it off, or were getting close to taking it off, when he went from IV to oral [administration of steroids], his body went out of whack and he had adrenal suppression, and adrenal insufficiency. So then all of a sudden his electrolytes went out of whack, his blood pressure dropped and like, got weird fast, so this time we were like, "Okay, well we do want to wean it again, but we're not in a hurry."

Savannah's highly detailed description of the specific biological chain of events that occurred when Jacob went on and off steroids reflected her particularly high levels of cultural health capital. That Savannah was able to converse with doctors at this level likely helped them to see her requests as informed ones, worth consideration. Without this display of exceptional cultural health capital, doctors may have been less willing to make these adjustments. Still, sometimes persistence was required. Todd and Savannah recounted another instance in which their close observation and research led to a medication change. When I asked her if she ever researched the medications she wasn't already familiar with, she exclaimed:

Hell yeah! We check every medication! I'm like, "Oh, this one has a lot of things." And I'm like, "I wonder if [a particular symptom] is from this!" And I'll email to the doctor, I'm like, "Do you think—?" And one instance was Foscarnet; one of the potential side effects could be penile irritation. And he was crying, like up to this point he had, over the previous week or two, he'd been crying intermittently. But we were figuring out more and more, we're like, "I think he's crying when he's peeing! Or just as he's getting ready to start." And the more we were watching the more we're like, "He's crying when he's peeing!" . . . So I look up his Foscarnet, and that's a potential side effect [the crystalization of urine] . . . [but] the doctor that was on during that rotation was like, "No, no, no, no, I've never seen that before." The doctor on the *weekend*, we tell him, like, "He seems to be doing good except for . . . [crying when he's peeing]"

Todd: He just says, "Oh yeah. Well, Foscarnet can do that!" (Emphasis original)

By digging deeper, the Marins gained knowledge that even some of Jacob's doctors lacked. By persistently raising the issue of pain during urination, they advocated for a medication change that helped to reduce their son's ongoing discomfort—and in turn, the emotional pain of watching their child suffer.

I personally witnessed Savanah's influence on Jacob's medication regimen during one of the clinic visits I observed. From my field notes:

Savannah asked about Jacob's vitamin K because, "Everybody's kind of wishy-washy about whether he needs vitamin K anymore." Dr. L said that he's doing well on Vitamin K, but Savannah pointed out that it's a $200 prescription every month, and that he might just "hang out low anyway" [in his Vitamin K levels]. Dr. L suggests that he may be doing better since he's being given some blended food along with breast milk through his feeding tube now, and offers Savannah the option of not giving him Vitamin K for a while and then checking his labs without it. Savannah said, "Yeah, that's what I was wondering."

Later, toward the end of the appointment, Dr. L reiterated, "So we're decreasing the Tachrilymous, hold the Vitamin K, we'll check the coags next week." She warned that even if the numbers were okay, Dr. S [Jacob's primary doctor] might want to keep him on it, but Savannah quickly offered, "No that's great, we can just check it out."

By speaking up, and by speaking knowledgably, comfortably, and confidently in medical lingo, the Marins gained providers' trust. The nurse practitioner even remarked to Savannah while going over his medication list, "You know better than we do [what his current meds and dosages are]." This encouraged the Marins' suggestions to be seriously considered and often agreed to by Jacob's doctors. It also let them signify their ability to hold providers accountable and to actually *hold* them accountable for mistakes when they occurred.

This was another significant advantage the Marins felt they derived from their constant surveillance. They were able, Todd explained, to "catch" problems or mistakes and make sure that things "would get taken care of." Often this just meant making sure that medications were given on time and that his schedule didn't get "off" (meaning that some medications would have to be given later in the night than would be ideal). But on a few occasions the Marins caught what they considered to be "true medication errors," and they were able to either prevent them from happening and/or hold the responsible party accountable for the mistake. Here again, Savannah's medical knowledge enabled her to successfully intervene:

> SAVANNAH: The couple times that he got the wrong dose or . . . was
> going to get the wrong order, like . . . the wrong flush before a med
> or something, it's like, "Okay, *this* is unacceptable" . . . if it [can] es-
> sentially cause a serious issue—
> TODD: We had that [something really serious] happen once. And, that
> one I, I wasn't very happy about that one. Actually went and talked to
> the nurse practitioner and did get them thrown off our team, it was
> just too serious for me to [handle] . . . but that was an instance like,
> if Savannah had not been standing there, that would not have gotten
> caught, and it was a really serious offense. (Emphasis original)

Savannah agreed that Todd would not have known things, "like, 'Oh, that's normal saline versus dextrose flush before a med.'" Savannah considered them lucky that such mistakes had only happened a couple of times during their six-month inpatient hospital stay and added wryly, "is that because we hovered like hawks?" To which, Todd, who was on the floor changing Jacob's diaper, turned to me and responded firmly and confidently: "Yes." The Marins took their role as captains of their child's medical care very seriously, and were clearly proud of what they had accomplished in doing so. Because of their efforts, they were able to prevent medical errors, more quickly reduce their sons' pain and discomfort, and feel good about themselves as parents.

Though Savannah's technical medical knowledge was a significant boon to their efforts, other care-captaining parents with less medical training also intervened to prevent medication errors. For instance, Vivian Patterson, a black mother in her early forties who worked in accounting at a large consumer goods corporation, kept careful records of every medication administered to her seventeen-year-old son, Shawn, when he was hospitalized for a pediatric brain tumor. When a nurse brought in a dose of three pills that Vivian knew should have been four, she called him on it. At first the nurse denied the error, but Vivian proudly told me that he must have gone out and "spoken to someone [who informed him], 'She really is paying attention, she is on the game'" because he came back and "owned up" to the mistake, and administered the fourth pill.

Holding practitioners accountable and, when parents felt it was warranted, getting practitioners who had failed to meet their standards "thrown off the team" helped parents to protect their feelings of confidence in their child's remaining providers and in their own ability to ensure their child received the best possible care. This was critical for maximizing hopefulness and minimizing their fears for their children's futures. Nora Bialy, whose son Benjamin was also hospitalized for a pediatric brain tumor, was deeply upset when an interaction with one of her son's providers threatened her confidence. At the hospital where Benjamin received his initial treatments, a provider came into Ben's room, and as Nora recalled,

> I knew more information than this person did—this person was supposed to know more information than I did—and I told this person not to come into a room unprepared to talk to me ever again. And to this day, that person actually does not come into the room and talk to me at all. . . . I was really upset about it, because I was like, "Oh my gosh." It was, you're at a point where your kid is seriously ill and this is a person who should be making you feel confident when they come in the room and when they're not—like I was just asking too many questions and too many times the answer was "I don't know." Like, "Are you kidding me?! *No.*" That's not, and I finally said it, "That's *not* the right answer! You need to know the answer!" (Emphasis hers)

Nora's increasing indignation as she recalled this incident demonstrates just how emotionally threatening any chinks to the armor of hope could feel. Even if providers' shortcomings or errors would have minor medical consequence for children, they shook the foundation upon which parents were building their hopes. Successfully catching "untrustworthy" practitioners and steering their children (and themselves) away from potential setbacks were points of pride families shared with me. Care-captaining then served not only practical medical ends, but played a key role in families' emotion work for themselves and their children. At the same time, this desire reinforced parents' perceptions that they needed to oversee every aspect of their child's medical care, putting an awfully heavy burden on their shoulders.

Parents with less cultural health capital—primarily poor and working-class parents—were not always so effective if they tried to engage with providers or hold them accountable when problems arose. Though many of the advantages parents gained by care-captaining were small ones, these cases of what I have elsewhere termed "microadvantages" could contribute to a smoother illness experience for children and provide emotional benefits to parents.[4] Catching medication errors might prevent a bad reaction and minimize children's discomfort, while helping parents feel efficacious. Getting access to supplemental therapies might help to reduce the impact of hospitalization on children's physical development, or keep them stronger and more active through lengthy courses of treatment.

Nora Bialy, for instance, requested a feeding tube for Benjamin when she believed that his nutritional status was declining. She guessed that his physicians hadn't proposed this option because "people get freaked out by that." But as a former dietician, she viewed a G-tube (a small tube inserted surgically into the abdomen so that nutrition could be delivered directly into the stomach) as a valuable tool to get more calories into Ben with less discomfort. Radiation burns on Ben's esophagus made swallowing extremely painful. Once on the feeding tube, Ben gained weight and his stamina improved. Clearly, the benefits parents could gain for their children through care-captaining could be quite tangible. But it also offered parents satisfaction and a sense that they had helped to improve their child's odds and ease their suffering.

Yet care-captaining required a lot from parents and could become highly taxing. The Marins devoted themselves entirely to coordinating their son's care, leaving no time for work, social lives, or even much rest. For Todd and Savannah, who were negotiating Jacob's illness together full time, doing so was manageable. For Simone Brady-Fischer, whose husband worked full time and remained home to care for their other children during the months she and her son spent at Kelly-Reed, the toll was even higher without a local support person to share the burden. That Simone consistently adopted a care-captaining approach despite shouldering the majority of the burden on her own further illustrates the important emotional needs it could fill.

Research Junkies: Managing Stress and Anxiety

"I'm a research junkie—or I've become one, since he's been sick," Simone Brady-Fischer told me. A white, forty-year-old, Canadian mother of five and high school graduate, Simone had worked for a local foundation in her hometown before taking a year-long paid medical leave to care for her youngest child, Max. Max was eight years old when a series of seizures led to the diagnosis of a congenital malformation that interfered with the flow of cerebrospinal fluid around his brain. Max, who was eleven years old when I met him and his mother, still suffered from frightening seizures, severe headaches, and a variety of behavioral problems.

During my first formal interview with Simone, Max was singularly focused on assembling a Lego kit that had just arrived in the mail. When Max became frustrated, he demanded that his mom build it for him. A petite woman with wavy dark hair twisted back in a clip on one side and a thick blonde streak on the other, Simone wore jeans, a beaded silver scoop-neck tee, and speckled pink and blue square-framed glasses. Simone and Max affectionately sparred with one another over who exactly was going to assemble the kit. When Simone said she would not build it for him but would help when she was done talking with me, Max groaned and sighed heavily, "I'm gonna have to do it myself. Alright, let's do it the hard way." Max began struggling with the kit while his mom continued our interview, but within thirty minutes Simone was the one deciphering the vague instructions and assembling the Legos. "You're a pain, you know that?" she said to Max. "It's a good thing I love you." "Yes, I love that I'm a pain." Max retorted. "That's just one of my talents." "I know it is," Simone agreed.

Like the Marins, Simone also worked hard to get her son to Kelly-Reed, and she regularly care-captained to influence Max's treatment.

Though Max's neurosurgeon in Canada decided that his case did not warrant surgery to correct the malformation and attributed his seizures and behavioral problems to other causes, Simone was dubious. After doing research that suggested to her that increased intracranial pressure, or pseudotumor (which was ultimately confirmed by a lumbar puncture at Kelly-Reed), might not have been visible on the MRI, Simone sought out a second opinion from doctors at a different top-ranked US research hospital, which offered remote consults. At her own expense she reported:

> We sent his MRI disc, I bought it, like, paid 200 bucks for it behind [the doctor's] back, and then sent $1500 to [a top-ranked US research hospital] and checked off all three of my options, like I could only have one option, but I checked off all three . . . either they send you a report directly, they have a conversation with your [home] physician directly, or you can have a conference call between the three of you, and I checked off all three boxes, and then I wrote beside it, "whichever will get treatment the fastest!" . . . I said, "I don't care what you do, whatever gets us results," and then like, coincidentally . . . within six weeks, after being so adamant that he wasn't doing surgery, we were having surgery [in Canada with the original neurosurgeon who had declined to operate] in eight days.

Simone's ability to do research to find the doctors who offered a second opinion and her comfort in challenging authority reflected the instrumental cultural health capital she deployed on her son's behalf. That she felt empowered to check *all three boxes* and write marginal notes expressing her distress and conveying a sense of urgency to those from whom she sought help was a significant display of comfort in negotiating with institutions and authority figures, which was rooted in her middle-class status and habitus.[5] Doing so also provided her an outlet for the anxiety she felt about her son's illness and an opportunity to feel she was doing something concretely to help him.

Though Simone and her husband, a white sixty-year-old provincial government official, did not have the advantage of Savannah Marin's medical background, they too negotiated with doctors about their child's medications. They were particularly concerned about the psychotropic drugs prescribed to manage Max's symptoms. Simone's narrative demonstrates her view of her and her husband's authoritative role in this process:

> [This physician] tried him on like every psychotic pill *that we would let him try*, basically. There were a few *we said no to* because we did some research, and were like, "Uh, no." Like the side effects potentially could be pretty harmful. [A headache psychiatrist he referred us to] even suggested that we put him on, like, artificial pot for his headaches. He was like eight years old then . . . I'm like, "No! My kid is not taking pot for his headaches!" Like, "What?!" It's bad enough he has to be on a prescription like . . . Tylenol 3 [Tylenol with codeine]. . . . And so we never saw that particular . . . headache psychiatrist . . . that suggested that we use the pot, we never saw him again. (Emphasis mine)

In Simone's view, she and her husband had the ultimate say over which medications Max would take and who would treat him. If they decided that the side effects were too severe (or too unnerving for them), they were willing to say "no" to the doctor. This was a very different approach than that adopted by the parents we will meet in the next chapter, who primarily care-entrusted.

At times, though, doctors gave the Brady-Fischers more or less leeway. When I asked her whether she always got the final say over Max's prescriptions, Simone said:

> Yes and no, Dr. Q is very adamant when he wants Max to try something . . . sometimes I'll agree to try something, and then I'll ask him, "How long do you expect me to give this before I tell you you're full of shit?" . . . So sometimes he'll say, "Well, give it a couple weeks and if it's not, if you don't think it's working, you're just going to do whatever you want anyway." I'm like, "Yeah" [shrugs indifferently]. He's like, "This drug is safe to do that with." He'll tell me if it's not safe to . . . just take him off a medication.

Though Simone conceded that when Max's home doctor was "adamant" that she try a medication she didn't just say "no," she presented herself as very comfortable in challenging him, and presented the physician as acquiescent to her ultimate ability to "do whatever she wants anyway."

In this way, Simone saw herself as having some degree of control over Max's illness and treatment, which may have been essential to her ability to cope with what was otherwise a frighteningly unpredictable situation.

Simone's care-captaining intensified as Max's headaches and seizures worsened. Still unsatisfied with the treatment Max was receiving in their home province in Canada and increasingly stressed by his progressing symptoms, Simone told me that she went to "every website that was reputable" and "listened to hours and hours of doctoral lectures, like from specialists [in this particular condition], online. And then after I listened to Dr. J's lecture, I knew he was the right doctor, 'cause Max's symptoms all fit what he specialized in, so I knew he was just the right one."

When I asked Simone, who acknowledged that there is "lots of crap out there on the Internet," how she identified "reputable websites" or distinguished good information from bad, she had a hard time articulating her thought process beyond telling me that "you have to definitely use your judgment." Yet she explained that when one of Max's doctors in Canada had challenged her online research, stressing the importance of making sure she read "reliable resources," she had retorted, "Oh, and would you consider the Mayo Clinic to be a reliable resource?" Simone reported that the doctor had to sheepishly admit that he would. Thus, not only is the impulse to *do* one's own independent research an important intangible component of cultural health capital, but the knowledge of what sources of information are either reliable or prestigious enough to be taken seriously is similarly taken for granted. Simone doesn't know *how* she knows that the Mayo Clinic's website will be respected by her child's doctor, she just "knows" that it will.[6] This automatic understanding of the hierarchies of prestige and resources within the healthcare system helped her to be successful in her care-captaining efforts because, as with Savannah's medical knowledge, it encouraged physicians to take her input seriously. Crucially, it also helped her to feel better about the care her son would receive as a result of her interventions. Parents who were less certain about hospital rankings and reputations sometimes felt unsure about whether they had obtained the best possible care for their children even after they had accessed treatment at Kelly-Reed, and this uncertainty exacerbated their feelings of anxiety for their children's health. For parents like Simone, the prestige of the hospital and physicians treating her son was a comforting victory.

After a lengthy weekend phone consult with Dr. J, a pediatric neurosurgeon at Kelly-Reed, Simone began fundraising over social media to help cover the entirely out-of-pocket costs of obtaining treatment in the United States as an international patient. The Brady-Fischers were required to wire over $9,000 to cover the initial estimated costs of Max's evaluation and treatment at Kelly-Reed before an appointment could be booked. After arriving and having her son's dangerously elevated intracranial pressure confirmed as she had suspected, Simone finally felt that Max was receiving the care he needed. She mentioned that Max was currently taking a medication she had concerns about, an issue she raised with Dr. J when she came to Kelly-Reed. But Dr. J had persuasively suggested that he take it for a while longer:

> There's one medication I really want him off of, and I've asked Dr. J already to take him off of it, and he said, "I don't want to do too many changes at once *because*, um, we won't really know what's working and what's not then." Which, okay! You gave me a *reason*. At home, I would have just gotten, "Just give him this medication and don't ask me any questions." He's given me a *reason* to keep Max on that medication right now. So I'll keep him on it for a little while. But I told Dr. P [Max's Kelly-Reed neurologist] again today, "I really want him off that medication." (Emphasis hers)

Although Simone strongly and repeatedly requested to stop a medication she disliked after getting to Kelly-Reed, she accepted the opinion of the prestigious doctors she trusted and the rationale for why he should stay on it for a while longer. Simone felt better about Max being on medications she had reservations about when the recommendation came from a physician she held in high-esteem and when she was given "a reason" that made sense to her. Accessing elite care—and the symbolic meanings attached to it—helped Simone to feel greater confidence in the care her son was receiving and helped to reduce her anxiety about his treatment.

Simone also found reassurance in her belief that she had the potential to hold providers publicly accountable if needed. When doctors at Kelly-Reed suggested that Max get ongoing treatment at an elite children's treatment center in Canada, but outside of her home province,

I asked Simone what had to be done for her home province insurance plan to cover it. She told me that "they have to approve it or not," but told me confidently:

> If they don't, I'm going to make a big stink in the media about it. CBC, in Canada, is like the equivalent of CNN down here. They're already all over his story on Facebook. They want to interview me, like, in the worst way. But I want to go up the ladder in the right way, because, in the end, these two negligent doctors—'cause don't kid yourself, he's not the only kid going through this at the hands of these doctors, these two doctors need to be called up by the college of physicians in Canada, and [told], "Hey!" Like, "Take this shit seriously, and now pay for his suffering that has happened."

As I chatted with Simone in the following weeks, she regularly reiterated that she was going to "make them pay" and spoke about the lawsuit she planned to bring once they were back home and Max had access to the care he needed. While Simone quashed her immediate desire to go to the press, calculating that trying to "go up the ladder in the right way" first might get her the quickest results, she could manage her stress and reduce her fear and anxiety that her son's access to the particular care she wanted for him was not guaranteed by planning to take steps to hold her province's health bureau publicly accountable if they did not approve her request. She also expressed a desire to hold the doctors she felt had not adequately treated her son accountable for what she deemed to be subpar care. In her view, their irresponsible actions had led to unnecessary pain and suffering for her child and might hurt other children and families in the future.[7] Importantly, Simone not only felt comfortable questioning and challenging a prestigious professional's competency, but also possessed a basic understanding of how to report them, to whom, and what consequences she might be able to create for them. These are all important, intangible components of cultural health capital, born of resources derived from her solidly middle-class status.

The intensity of Simone's anxiety for her son was particularly apparent during an appointment for a second lumbar puncture at Kelly-Reed—which I observed—to evaluate a new medication's effectiveness in reducing Max's intracranial pressure. When Simone learned that Max was not going to receive general anesthesia (full sedation) prior to the procedure, she was very concerned that anything less would be too painful for Max to tolerate. She insisted to the nurse that "Dr. J did want him to be [fully] sedated for the procedure" and forcefully told her, "He has a *very* high tolerance for medications" (emphasis hers). The nurse told Simone that she could discuss the medications Max would receive with the "physician in charge today." When this doctor came in to speak with us, he offered Simone the option of rescheduling the procedure so that Max could be fully sedated, but gently encouraged her to consider moderate sedation instead. The doctor gave her a detailed explanation of the drugs they would use (Dexmedetomidine and Ketamine), outlined the physiological effects of each, and explained that the advantage over general sedation was that no airway support would be required. Simone began to soften toward this idea, but asked, "What are the risks if he moves during the LP?" The doctor assured her that the risks were not severe and that they often performed LPs on "uncooperative" patients.

After a few more questions about what Max might feel during the procedure, and reassurance that he would not feel much, if anything, Simone consented. Max did require a number of nurses to hold him down as he resisted the initial shot of Ketamine, but he quickly drifted off while an IV was placed. Simone relaxed a bit while we watched him move slowly through the MRI he was scheduled for before the lumbar puncture was performed. But she became visibly nervous and on edge afterward, as we stood out in the hall while the neurosurgical team entered and positioned Max for the procedure. "This is the part I'm most worried about," Simone told me. "I can't watch," she said, and stepped back to a set of chairs on the opposite side of the hallway. A few moments later, Simone rushed to the bathroom to vomit. When she returned, hopeful that the procedure was over, she asked me anxiously, "Has he been quiet? Did he scream?" I told her that he hadn't moved a muscle. Simone seemed to exhale with her entire body

When Dr. J, who had been paged to perform the short surgical procedure himself, emerged, he reported that Max's intracranial pressure was significantly reduced (confirming that the new medication was working). Simone was surprised, given Max's ongoing seizures, but thanked him profusely and told him she would cry when she got home that night, "a cry of relief." Dr. J put his arm around her, telling her, "I know it's been very challenging and there are no easy answers." He promised to call as soon as he reviewed the MRI images.

Though the families I met—whether they care-captained or care-entrusted—generally "kept it together" and remained tightly focused on the immediate tasks involved in coordinating care and planning next steps (from the next appointment or consult to what to do for dinner), Simone's embodied anxiety during Max's procedure reveals the depth and power of the emotions that course just beneath the surface. For care-captaining parents, the broader context of fear and uncertainty could be made more tolerable in part by intervening in ways that could—at least in theory—hurry along the hoped-for resolution. Simone's relentless efforts to seek better and more promising options for her son hint at this underlying dynamic. She could not bear to leave any stone uncovered if hope for her son's improvement might be lurking beneath it. As Simone had joked, she was a "junkie," and care-captaining was her addiction.

Simone admitted that she often couldn't sleep due to her worries about Max. It was during these sleepless nights that she stayed up for hours doing research on doctors, treatments, and international care options. Sociologist Jacqueline Clark's study of breast cancer support groups found that middle class women's information-seeking and online research helped them to manage the fear and anxiety they felt about their futures by becoming "lay-experts" on their disease.[8] The research care-captaining parents did was instrumental not only in helping them to access care but also in managing the emotional upset sparked by frightening diagnoses.

But sleep deprivation took its toll. More than once, Simone caught herself nodding off while driving, until she hit the shoulder or someone honked at her. Eventually, she recounted, "My husband dragged me to my family doctor 'cause I was like slurring, and walking like a drunk person." Simone's physician put her on anti-anxiety medications to help her cope.

Navigating a child's serious illness, no matter how much cultural health capital one possesses, is a massive undertaking. It is an enormous amount of work for parents, and care-captaining requires exceptional commitments of time and resources, stretching even families with significant financial resources to the max. This can wear heavily on already profoundly stressed family members. That parents like Todd, Savannah, and Simone sustained such efforts for long periods of time speaks to the important emotional as well as practical functions those efforts serve. Despite the time and energy required, care-captaining can help parents feel a degree of control over frightening and uncertain circumstances. It pushes families to actively seek—and sometimes find—new possibilities on which to pin their hopes, providing them with a path for moving forward. For some parents, cord blood–derived stem-cell transplantation at a highly ranked state-of-the-art facility can be, returning to the metaphor of hope as a rope flung into the horizon, the hook they need to anchor their hopes and pull themselves and their child toward safety.[9]

Keeping Calm and One Step Ahead

A sunny late-spring afternoon at the Ronald McDonald House can be something of a homecoming. A young Puerto Rican couple in their early-thirties, Edward Rivera and Juliana Cruz already knew many of the staff at the house from the eight months they had stayed there two years earlier. I had heard stories about the fantastic meals Edward, a restaurant owner, had cooked and shared with everyone. This time, in addition to their daughter, four-year-old Sophie—a plucky girl with bouncy ringlets and lots of energy—they brought their brand-new infant son, Noah. Noah was a happy, mellow baby with big brown eyes who sucked his pacifier serenely in his infant car seat while his parents reminisced with the staff and passersby cooed at him.

Both Sophie and Noah were born with a rare genetic condition that kept them from producing an enzyme needed for neurological function and normal physical development. Without stem-cell transplantation, they were unlikely to live for more than a few years. When Edward and Juliana learned that Noah, too, had inherited the disease, they once again left their home in Puerto Rico, Juliana's job in a pharmaceutical laboratory, and the two restaurants Edward owned and managed to travel to the United States for the transplant. They were hopeful that the outcome would be as successful for Noah as it had been for their now happy and healthy little girl.

I got to know the Rivera-Cruzes over the next few weeks while they settled in at the Ronald McDonald House before Noah was admitted to begin the process of transplantation. Ten days after Noah's cord blood transplant, I visited the Rivera-Cruzes on Unit 27. Juliana sat perched with one leg tucked underneath her on the edge of the full-sized hospital bed that dwarfed three-month-old Noah. Noah was nestled against a pillow and tucked under a colorful fleece blanket. An oxygen mask on a long plastic accordion-style tube, strapped to a tightly rolled receiving blanket to hold it in place on the mattress, rested a few inches away from his face. Juliana, who had been sleeping at the hospital for several weeks by this point, wore a gray hooded sweatshirt, black and white striped leggings, and a pair of squarish tortoise-shell-rimmed glasses. Her straight, light brown shoulder length hair was pulled loosely back, but fell across her forehead each time she leaned over to comfort Noah when he squished up his face to cry. She kissed him and assured him, "Oh, *yo se mi amor*. I know baby, I know. I'm here with you." When Noah looked particularly pained, Juliana pressed the nurse call button on the bed's side rail, and the nurse came in for a "button push," sending a dose of intravenous pain medication into Noah's central thoracic line.[10] When his pulse oximeter beeped (because his blood-oxygen saturation dropped below 90 percent), Juliana calmly picked Noah up and cradled him in one arm while she held the oxygen mask over his nose and mouth with the other until his blood-oxygen levels rose again.

Though Juliana had no medical training, she was entirely at ease participating fully in Noah's care. She swabbed his mouth regularly with a fluffy green sponge on a stick to combat his mucositis (a painful oral side effect of chemotherapy) and to prevent infection and bleeding. She kept careful track of how much breast-milk he consumed, pumping and bottle-feeding in measured ounces in order to do so. She directly requested pain medication whenever she deemed it necessary.

Juliana had beefed up her cultural health capital years earlier, when Sophie was first suspected of having mucopolysaccharidosis (also known as MPS, or Hurler's Syndrome), a rare, usually fatal genetic metabolic disorder that was also passed on to Noah. When Juliana first heard this, she told me, "I was in shock. I said, 'What is she talking about!?'" The neurologist she had taken Sophie to see because of her developmental concerns encouraged her not to mention this terrible hypothesis to the geneticist with whom she had an appointment later that day. But Juliana, a first-time mother with bachelor's degrees in both chemistry and mechanical engineering, "was afraid." As soon as the geneticist saw Sophie,

Juliana told me, "he already knew that she has the syndrome" because of its unique facial features and spinal curvature. It would be several weeks before genetic testing, express-mailed from the Rivera-Cruz family's home doctors in Puerto Rico to the United States, confirmed the diagnosis. During the wait, Juliana told me: "I was searching online [before the appointment with the doctor to get the results and go over treatment options] . . . and I was like, oh, freaking out! But, you know, *I stayed calm in that way too*, [because] I knew about the cord blood transplant [before the appointment]" (emphasis mine). Though Sophie's neurologist ultimately informed them of the possibility of a cord blood transplant at Kelly-Reed—making Juliana's research less instrumental than others' in getting them access to life-saving care—learning that there was hope for potentially saving her daughter while they waited on the official diagnosis helped Juliana to manage her anxiety, plan for major upheaval in their lives, and find some "calm" in a moment of terror.[11] Doing research allowed Juliana to do something that helped her cope, gave her reason to have hope, and let her feel a greater sense of control over the situation.

It also gave Juliana and her husband, Edward, a chance to develop a basic understanding of what their options were and the pros and cons of each prior to meeting with the doctor. Even before the official results came back, Juliana already knew from her research that there were only a few hospitals in the United States offering the transplant for MPS and that Kelly-Reed would likely be the best option. She told me that she brought all of the information she had gathered to that next appointment. When the doctor told her there were two possible treatments—the other being enzyme replacement therapy—she was able to immediately agree with the doctor, who recommended the transplant, because she had been "reading about that" as well, and "already knew that enzyme replacement doesn't work on the brain." In this way, the doctor confirmed the information they gathered and reassured them that a cord blood transplant was the best option in his opinion. They began the process of admitting Sophie to Kelly-Reed immediately.

The thought of spending six months away from their friends and family in Puerto Rico was still overwhelming, but Edward and Juliana were able to brace themselves for this possibility while they waited for results. As Juliana put it: "[It was] that, [or] if you don't do it, your girl must die. At the age of five. So, if you have a balance [Juliana gestured her hands in the air as if weighing on an imaginary scale], you say, 'Oh, *we need to do it*'" (emphasis hers). The Rivera-Cruz family traveled to the United States to begin Sophie's pre-transplant work-up just two weeks later. Though it was a long and grueling process, Sophie had come through the transplant beautifully, was fully recovered and developing well, and could now serve as a poster child for the miraculous potential of stem-cell transplantation for her baby brother, Noah.

When Dr. Coleman, who was on rotation the afternoon I stopped by to visit Noah and Juliana, came through on rounds, he was delighted to see Noah's engraftment rash appearing "right on schedule." This accounted for Noah's increasing discomfort, but meant that his body was accepting the donor stem cells, which were beginning to grow and multiply. The transplant was proceeding smoothly. Unfortunately, there was a rough road to come for Noah, one that we will return to in the chapters ahead.

For the Rivera-Cruzes, the ability to verify physicians' treatment recommendations with their own independent research helped them to make confident decisions, brace themselves for the massive upheaval they would bring, and move swiftly. Participating intimately in Noah's medical care allowed Juliana to enact her deep love and care for her son, as it had for Todd and Savannah. Care-captaining provided an outlet through which Juliana, like Simone, could channel her anxiety, though for Juliana, its effects appeared to be more effectively soothing. Juliana had the benefit of one successfully recovered child under her belt already when I met her, which also helped to bolster her hopes that Noah, too, would be okay, even if it took a great deal of time and dedication to get there.

Physician's Perspectives on Care-Captaining

In their 1998 ethnography of two neonatal intensive care units, Carol Heimer and Lisa Staffen found that parents who questioned providers, requested changes, or hovered over their children were often seen as "pains in the neck."[12] Battles around who was responsible for children's care and medical decision-making could lead to conflict between parents and providers and "some pushing and shoving over where one party's responsibilities end and the other's begin."[13] This was especially the case when parents attempted to get involved in directing medical care, rather than simply participating in dressing, bathing, or feeding children. I expected to hear similar frustrations from the physicians I interviewed about being second-guessed and constantly pestered by care-captaining parents. I was surprised when, a year after wrapping up my initial fieldwork, I returned to interview the physicians on Unit 27 and they told me that they actually *preferred* parents who regularly care-captained. They quickly agreed that parents who did so could gain tangible medical benefits for their children.

Of course, at its most basic level, the primary advantage care-captaining parents could gain was getting their children access to the highly specialized expertise and novel technologies available at hospitals like Kelly-Reed. Dr. Vogel, a petite athletic white woman in her sixties who had served for years as the head of the pediatric transplant program, told me:

> Parents reach out to me from afar, and say, "I've been told this or that, I've been told whatever isn't an option, do you think that's true?" And usually we have options that their home doctors might just not know about. . . . You know, half of our referrals come from a family, not from a doctor. And a lot of the referrals are families whose doctors said, "No, there's nothing you can do," and they get in touch with us or another center anyway. A lot of the families that are considering coming here are talking to every center in the country, and comparing notes. . . . I do think in general, families that do research probably get better access to higher quality care.

Physicians also recognized that care-captaining could provide children with advantages even after families got to Kelly-Reed. Dr. Vogel admitted: "I mean there definitely have been times when parents brought things to our attention that were important, or options for their kids that we wouldn't have thought of that at least were viable options." Dr. Fadian, a stout jovial white man in his fifties who had been overseeing pediatric stem-cell transplants for over twenty-five years, recognized this as well. He recalled a mother who was "doing all kinds of PubMed searches and came up with a medication to try in a certain clinical scenario we were in with her son. Has very few patient reports on it. But yeah, there, every once in a while, the parents do come up with something that is really helpful. . . . A lot of parents do do PubMed searches, and [there have] been scenarios where it's actually been helpful."

Even when care-captaining occurred in smaller everyday ways, physicians viewed it as important and took parents' input seriously. Dr. Newell, a white woman in her late thirties who had completed her fellowship with the pediatric transplant program six years earlier and then joined the team as one of the primary attending physicians, explained:

> Parents who are invested are invaluable to the care of the child because you get a much clearer picture of what is going on. Obviously you can trust that they're compliant with medications and with treatments, so you just have a better sense of how the child is truly doing, how they're truly responding to treatment. . . . They're in that room 24/7 with the child, so they are going to be the ones who say, "Something's off." And certainly there's been times when I've made medical decisions based on the fact that Mom says, or Dad says, "She's just not acting right."

Dr. Newell's language here is revealing. Framing medically involved parents as "invested" indicates that care-captaining conveys parents' commitment to their children most clearly to physicians. In a different study of physicians caring for pediatric cancer patients, sociologist Elizabeth Gage-Bouchard similarly found that physicians appreciated parents who used an interactional style akin to care-captaining, which she calls "vigilant advocacy," because although these parents were demanding, their demands were seen as "appropriate."[14] Within the contemporary healthcare context, intense participation in the medical arena by patients and caregivers has taken on new meanings. Yet because care-captaining requires so many largely class-based resources to accomplish successfully, poor and working-class parents are at a significant disadvantage in demonstrating such investment, as we will see in the next chapter.

But Dr. Newell points to the practical medical benefits parents who are able to constantly monitor their children's health and communicate effectively with physicians about their observations could obtain as well. Since all six physicians cared for one another's primary patients when they took their turn on "service" on Unit 27, this was especially important. Dr. Fadian explained that he appreciated parents who could bring him up to speed if he hadn't seen their child for some time. "You know if I was here in the [outpatient] clinic and I haven't seen this kid in two months, the parents will fully relay his history." Parents with less cultural health capital who primarily care-entrusted may not have recognized that they could or should play this role when the rounding physician came into the room.

Beyond these "additive" components of care-captaining, several of the doctors noted that care-captaining parents could prevent medication errors. Dr. Fadian explained: "We don't have many, fortunately, but the parents again are part of the team, and they're picking up on things. . . . It helps keep the nurse, keeps everybody on the . . . I don't know if I'd use the word 'on their toes,' but more 'in tune' to make sure things are right, which they need to be." Dr. Coleman, a tall, trim white man in his fifties who served as medical director for the transplant program, also viewed parents' efforts to negotiate medication dosages as advantageous for children. Dr. Coleman explained that he, more than some of his colleagues, wanted to actively reduce medications after transplant:

I very much value those parents who are of the same mindset of, you know every Monday, Monday's my clinic day, so every Monday, "What medicines can we stop? What medicines can we wean?" Because that's, that's how I want [to proceed], and not all the practitioners are of the same mindset, not all the physicians. So a lot of times if I've done my two weeks [on Unit 27 and away from clinic] or been at a conference and I come back, I mean this past Monday I'd come back and I'd expected a kid to be weaned last week when I was away at a conference. And I came back: wasn't weaned. Um, "Why not?" "Didn't think of it." You know? "But we're weaning every week. If there's not symptoms, active symptoms of GVH, we wean." And so that's when a parent can be a good partner, because they'll be the ones who say, "What are we weaning this week? What can we get rid of?" This med, this fifteen medicines, "What can we get rid of today?" So [that's] when parents, and the adolescent patients, can be very big advocates.

Physicians admitted that they found care-captaining to be problematic if taken to an extreme, or done badly. Several recalled parents who were administering alternative treatments or supplements, which could be dangerous if parents were not completely transparent with physicians about these interventions, given the potential for interactions with other medications. But overall, they found such instances to be few and far between. On the whole, physicians valued not only the medical benefits care-captaining could produce, but also recognized its emotional advantages—for both patients and themselves. "A lot of our parents are pretty up on things," Dr. Fadian told me.

> A lot of them read a lot, and know a lot, and actually I enjoy it. . . . They're part of the team, and everything has a reason why we're doing it. And we want you to know why we're doing it and how we're doing it. So you know, we can all work together . . . because even if you do everything right, transplants don't always work out good. And so in that sense, the [medically involved] parents, they understand, this is where we're at in 2014. And it's where medicine is . . . and that way they understand we're doing everything we know to do. And so I guess if they're involved and they understand, there's less, I don't wanna use the word 'frustration,' but there's more [a] sense of closure because you know that they understand what's going on.

In Dr. Fadian's view, there were fewer opportunities for misunderstandings when parents had a higher level of technical comprehension of their child's medical situation and the limits of medical knowledge. This seemed to him to provide a better foundation from which to approach moments when transplants were failing and children were dying. This was not an infrequent occurrence, so cultivating relationships with parents that could weather bad outcomes could help doctors feel better about these situations and smooth interactions with families at these difficult times as well.

Though all the physicians I spoke with told me they preferred care-captaining in general, they cautioned that it could become an undue burden on parents if taken too far. Dr. Newell explained that in her view,

> I don't want the parents to get so bogged down in details that (a) they can't function and (b) they are not able to be there for their child in a sense. Because that can be not healthy. It can be not healthy for the child

in the sense that they have a parent who is, you know, focusing on all these details and not able to sleep, and may not be playing with the child because they are so busy looking [at the monitor]. . . . And most of the time that's not the case, but there is a line where it is not a healthy thing for the parent because they need to be the parent. They don't need to be the doctor or the nurse. They are the only one who can specialize in the parenting of that child. That is their most important job and one job that none of us can fill. Um, so as long as the child remains the focus and it is a healthy balance, then it's a benefit . . . [but] if we're having to spend hours in the room going over every single [thing], that can take away from other families or, you know . . . I want to make sure that we are not just, you know, looking at every single tree when there is a forest.

Similarly, Dr. Fadian articulated his observation that parents' care-captaining could become a problem if they "are just into minutia. I mean they just keep coming up with things, [and it] actually impedes medical care, because you're spending a lot of time talking about stuff that's really of no clinical consequence. But they don't know that, the difference. Or sometimes they'll do that, they'll direct their attention to minutia because they don't want to deal with the big problem. You know, their child's got a life threatening infection, right? And they know it."

Physicians recognized then that parents' fears and anxieties were also driving their efforts to intervene. Because of this, physicians saw going with parents' requests when they deemed them reasonable to be a way to *help* parents accomplish their emotion work. Dr. Ravipati, a slender Indian man in his fifties, explained frankly, "Their perception about certain things [does] make us do things differently. But a lot of times it is more to help them cope with it and us finding that, 'Okay if we do this it's not going to hurt.'" Similarly, Dr. Newell told me: "If it's a decision that truthfully you could choose one medicine or the cousin, you know, Advil or Tylenol—it totally doesn't matter. Those are just decisions that are fine to make, and are fine to give to the parents, or at least let them, listen to them strongly, sometimes. And that could be helpful for families." Dr. Vogel was adamant that if parents' requests were misguided, she would not concede, but suggested that doing so when the "correct" decision was murky served its own purpose:

Some parents micromanage things, and negotiate medication doses and things, to an absurd point, where they don't know what they're doing, and they're actually getting in the way of their child's care. . . . And I'm older, I've done it a long time, I don't have any problem sitting down with a family and saying, "You know, I know where you're coming from and I know why you're worried, but this isn't the right decision and I'm not going to let you make us do that. It's actually getting in the way of what we think is the right way to care for your kid." [But] on the other hand, sometimes nobody knows. So what's the difference? Don't make it a battle, you know? . . . There are times when the parent's right, because they know their kid better than we do. There are times when we're right, there are times when nobody's right or nobody's wrong. We just have to figure it out and do the best [we] can.

Dr. Vogel, recognizing the emotional benefits for parents when they felt efficacious in helping their children and the emotional dynamics underlying parents' efforts to intervene, prioritized parents' wishes at times when she herself did not feel that there was a clear "best choice." Accepting parents' input at these times may also have helped *physicians* to make tough choices and to feel better about the choices they made. In the context of medical uncertainty, parents' requests could provide physicians with a concrete data point to tip the scales when they themselves were in difficult decision-making positions. At such moments, choosing option X over option Y could at least have the known benefit of pleasing family members and helping them feel better. This may have helped physicians perform a bit of emotion work for themselves, as they coped with the high stakes of making decisions that impacted the survival of the children in their care.

That parents—especially middle-class parents—increasingly see themselves as "experts" regarding their children and feel entitled to the final word on medical decisions may not be as highly valued by physicians in other contexts. In Jennifer Reich's research on parents who refuse or renegotiate children's vaccination schedules, for instance, the fact that "parents see themselves as experts based on what feels true for their families" is not particularly appreciated by well-children's physicians.[15] But in the context of children living with serious, life-threatening illness, families' possession of a decent amount of cultural health capital and a willingness to care-captain can benefit children, parents, and physicians alike in multiple ways. It can smooth interactions between patients and physicians because it allows parents to "do parenthood"[16] in a way physicians understand, helps physicians feel they can communicate more clearly, and regularly produces concrete advantages physicians recognize. Physicians feel more confident that if a child's health deteriorates, parents will understand why and be less likely to blame them for this failure.

Care-captaining is not infallible: it comes at a cost to parents of the investment of even more time and energy during an exceptionally stressful moment in their lives, and it can sometimes backfire. Todd and Savannah Marin admitted that during one of Jacob's stints in the PICU they hemmed and hawed for so long about whether or not to consent to intubation for mechanical ventilation that they could have prevented him from receiving what turned out to be a life-saving intervention in time.[17] But on the whole, parents' care-captaining often got children better care, could minimize suffering, and helped parents to present themselves as devoted parents and "partners in care" to their child's providers. Parents with less cultural health capital could not do this quite so easily or successfully, as we will see in the chapter ahead.

4

Care-Entrusting

Staying on the Medical Sidelines

I trust their judgment. If they say, 'No, don't take this [medi-
cation] no more?' Okay. She doesn't need it anymore.
—Jeanetta Moore, mother of five-year-old Kaelyn

Unlike the families in the previous chapter who regularly worked to
steer their children's health care in the directions they deemed best,
the families I introduce next generally felt most comfortable turning
the helm over to providers and letting them determine the appropriate treatment plans for their children. Poor and working-class families
in particular tended to almost exclusively care-entrust, lacking the
resources many families in the previous chapter were able to invest in
regular care-captaining. Families who primarily care-entrusted tended
to devote their caregiving efforts to nonmedical matters instead. Believing their children's medical team was best equipped to see their children
safely through to the best possible outcome could let families without
much cultural health capital feel hopeful that everything was going to
be okay in the end. Sometimes however, care-entrusting families who
lacked cultural health capital weren't able to communicate effectively
with their children's providers and were left with a murkier understanding of their child's treatment or health status at any given time.

Providers who recognized this dynamic voiced concerns about parents who care-entrusted during key moments they considered particularly treacherous. At times, they interpreted care-entrusting as a lack
of interest. This could lead to more challenging interactions between
parents and physicians, and increase worry and concern on all sides.
Nonetheless, although care-entrusting, like care-captaining, had pitfalls,
it generally provided families without much cultural health capital or
other class-based resources required to effectively care-captain an alter-

native strategy for managing anxiety and generating hope throughout their child's illness and treatment process.

Deferring to the Doctors: "If That's What You Think Is Best . . . Then I Will Do It"

I was at the front desk the night Lakira Harris and her eight-year-old son, Jayden Lacoste, arrived, shivering in heavy winter jackets and laden with bags and suitcases. A black thirty-two-year-old single mother of four, Lakira was tall, slim, and quick with friendly banter to put everyone around her at ease. Lakira and Jayden, fresh from their southeastern home state hundreds of miles from Kelly-Reed, were floored by the cold weather. A few months later, Lakira, who wore her dark curly hair long and favored sandals and sundresses, looked sunny and radiant when I visited them on Unit 27. But on that first night at the house, though her affability shone through as she expressed her gratitude that they had "made it this far," she teared up easily. It was clear that the travel, sudden change of climate, and anticipation of the daunting treatment ahead had taken a toll. Jayden, a sweet, sheepishly charming and playful boy with close-cropped hair and a quick wit of his own (the nurses on Unit 27 would soon speculate openly about what a "heart-breaker" he would be one day), looked tired as well, but eagerly scampered off to make construction-paper penguins with the evening activity group while I helped Lakira get settled.

Jayden was diagnosed with a severe case of sickle-cell disease before he was born and had been in and out of hospitals with vasso-occlusive crises (the obstruction of vessels by sickled red blood cells) ever since. But unlike the routinely care-captaining Marins, Brady-Fischers, or Rivera-Cruzes, Lakira had not researched doctors and treatments across the country (or globe) in order to "decide" to come to Kelly-Reed. Like the Hendersons, she simply followed her local physician's referrals. Only through a physician's efforts to seek more advanced treatment options for Jayden did she learn of the possibility of cord blood–derived stem-cell transplantation at Kelly-Reed. She explained:

> Dr. B called me one day and told me that there was an opening for Kelly-Reed, and that they had, uh, research money for stem-cell research. And

he asked me if I wanted to go, because he felt like it was best for Jayden, in his case, best for him to go. And um, I prayed about it, and I was like, "If that's what you think is best for my child, then I will do it." And that's how we got here. It was all the doctors rooting for me and my son.

Getting to Kelly-Reed was easier said than done. As a single mother with no one to come with her to care for Jayden's siblings at the Ronald McDonald House while Lakira stayed on Unit 27 (a hospital requirement), Lakira had to arrange for her other children (separated under this arrangement) to live with friends or relatives while she was away. Financially, Lakira had few resources to begin with, and even fewer since "quitting" her job as a security guard due to Jayden's frequent hospitalizations. This meant she couldn't afford to fly Jayden's siblings up for visits and didn't see them for months at a time. But Lakira repeatedly told me that she would do whatever it took to get Jayden better. She explained that living with Jayden's illness meant living "on pins and needles. Pins and needles. Every time he got sick. Every time somebody in my house got sick." Lakira felt trapped in an endless cycle of her son's hospitalizations and constantly feared the next minor event that might escalate into a major health crisis. Getting Jayden to Kelly-Reed was a profoundly emotional victory for her in these early days. "From the time he was born, I was praying for a miracle" she told me:

> 'Cause I didn't want to lose my baby [Lakira teared up, dabbing her eyes with a tissue]. Every year I saw on the news, they were coming up with new research. And then, one year um, it was an older boy that went through the bone marrow transplant and he succeeded. And, I was jumping up like that was my child, and I was like, "Jayden, they found a cure!" [Lakira began to choke up.] And I was like, "I wanna be a part of that" [Her voice shook as she began to cry.] And I'm just so happy that he's here [whispering, as her voice cracked]. I mean, I had to leave my family, I had to sacrifice a lot of things. My education, my job, you know? But it's all well worth it. To see my baby healthy. And to see that he can have a normal life? I'm so happy [whispered, sobbing.]

The following week I accompanied Lakira and Jayden to their patient education session prior to the transplant—a meeting during which a nurse coordinator spent two hours going over the consent forms, risks, and treatment protocols with her. A stem-cell transplant was the only way to "cure" sickle-cell disease, the nurse explained. Lakira nodded, indicating she understood this. The alternative, the nurse reminded her, was to continue with blood transfusions "which he may need for many, many years," or other treatments. But there is "no other *cure* for sickle cell— that's why you're here today." The nurse continued providing detailed explanations of each step of the transplant process, and described several of the medications used, along with their potential side effects. Lakira nodded and "mhmmed," and voiced occasional awe at some of the more unusual medications—for instance, anti-thymocyte globulin, which is derived from the antibodies of rabbits or horses—as the nurse continued her overview of the process. But she asked few substantive questions. After the nurse finished going over the many pages of three different institutional review board (IRB) protocols and consent forms that would be sent home with her so that Lakira could examine them closely before they were to be signed at a meeting with Dr. Ravipati later in the week, she warned her that some parts would be "a tough read": those that explained the potentially fatal risks of the procedure. Lakira assured the nurse that she planned to become "a spokesperson for other parents" who might be "afraid to do this because they're afraid of losing their child."[1]

Though Lakira expressed little but confidence and optimism to the nurse during the education session, she had lingering questions that she did not voice. While we walked to Jayden's next appointment, she remarked that I had "asked some really good questions." She also asked me if understood a component of the protocol she was unclear about, revealing that her acceptance of the nurse's explanations was in part a performance: Lakira did not want to admit to the nurse that she had not fully understood, but was willing to ask me privately afterward. Lakira was not uninterested in understanding the details of her son's treatment, but may not have felt comfortable appearing to medical professionals as failing to understand them. This did not seem to weigh heavily on her, though, as she viewed the medical professionals who were treating her child as the ones in charge and her own role as that of Jayden's cheerleader from the sidelines.

Still, Lakira didn't have as strong a grasp of the medical details involved in Jayden's transplant as the families in the previous chapter had on their children's treatments. She kept all the paperwork she was given regarding the trial protocols and medications Jayden was receiving in a plastic file tub she purchased for this purpose. When I asked her questions about something, Lakira might sort through the tub and hand me a sheet of paper in an attempt to offer an answer. But she generally expressed a sense of being overwhelmed by all of this information. Though this didn't concern her on a daily basis, her lack of clarity did start to trouble her on the day of Jayden's transplant.

The transplant—which involved a series of infusions of the donor cord blood over a period of about eight hours while Jayden colored, played games, or watched television—began with a celebratory mood. Lakira posed for photos with Jayden, who reluctantly held up the first bag of blood, and the nurses told him today was his "new birthday." But a few hours later, the mood changed when Lakira received a phone call from someone at the local sickle-cell foundation in her home state with whom she had been in contact before coming to Kelly-Reed. The caller asked her a series of questions—such as how many other families had participated in this study and what a transplant with "manipulated" cord blood (the particular clinical trial Jayden was enrolled in) entailed. The caller suggested that Jayden might be one of the first children to undergo transplantation using this type of cord blood and that Lakira should ask about survival rates. Lakira said she would request this information, but was distressed when she got off the phone. She told me she was upset that people at a foundation she felt had encouraged her to pursue this option were suddenly "second-guessing" it and "scaring her" now. She got out a small notebook and wrote down a few questions she wanted to ask Dr. Ravipati, Jayden's primary physician at Kelly-Reed and head of the study. An hour later, when Jayden went for a walk in the hall with a physical therapist, Dr. Ravipati poked his head into the room. Lakira grabbed her notebook and tried to ask him her questions, including the question about survival rates, but she phrased them as things that "the lady at the sickle-cell foundation wants to know," and added, "I told her I didn't know the answers." From my field notes:

> Dr. Ravipati told Lakira that if they want to know about the procedure, they should be contacting the doctors, not her, and that she should tell them to page him or email Dr Vogel, and they would make time to speak to them.

Lakira said, "Okay" several times, and then told Dr. Ravipati that they were "kind of scaring her" so he reiterated that if she was "not comfortable with their questions" she should tell them that "Jayden is doing fine" and to contact the doctors. Lakira said, "Alright, thank you Dr. R." Shortly after he left, I asked Lakira if she felt like Dr. Ravipati had answered her questions. She gave me an exasperated look, and said, "No! I feel like he kind of brushed me off."

Because of Lakira's presentation of her questions as coming from the foundation and not herself, she did not successfully communicate to Dr. Ravipati that she was worried about her son and wanted to know more. Instead, he responded only to his concern—one that I also shared—that the foundation was asking her for information (including copies of his signed protocol and medication records) that would be more appropriate for them to request directly from the program itself. Yet when he responded to that issue alone, without answering the questions that worried Lakira and that she now felt she *should* know the answers to, she did not ask him again or clarify that she wanted him to give *her* those answers now. Rather than pressing him for a response (as a care-captaining parent would have), she demurely acknowledged his instructions and thanked him anyway.

This deference was common among primarily care-entrusting parents, particularly during interactions with physicians.[2] Unlike care-captaining parents, who were regularly checking up on things and requesting even more information than they expected to receive, care-entrusting parents rarely pushed for information, even information they were told to expect. For instance, when I asked Nicholas Henderson how Elijah was doing one day, he remarked that they were supposed to have gotten a call with his labs that afternoon but hadn't heard anything yet. I went to the clinic with them the next day, and about halfway through the visit the nurse practitioner remarked that they "didn't call yesterday because his labs were fantastic." Nicholas simply nodded and asked for no further information. I wondered if anyone would have dared not to provide the Marins with a promised lab update simply because there were no concerns.

Mary Shaw, a white, fifty-eight-year-old custodial grandmother to her seven-year-old grandson, Aaron, also left medical decisions to the doctors and voiced no second thoughts about doing so. A plump woman with short graying hair and round glasses, Mary spoke softly but matter-of-factly. With a thick regional accent, she recounted Aaron's diagnosis of a rare genetic glycogen and lysosomal storage disorder that causes neuromuscular degeneration and, without newly developed treatments, is fatal within the first year of life. Even with the clinical trial-based enzyme replacement therapy developed by researchers at Kelly-Reed, Aaron was given a life expectancy of five years. Thanks to weekly infusions, for which Mary drove three hours a week and Aaron missed two days of school, he had already beaten this estimate by over two years.

Aaron was doing well and attending public school the rest of the week. But he wore braces on his legs, used assistive devices to walk significant distances, and struggled to speak clearly due to weak jaw and facial muscles. Mary had helped care for Aaron since birth. She was assigned full custody a few months after his diagnosis, when Aaron's mom (her son's girlfriend) failed to care for him properly and soon thereafter was incarcerated on drug charges. Mary told me that they simply followed a series of referrals from the local doctors who identified Aaron's condition after he started struggling to breathe during the first weeks of his life. These referrals led to Dr. T, one of the Kelly-Reed researchers who oversaw the clinical trials that extended Aaron's life.[3]

Mary continued to follow her referrals to related specialists, including speech, occupational, and physical therapists over the years. She assured me, "She'll tell me, 'Well, he needs to see this [specialist],' and whatever she said I need to see, he's seen." When I asked Mary what medical decisions she'd had to make, for instance, about medications or which treatments to pursue, she told me proudly, "I always leave it up [to them]. I says, 'What you think [we should do] is the way I want to go.' [That's] the way I leave it with them." Mary viewed her grandson's medical team as the experts who possessed the knowledge required to make good medical decisions for her grandson, and saw her job as ensuring that their orders were carried out faithfully.

Tariq Khalid, a South Asian father of three in his late-forties who worked from home as a computer technician, also felt strongly about care-entrusting throughout his sixteen-year-old daughter Nazia's treatment for aplastic anemia. Tariq told me that the doctor at the research hospital nearest to their home suggested he take Nazia to Kelly-Reed, several states away, for a sibling-donor bone marrow transplant to treat this life-threatening condition, "because they are the best place to go for the transplant. They do a lot of transplants. They are good. . . . The doctors told me to go there? I go there."

Tariq, a tall man with a receding hairline, close-cropped gray hair, and a stubbly beard and mustache, took comfort in knowing that his daughter's treatment was being done in the "best" place to receive a bone marrow transplant. He emphasized the importance of following doctors' orders throughout our interview. For Tariq, *doing what the doctors told him to do* helped him feel that he was doing everything he could to get the best possible care for his ill child. He was proud to report his obedience, and further explained that it would be foolish for him to get involved in decision-making about his daughter's medical care because of his lack of expertise.

When Nazia first became ill and the local doctor phoned with results of the initial blood test to tell him that her platelets were low, he recounted, "At that time I [didn't even] know what a platelet is, or what is the normal [range]." Tariq succinctly articulated his care-entrusting philosophy: "A lot of times we think the doctors are in the wrong, [or] something is unusual, [but] we should not think about that. We should follow the doctor. We should follow the doctor, and you know, it is difficult, but we came here, we have to trust in the doctors, and listen to what they say." His wife, Mayaddah Tahir, a stay-at-home mom in her mid-forties who wore a traditional hijab, echoed his sentiments about trusting the doctors, who knew best. When I asked if they'd done any research on their own, she told me: "Why look online when you have doctors who can explain in front of you? We just ask the doctors and they explain it to us." She told me that she felt it was not helpful to go online because you'll find "bad information" or a "worst-case scenario."[4] Deference, for some families, could be a highly effective emotional strategy that gave them confidence in their children's care. But sometimes this strategy left room for lingering feelings of uncertainty and doubt, as was the case for Lakira Harris when she realized mid-transplant she lacked information others expected her to know.

Other care-entrusting families also felt great confidence in the healthcare providers they turned their children's care over to, despite occasional difficulties communicating with them. Sometimes, as we'll see in the pages ahead, this led families to direct their advocacy efforts into the realm of "loving care" rather than the medical arena. For families with little cultural health capital or financial resources to invest in their child's illness, such efforts allowed them to feel they were doing the things they could to help their children regain health, even when they saw themselves as unable to engage more directly with children's medical treatments.

"Her Family Is Her Medicine": Focusing on "Loving Care"

Pauline Donnoly nursed a cigarette while we sat outside rocking on the second floor "smoking porch" at the Ronald McDonald House in the muggy late-evening air. The central air conditioning unit next to us whirred in the background, kicking on and off as we chatted. A slender, white, fifty-eight-year-old grandmother with straight chin-length white hair, Pauline was dressed youthfully in a long flowing white cotton skirt, a peach-colored sleeveless crocheted cardigan, and flip flops. Her deep gravelly voice betrayed her lifelong tobacco habit. Pauline's biracial (white/Filipina) granddaughter, Isabelle Santos, bounded onto the porch intermittently in her trademark pink cap and an oversized green t-shirt to see if we were done talking yet. A skinny, spirited, and sometimes defiant seven-year-old, Isabelle often wanted to play Uno with me during my volunteer shifts, and I promised to go inside to play with her as soon as her grandmother and I finished talking. As dusk turned to night, Isabelle became exasperated with the wait and tried to take my tape recorder from me. When Pauline asked me how many years I had left in school as we wrapped up, Isabelle answered for me, proclaiming into the microphone, "130!"

Isabelle was diagnosed with a rare form of kidney cancer when she was three years old. After a weekend-long stomachache, Pauline took her to the pediatrician, who, fortunately, took action more quickly than the Hendersons' local physicians had. The pediatrician quickly sent Isabelle to a nearby coastal teaching hospital where the diagnosis was confirmed, and she underwent surgery to remove the mass. When Isabelle's mother (Pauline's daughter, who still had legal custody at the time) failed to take her to her first chemotherapy appointment or respond to calls from the hospital, Isabelle was placed in foster care.[5] Pauline described the time that Isabelle was in foster care as more harrowing than her illness. She fought hard to get custody of Isabelle assigned to her. When Isabelle caught pneumonia while undergoing chemotherapy, Pauline was horrified to see how "tiny and frail" her granddaughter had become. Though Pauline had been trying to work through the bureaucracy of the Department of Social Services (DSS) to obtain custody for months, this incident rattled her so much that she decided to escalate her efforts:

> I'd already called everybody, I'd had people praying forever anyway, but I called different ones that morning, I said, "Be in prayer." And I got on the phone with the law office . . . and I started talking to this woman who was a mediator for children . . . and I told her, I said, "[Isabelle's] family is her medicine." I said "If she doesn't get back with her family, she's going to die." I said, "Do you have children?" "Yes ma'am" [she replied]. I said, "Do you have any small children?" "Yes ma'am, I have a three-year-old son." Well I gave her a good picture, and that hit her hard. She said, "I'm gonna call you back in a few minutes." And a couple of more phone calls, and [she said] "When she's released from the hospital, we are gonna say that she can go back to the family."

Once Isabelle was at home with her, Pauline poured herself into providing as much restorative nutrition as she could. She cooked huge homemade meals—"with fresh vegetables" she assured me. She attributed Isabelle's frailty during her time in foster care to being fed "only microwave meals" or "just a cup of something here, and a little half a sandwich there. Pauline explained further that the foster care provider "didn't feed her. I mean, of course she fed her, but it wasn't a meal you're gonna sit down and drool over." Pauline took great pride in Isabelle's response to her cooking:

> The first night she sat down to the table . . . every bite she'd take, she would turn to me and tell me, "Thank you." And it broke my heart [Pauline began to choke up]. 'Cause she did it for like a *week*. It was like she hadn't had any food! And every time I gave her something, "Mimi thank you, it's so good," she said. "It's *so* good." And she's always loved to eat. . . . Seems like it was two weeks, all she could do was thank me, honey. She couldn't wait for me to cook the food, she loves food, she would eat, and

eat, and eat, fix plates and go to the table and sit down and she would thank me and she couldn't hardly stand it. And so, after that we just, everything started kind of meshing and coming together. (Emphasis hers)

Isabelle completed her chemotherapy a year after her initial diagnosis and was given "a clean bill of health."

Unfortunately, a few years later, just before Isabelle's seventh birthday, she again had a weekend-long stomachache. Pauline took her to the pediatrician right away, and they quickly determined that the tumor had come back. When they asked which hospital to send Isabelle to, Pauline named the same coastal teaching hospital which had performed the initial surgery. She explained, "That's where everything's been done before." But because Pauline had moved across state lines since the original treatment, that hospital claimed that they could not take Isabelle's now out-of-state Medicaid insurance. At that point, Pauline deferred to the local doctors to identify a new treatment facility. Another in-state teaching hospital was "full," so they were sent to Kelly-Reed. Pauline admitted that at the time she hadn't really understood the differences between hospitals and pointed directly to her lack of cultural health capital in turning this decision over to Isabelle's healthcare providers: "I mean, if you think about it, you don't really have the knowledge base. If I had had time to have sought out different hospitals, *I still wouldn't have known what I was looking for, or what would have been right*" (emphasis mine).

Because Pauline would have felt uncomfortable attempting to make care decisions she did not feel equipped to make, care-entrusting protected her from feeling even more anxious and inefficacious. Pauline continued to care-entrust after they arrived at Kelly-Reed. When I asked her if she had to make any decisions about treatments, medications, or testing, she told me:

No, they tell you, because it's all protocol. And they've got the whole thing laid out . . . and so, you know, you do this, and this, and this, and this, to the point when I talk to the doctors I don't know if they know any more than just reading the chart and seeing where she is. I mean, I say that? [Pauline's inflection indicated that she was reconsidering her statement.] I wish it was a little bit more, I wish it did have a little bit more information from them, but um, you don't get a lot of information, you're just going through the program.

Despite her suggestion that more information could be helpful, Pauline did not feel qualified to question physicians about her granddaughter's medical treatment or offer her own input about it. One area Pauline did continue to feel strongly about—and was willing to speak up for—was keeping Isabelle well-nourished. She raised concerns about her eating—or lack thereof—to multiple members of Isabelle's medical team. Pauline was puzzled that the doctors didn't seem to be concerned about Isabelle's nutrition or particularly interested in Pauline's desire to provide Isabelle with additional nourishment. Pauline told me:

> There'd be areas that I'd want answers about . . . she's not eating, things like that, things that would be important for her body. I was really kind of big on trying to give her supplements, and different um, nutritional things, and they, they were opposed to that, they felt like she didn't need, [that] she'd be all right, you know? . . . I was wanting to try to keep her going as good as possible while all this was coming along, so she could maintain that . . . They just never saw necessity in it . . . so they kept reassuring me she'd be alright, when it's all said and done, she'll, you know, "She'll be sick now, she won't be sick later." . . . [But] you kind of just want to give it to her—[so] when you're sick you're not starving to death and that kind of stuff.

Lakira Harris also took satisfaction in offering her son food-related pleasures. Because of their weakened immune systems, transplant patients cannot eat food that has been prepared more than one hour previously due to the risk of foodborne illnesses their bodies have no protection against. This limited the menu available to them. Lakira would make special trips to the cafeteria to ask them to do her the favor of making a fresh batch of her son's favorite curly fries. She also focused on other joy-related nonmedical matters by, for instance, keeping careful notes on the whiteboard in his room on Unit 27 to document each "Bead of Courage" Jayden earned that day. "Beads of Courage" were colorful, artsy glass beads that children earned for undergoing unpleasant treatments (anything from a "needle prick" to a surgery), dealing with symptoms like pain and vomiting (for which they might receive a "bumpy day" bead), or small accomplishments, like walking a lap around the unit or completing a tutoring session with a local teacher. Lakira made sure Jayden got every bead he was entitled to, and he soon had multiple long strands of beads hanging from his IV pole as a testament to her efforts.

Care-entrusting parents often advocated for children in nonmedical ways but usually avoided straying too far into more technical matters. Though Pauline spoke up about her desire to see Isabelle eat well, she rarely raised questions about medical issues, even if she had them. When I asked her if Isabelle was now considered to be "in remission," she told me she wasn't sure:

> To be honest, they've not really said yes or no. I mean, in short he was saying, "Well, you know, there's no guarantees in anything." And so, I've been getting those kinds of remarks. . . . I did talk with Dr. Y one time, a couple of months ago, or maybe 6 months ago, right at the end of the chemo . . . 'cause he's the head doctor. He said, "Well, there's really no numbers or anything we can tell you anything about" because, um, what she's got, they don't, they can't read your hormone level or whatever numbers would show [that, or] would help you to know. In her case there's, as far was what he could tell me, he, uh, didn't have any information, that would define, here or there.

Pauline also mentioned that she requested but still hadn't received what she referred to as the "PET report," which she told me was "supposed to be a finality of everything."[6] Ultimately, she said, "I've not gotten anything concrete . . . and that kind of puzzles me. And I was hoping that I could get something today. But I haven't gotten a call back."

While Isabelle's doctor may not have been able to guarantee that Isabelle was entirely out of the woods, Pauline's difficulty getting records and reports—which she didn't have a firm understanding of—stood in contrast to higher cultural health capital families' ease in accessing such information. For instance, Jacob Marin's nurse practitioner ordered a DVD of these sorts of electronic records and images for Jacob's mother, Savannah, to take back with her to her home state when they left the Ronald McDonald House. The nurse hoped it would be ready before Jacob's final outpatient visit, but promised to have it shipped to the family via Fed-Ex if it was not. The Marins, who had care-captained intensively throughout their son's illness, were assumed to want this level of information and were provided with it automatically.

Pauline and many other low cultural health capital families still felt very positively about their experiences with most providers at Kelly-Reed even though the communication between them was not always ideal. Despite the occasional difficulties she alluded to, Pauline told me: "Oh, I think they're great people. They all present themselves well. I think, um for as much as they do, and trying to do it all, I think that they hold up well. I don't know what the word is, um, you're hoping, I mean you're *hoping* they're doing [a good job], and I feel *confident* that they are" (emphasis mine). Though Pauline thought "they're great people" who all "present themselves well," and clearly wanted to have faith in the doctors in whose hands her granddaughter's life and future lay, she also expressed a hint of uncertainty, recognizing that she had no way to really know. Because Pauline lacked the skills, tools, or knowledge she would need to double-check doctors the way families with much more cultural health capital did, she instead *hoped* that Isabelle was getting the best care possible. By shifting the bulk of her attention toward nonmedical matters and not digging too deeply into any of the medical questions that occasionally "puzzled her," Pauline was able to avoid focusing on that which might arouse uncertainty or anxiety and maintain a steady and optimistic emotional state for Isabelle and for herself.

Performing Parenthood Differently

Marcus and Jeanetta Moore also felt great confidence in their daughter's medical team and turned all medical decision-making over to them. Black working-class parents of two school-aged daughters from a rural coastal area, the Moores weren't expecting to have any more children when, in their early forties, they learned Jeanetta was pregnant with Kaelyn. They also weren't expecting their third child's infancy to be much different than their previous two. But a few days after bringing Kaelyn home from the hospital, Jeanetta told me, "She started shaking, and my husband and I—it's been a long time since we had a child—[so] first we thought she was having chills, but it would stop, so, you know, we overlooked it." But when one night she "kept doing it," Jeanetta decided to call the pediatrician and was advised to bring the baby to the hospital right away. Once there, tests revealed that her calcium was low. But the doctors told Jeanetta they couldn't treat Kaelyn for "what they thought she might have" so they were sent on to a larger regional hospital.

Doctors at the regional hospital suspected a more serious problem, but they sent them home with seizure medications while they waited for the results of more tests. Back at home, newborn Kaelyn began to break out in a rash and "started scratching all the time, she would just dig into [her skin], a little tender thing, she would just scratch and scratch and I was like 'What?!'" So Jeanetta took her back to the doctor, who said, "Well, maybe she has eczema."

So the Moores were sent home, this time with medication for eczema. When the problem continued, Jeanetta told me, "They thought she might have an allergic reaction to her milk. [The doctor] kept changing the milk and everything. In the meantime I was trying to work and raise my other two girls." Jeanetta recruited her sister-in-law to help out, but the rash continued to worsen until Kaelyn completely "turned red." Jeanetta brought her to a dermatologist at the regional hospital, who saw her and said, "Oh my gosh! She looks like a child that has [a rare chromosomal deletion disorder]!" After drawing blood, they told her: "'Her T-cell count doesn't look right. Something's wrong with her, I'm going to have to send you to Kelly-Reed.' I said, 'To Kelly-Reed!' She said, 'I'm going to have to send you to see Dr. E'" (a specialist in severe combined immunodeficiency disorders). The Moores never did see Dr. E, however, because the first doctor who examined Kaelyn at Kelly-Reed told them, "I know who you need to see; you need to see Dr. Oliver."

Dr. Oliver met with the Moores, examined Kaelyn, collected blood, and by the time the Moores made the several hour drive back home, called to confirm the diagnosis of the rare chromosomal deletion syndrome the dermatologist at the regional hospital had suspected. Incredibly fortuitously—and in no small part due to the fact that they resided in a rural area only a few hours' drive from Kelly-Reed—they had already been connected to the only doctor in the world who could perform a specialized tissue transplant to cure this condition and restore immune function.

Because the procedure was still considered experimental at this time, neither Marcus's insurance nor Medicaid would pay for it. The Moores were very concerned about how they would raise the money to obtain this life-saving treatment for their daughter, but Marcus was reluctant to ask others for help. Jeanetta recalled telling him: "You used to do the March of Dimes walk, and you would raise almost a thousand dollars for them. That's helping people. You helped someone. So maybe somebody will help us." Jeanetta did interviews with local newspapers, and even appeared on a national television morning show that visited the Ronald McDonald House while they were staying there. Their home community held a variety of fundraisers including a "chicken and fish fry" at the local hospital, a raffle at their older daughters' schools, local church campaigns, and a website through which anonymous donations could be made to a local foundation that would set the money aside for Kaelyn's transplant.

While they waited for the transplant, the Moores were meticulous in keeping Kaelyn protected from illness in her immune-compromised state. Jeanetta explained: "When we came home from school or work, we'll start right at the door, we'll strip our clothes, go take a shower, put on new clothes. 'Cause I was trying not to bring any germs in the house. I wouldn't let nobody come in the house to see her, and wouldn't take her out so nobody can see her." During visits to the hospital, Jeanetta put a plastic cover over Kaelyn's carrier "so she couldn't pick up no germs." The Moores ultimately raised the $20,000 they needed to cover the costs of treatment,[7] and Kaelyn received the transplant when she was nine months old. The procedure was successful, allowing Kaelyn to develop a normal immune system and the chance to venture safely into the outside world.

Like the families who regularly care-captained, the Moores did an incredible amount of work on behalf of their daughter and ultimately accessed cutting-edge, life-saving treatment for a perilously-ill child. However, unlike families who care-captained, the Moores did not turn to their social networks for medical advice or immediately begin scouring the Internet for information. They did not request particular tests, push for quicker referrals or appointments, or question the efficacy of the drugs or diet changes prescribed before Kaelyn was accurately diagnosed. For each new symptom Kaelyn developed, the Moores placed a call to their daughter's pediatrician and followed the instructions they were given.[8] They turned to kin networks for support in caring for Kaelyn and her siblings and sought help from their community,[9] rather than fiercely negotiating with Medicaid or her husband's insurance company to obtain coverage for a prohibitively expensive medical treatment.

Kaelyn's mother, Jeanetta, a heavy-set, no-nonsense, well-organized woman who was a direct and firm disciplinarian with all of her children, believed her role was to be respectful of and deferent to Kaelyn's providers at Kelly-Reed. When I asked if she ever asked physicians to reconsider a medication or adjust a dosage, Jeanetta told me flatly: "I trust their judgment. If they say, 'No, don't take this [medication] no more?' Okay. She doesn't need it anymore." When I asked Jeanetta if she ever sought a second opinion, she proudly explained that if she wasn't sure about a particular *local* provider's recommendations, she turned to Kaelyn's doctors at Kelly-Reed, which she considered to be Kaelyn's "medical home." She left any new referrals up to them: "If I'm not happy with something locally? I'll call, the nurse, Dr. Oliver's nurse practitioner, Cynthia, [and say], 'Well, I don't agree with something [another] doctor said.' I'll say I want a second opinion. Then she'll refer me to someone."

Jeanetta did not do her own research or seek out other local options. She viewed this as something for which medical experts were responsible and best positioned to determine. She also felt best about deferring to Dr. Oliver and other Kelly-Reed providers when she encountered conflicting opinions about Kaelyn's therapeutic needs in her post-transplant development, despite the huge amounts of time and travel required to follow them. Doctors at Kelly-Reed told her that Kaelyn needed regular physical and occupational therapy to help her to continue to overcome related cognitive deficits. Without these therapies, children with her condition struggled to catch up with their peers. But back at home, Jeanetta had a hard time accessing these services both because of a shortage of them in her rural coastal community and because the doctors there "don't think she needs them," she reported. Jeanetta, attempting to follow the recommendations of the doctors at Kelly-Reed, continued to ferry Kaelyn back and forth to Kelly-Reed twice a month so that she could access these therapies more regularly. Jeanetta told me that without this, Kaelyn—who was sitting at the table next to us drawing pictures of a house, her sisters, and some flowers on the back of my consent forms—"wouldn't be doing what she's doing right now."

Though Jeanetta's dedication to her daughter was plainly apparent to me, this was not always the perception of others. Jeanetta's parenting style may have appeared overly strict to white, middle-class providers and staff at the Ronald McDonald House. For instance, during a physical therapy appointment I observed, Jeanetta regularly admonished Kaelyn to behave, telling her firmly: "Sit down and stop squirming" or "Pay attention to Miss Brittany." The physical therapist, alternatively, adopted a "positive parenting" approach. She avoided saying "no" and cheerfully redirected Kaelyn rather than scolding her. When Kaelyn seemed uninterested, she even abandoned an exercise, telling her, "That's okay, we don't have to blow bubbles right now." This clash between child-rearing philosophies, itself rooted in racial and social class differences, widened the divide between Jeanetta, Kaelyn's providers, and Ronald McDonald House staff.[10]

I was initially puzzled by the Ronald McDonald House staff's chilly attitude toward Jeanetta. In time, I learned that some thought she was "milking the system" by continuing to stay there regularly to obtain medical treatments they believed she could access closer to home, and thus deemed her use of their services unnecessary. When a generous Ronald McDonald House patron donated an iPad over the holidays during my second year as a volunteer, I suggested it might be especially beneficial to the Moores. Jeanetta had mentioned to me that Kaelyn's speech therapist wanted her to use a special speech therapy "app" to enhance her communication skills and foster language development, but Jeanetta could not afford one. This idea was not appealing to the staff person I proposed it to, who told me, "I don't know, we need to make sure it goes to a really deserving family." Class-based differences in childrearing were likely compounded by racialized "controlling images" regarding dependency and overuse of social services, which contributed to staff's difficulty in viewing Jeanetta as a "deserving" parent.[11] I suspect that had a white middle-class family like the Marins continued to request stays at the Ronald McDonald House to access the "best" possible developmental therapies for their child, staff would have seen this dedication as noble.

Physicians' Perspectives on Care-Entrusting

Though families who primarily care-entrusted believed that they were doing their best to please and respect their child's healthcare providers, this approach could, ironically, raise concerns for physicians. First and foremost, the physicians I interviewed recognized that without some care-captaining, kids may not make it to needed treatment to begin with. If, as Dr. Coleman put it, "they never get referred because they're somewhere where the general pediatricians, the general family medicine doctor, has no clue," kids could miss out on the opportunity to access life-saving care. This would almost certainly have been the case for Aaron Shaw and Kaelyn Moore had they not encountered local doctors who recognized rare conditions quickly and knew exactly where to send them.

Dr. Vogel explained that sometimes even these referrals were not enough. Although the program employs staff to negotiate between the hospital and both state Medicaid and private insurance companies, less "aggressive" families may drop out along the way when extra advocacy is required to access treatment. She explained: "Let's say it's Blue Cross/ Blue Shield, and you have to appeal. You know, there are certain parents who will actively work on that very aggressively. And then there are other parents who just don't want, you know, they take that as overwhelming." But even once families made it to Kelly-Reed and obtained access to all the same treatment options and highly specialized expertise, physicians worried that care-entrusting families may not provide them with the same level of information that care-captaining families did, as we saw in the previous chapter. Dr. Coleman elaborated: "The ones who just, you know, blindly follow things; yeah, in some ways that's easier, but you never are quite certain that if something was off that they would help you figure that [out]. Something that, [whether] there was a side effect, or not effective therapy. You just don't have the certainty that you do with the family that's always questioning." Notice that Dr. Coleman felt less certain—and thus worried more—about children whose parents care-entrusted, a fact that points again to the role parents' care-captaining can play in helping physicians manage difficult emotions.

But most of all, physicians expressed concern that care-entrusting might not offer the same emotional benefits of care-captaining for parents themselves. Dr. Ravipati told me that care-entrusting parents were in an even more difficult emotional position if their children died:

What happens is when families trust the doctors completely, they don't have—sometimes they don't understand what we are saying. Like we say that there's a chance of dying, there's a chance of infection, there's a chance of organ toxicity, and they just hear it and they don't really visualize it. And then when it actually happens they feel like, "Oh, we didn't know about this." You know. "We wish we knew about this, we wouldn't have proceeded with transplant." So that kind of feeling occurs in the family. On the other end, the families who have worried and proceed know about it, before transplant, and are already expecting it. And they understand and they don't feel it, sometimes, I mean they don't feel as bad. Or at least they feel like this was expected.

Dr. Fadian echoed this sentiment even more emphatically:

The reason it's so, at least to me, it's so important that they understand what we're doing—it gets back to that if there's a bad outcome, you want the parents to understand that they have truly done everything they could for their child. And that's what the parent wants to know . . . that I did the right thing for my child, and I've done everything humanly possible. That's why it's really important for me to make sure they understand. Because if things don't turn out okay, I don't want them . . . They're going to grieve. They're going to grieve for years, no matter what. We all know that. But they've got to know that they really were doing the best they knew to do. And what was humanly possible was done for their child. And it's just the fact of life that some children don't survive. So I guess that's what I come back to. So even if they don't really want to know a whole lot, that's fine, unless we're in a very clinically serious scenario, then they need to know. Because I don't want them coming back and berating themselves. That's important.

Dr. Newell shared this perspective as well. She worried about care-entrusting parents not correcting problems or providing them with additional information and suggested that parents might feel regret if they did not participate more:

I don't want them to feel like they have no control because this is their child and this is a team that they're working with. And just because I've had the training doesn't mean that I don't—you know, I welcome their input. And I do want them to feel comfortable saying—if I make a decision based on information that the nurses gave me, or the trainee, you know, the residents or fellows give me—I want them to feel comfortable saying, "You know what? Actually, I disagree! The stools look like this," or you know, "She *did* eat that much."

I also don't want them to walk away from this with regrets. And if they hand things over completely to us, they may not feel like they have had the opportunity to make, you know [decisions]. This is a partnership and I just don't want them to feel like we steamrolled them. And I hope they never feel that way and I hope they feel like if they did have concerns that they could bring it up with me or whoever the doctor was who was caring for the child. I don't want them to be that afraid of us, you know! (Emphasis hers)

These physicians' concerns that parents might struggle while grieving if they didn't play a significant role in overseeing their child's care were likely rooted both in a desire to help better emotionally position families for the loss of a child and to protect themselves from potential fallout if families expressed anger or distress about how their children were treated.

Doctors also worried about care-entrusting parents' abilities to get children the emergency care they need from local doctors who are not familiar with rare diseases or children's post-transplant needs after they returned home. Dr. Oliver offered an example:

There's one . . . patient, and she ran out of calcium. Well, the kid's now been in the hospital about four days because of low calcium. And I told her, now—of course, the initial time this happened, she went to the emergency department and I told her that she always needs a calcium level [to be checked if they go to the emergency room]. She said it, and the guy just ignored her. And then the next day [her child] had to be admitted with, like, life-threatening low calcium. And I told her that from now on, when she's in the emergency department, if they don't do it, call me on my cell phone right then. Don't go home and call me, call me right then and I will talk to the people. And so she has subsequently done that.

Unlike care-captaining parents who would not simply request a calcium level but demand it (or, as Dr. Oliver later noted, would call her—the primary physician—right away), this parent simply deferred to the physicians in the emergency room when her attempt to follow Dr. Oliver's orders did not succeed. Given her lack of cultural health capital and inability to assert herself the way that many care-captaining parents could, local emergency medicine physicians may not have taken this parent's input or request seriously, putting her child at greater risk.

Dr. Oliver also worried that this mother did not fully understand how vital it was to ensure that her child's calcium never ran out. Physicians thus viewed parents' abilities to understand the complex medical challenges their children were facing as critical and worked hard to find the best way to convey as much information to parents as possible. When I asked physicians how much technical information they provided to parents, they told me their goal was to provide as much as possible, but they tried to match the information with a parent's level of understanding. Dr. Fadian elaborated:

I ask the parents, "What do you know about the disease?" and then I'll let them tell me what they understand. And from how they describe it, and the depth of their knowledge, that helps me understand how to explain transplant to them. And . . . if I'm talking to them . . . and I'm doing a consent . . . and then you know, they're picking up their phone, rolling their [eyes], you know, you can see body language. Then I know I'm giving too much detail and I back off.

Dr. Coleman also tried to read patients and adjust the level of detail he provided:

[I start] the way most teachers start, you know? You start off slow and if they seem to understand what a cell is, then you start talking about genes. If they seem to understand the genes, then you go to the details of the genes. If they understand the details of the genes, then you go up a little higher. Until you realize, "Oh, I've lost them." And usually it's the, you know, one of the nurse coordinators is kicking me under the table to say, "Get off the lecture stage professor, and come back down" [laughing]. But I think, um, I think just the way I was raised, the odd jobs I had as a teenager and as a college student, you know, I think I can talk with almost anybody. You know, I've worked in factories, I've worked dorm crew. I've worked all sorts of odd jobs here and there. And I think I can usually relate pretty well to any, uh, socioeconomic status, any family. And pretty quickly judge their level of understanding, and how much they want to understand.

Dr. Fadian's and Dr. Coleman's descriptions suggest that it is less likely that families with low levels of cultural health capital will develop significantly more of it. Because they adjust the information they provide to a family's level of understanding and interest—which is almost certainly a reasonable, effective, and sensitive approach when interacting with overwhelmed parents—families with less cultural health capital (primarily poor and working-class families) don't have their knowledge pumped up in the way that families with even a vague grasp of physiology—whom physicians perceive as capable of learning and understanding more—might. Dr. Coleman was careful to make it clear that he understood why some parents care-entrusted entirely. He did not see this as a sign of irresponsibility, but explained that he still prefers the care-captaining approach:

> Some families . . . all they can do is say, "Yes doctor, yes nurse." "Whatever you say." And they do it. You know—but if the follow-through is there, then they're doing everything that they can do with their resources, with their intellectual and financial resources, they're doing everything they can. Yeah. No, I think we've had plenty of you know, grandmas who are raising the kids, they have few resources, but they—you say be here at 10:00 a.m., they're there at 10:00 a.m. You say give these pills, they give those pills. That's a great partner to have too.

Similarly, Elizabeth Gage-Bouchard found that physicians treating pediatric cancer patients appreciated parents who used what she terms a "trusting advocacy" style of interaction, in which parents are deferential (asking few questions and making few requests) and highly compliant.[12] The physicians in her study referred to such families as "good" ones. But Dr. Coleman modified his appreciation of such care-entrusting families by again pointing to what he saw as the emotional benefits of care-captaining, adding: "I *prefer* a family who has the intellectual resources to go and, you know, search for other options, for other things that might work better for their family. If they want to try, you know, herbal therapy, acupuncture, anything else that will make them feel better." Rather than view families with more questions, requests, and opinions as frustrating, the physicians I interviewed enjoyed interacting with families in these ways and believed it would benefit them in both the short and long term.

Physicians took their assessment of parents' medical savvy into account in making treatment decisions as well. I asked Dr. Ravipati how he decided when to remove a child's central line, which makes it easy to deliver infusions and draw blood without reaccessing a vein each time. This is especially beneficial given the regularity with which blood is drawn from transplant patients and intravenous medications are administered to them, even after they return home. But if the central line becomes infected, this poses a significant risk to children who are still immune compromised. So there are advantages to leaving it in (removing it prematurely could result in additional surgery to put it back if the child is readmitted) and to taking it out (as it reduces infection risk). Dr. Ravipati explained that when the decision was borderline, he considered factors on the parents' side: "If I feel like the parent is not very capable of handling the [central] line, will not be compliant with coming to the hospital for fever and all that, and put the child at risk that way, then I would be more inclined to remove it." Similar to the calculations physicians made in Lutfey and Freese's study of two diabetes clinics, Dr. Ravipati's assessment of families' likelihood of compliance led him to adjust the level of risk he deemed reasonable.[13] To the extent that children without a central line may have to endure the additional discomfort of regular "needle sticks" for blood draws and injections, this introduces additional inequalities into the treatment process for the children who must endure them, and is a tangible, ongoing microadvantage for children who do not. Yet within the broader context of significant social inequalities around the resources families can bring to the provision of home medical care and the genuine threat of infection or death, such calculations might well, as Dr. Ravipati believes, be the safer choice.

Though physicians understood why parents, particularly poor and working-class parents, would choose to adopt a care-entrusting approach to managing a child's serious illness, care-entrusting parents' behaviors were sometimes perceived by healthcare providers as evidence that they were *not* as invested in their children and their children's health as care-captaining parents were. Dr. Coleman described particularly problematic signs of non-investment as

> leave the kid in the crib and not, not be involved at all. Be on their cell phone all the time. Disappear for hours and hours without letting nurses know where they're going. Um, you know, showing no maternal instinct kind of things. I mean it's pretty easy for anybody to tell if, if the child's crying and the mother goes over to the crib, picks them up and comforts them, and the child quiets down, and they interact with the child, and they read to the child. You know, those are all good things. If the child's crying and it's left in the crib and mom's over in the chair, watching TV, or the dad's on the video game, and not paying attention to the kid, those are all red flags.

Though Dr. Coleman mentioned the possibility of fathers appearing to pay too little attention to an ill child, he focused primarily on the behaviors he expected to see from mothers. Mothers have long been held to far higher standards when it comes to caring for children, in sickness and in health.[14] In fact, the ability to meet children's medical providers' expectations of appropriate mothering has historically played a powerful role in whether or not one is deemed to be a "good" or responsible mother, a standard that sociologist Jacquelyn Litt has shown to be even more stringently applied to black mothers, while simultaneously being more difficult for them to meet.[15]

Dr. Fadian echoed Dr. Coleman's concerns. He explained that care-entrusting itself wasn't a problem; "It's the ones who are negligent. And that's where you have children's services involved. Of course, then you probably have parents who are on the borderline there." I asked him to elaborate on what kind of negligence he observed: "To have DSS involved? Sleeping 20 hours a day, being gone from the unit, not participating in the care of your child, who's two years old. I mean this is, this is not just [important] in transplant, this is just parental neglect, [from my perspective] as a pediatrician." Parents also expressed alarm and disdain for other parents who were not always present or deeply engaged. However, even if these behaviors could be an indication of abuse or neglect (and certainly, this is a genuine issue physicians encounter at times and must address), they could also be coping strategies that overwhelmed parents who prefer to care-entrust use to manage feelings of helplessness when their children are especially sick and suffering.

For instance, when I took Chanise Rowland, a black mother of five in her late twenties, to visit her five-month-old daughter, Anaya, in the pediatric cardiac intensive care unit (PCICU) a few weeks after Anaya's emergency open-heart surgery for a congenital heart defect, Chanise engaged very little with her daughter's healthcare providers. The nurse greeted her cheerfully when we arrived and told Chanise that "Anaya has a new little hat on" because a few hours earlier they had placed a peripheral IV in her forehead and removed her transthoracic line. Chanise responded simply "Ok!" The nurse went on to explain that she'd had a fever, and they had administered two different antibiotics and were doing blood and urine cultures which should come back soon. Chanise asked, "When will she probably be going to the floor [getting out of the PCICU]?" The nurse said that if everything came back okay and the fever stayed down, it could be as early as the next day. "Wow, okay!" she replied happily. Chanise spent about twenty minutes sitting by her daughter's bedside, speaking a few short phrases to her, and made clucking sounds as directed by a sheet Anaya's speech therapist had taped to the wall. But aside from these small efforts, there was little for her to do. I asked Chanise a few questions, which she in turn asked the nurse or the nurse overheard and chimed in to answer. When I asked, for instance, about the transthoracic line, the nurse explained it to me. Only then did Chanise say, "Oh, that line," revealing that she hadn't fully understood the initial update the nurse greeted her with, but had asked for no clarification. Anaya's father, who stayed downstairs in the cafeteria, came up for a moment to take a quick look at Anaya before leaving again. "He can't hardly take stuff like this" Chanise explained. A few minutes later, Chanise was also ready to go back to the Ronald McDonald House.

To nurses, doctors, and other parents, Chanise may have appeared to be one of those parents whose behavior indicated a lack of interest and bordered on irresponsible. Anaya likely would not have made it to Kelly-Reed before going into cardiac arrest had it not been for the efforts of a physician at their regional hospital who, Chanise explained, "stayed right up on her" and insisted that she be medically evacuated to Kelly-Reed on a Friday afternoon, rather than waiting until the following

Monday as planned. This physician's advocacy turned out to have been crucial when Anaya "crashed" a few hours after arriving at Kelly-Reed and required immediate open-heart surgery, which the local hospital would not have been able to perform. Chanise teared up recounting how overwhelmed she felt in the wake of the sudden many-hours-long surgery, after which a nurse reassured her that Anaya was going to be okay, because if they had still been at the regional hospital, "You wouldn't have a little girl tonight."

Chanise described to me her efforts during Anaya's first months of life to keep strangers out of the house and to never let her cry (which might stress her fragile heart). It was apparent to me that she cared deeply about her daughter. However, once she placed her in the care of medical experts, she viewed her role as minimal at best. For Anaya's father, witnessing his daughter's suffering was too emotionally difficult for him to handle even for a short period of time. This was the case for other families as well. Care-entrusting offers different, but important emotional benefits—so much so that even parents with much more cultural health capital sometimes find themselves blending care-captaining and care-entrusting for exactly this reason.

Conclusion

Families with limited cultural health capital often took a very different approach to managing a child's serious illness than the families who became intensively involved in steering their children's medical care. They chauffeured their children to professionals who could direct them where to go and what to do, and then followed these instructions, shepherding their children through the treatments doctors prescribed. In this approach, families *stayed on the medical sidelines* and deferred to doctors in making medical decisions. They did not seek to become active members of their child's medical team or work to influence the daily provision of their child's care. They generally did not question medical directives. Some care-entrusting parents engaged in limited, occasional online research about their child's illness, but this research was, for the most part, not undertaken with the idea that they might seek different providers, question medications, or select different treatments; rather, it remained at a more basic level. Parents who adopted this approach did not conduct PubMed searches or listen to lectures given by international scholars conducting research on their child's particular disease. At most, they consulted Wikipedia, public forums, or perhaps WebMD.

Those who care-entrusted still advocated for their children, but their advocacy was less medically technical. Families spoke up to improve their children's comfort, requesting, for instance, that a nurse tape down the tube connected to a child's accessed port so that it wouldn't tug on him,[16] or asked for medications to be spaced farther apart if their child became nauseous from too many drugs administered at one time. They also expressed a desire to participate in caring for their children in the nonmedical ways they felt most competent in, whether preparing home-cooked meals or offering vitamin-supplements to an older child or bathing a baby in the neonatal intensive care unit (NICU). Families who stayed on the medical sidelines still engaged in an enormous amount of work to obtain care for seriously ill children— ferrying them to and from treatments and hospitals far from their homes, rallying social and material support, engaging in rigorous cleanliness rituals to protect their children from germs or other harms, and even, when necessary, leaving jobs and schools behind and their other children in the care of kin support networks—so that a sick child could receive potentially life-saving treatment far from home. Still, they rarely crossed into the medical realm, which they left in the hands of medical professionals. This approach sometimes left them vulnerable to the judgments of others who viewed care-entrusting as less committed parenting.

Yet the emotional benefits of a care-entrusting approach were very real, especially for poor and working-class families who lacked the cultural health capital and other resources that are necessary to be *effective* in care-captaining. Even parents who could more easily care-captain sometimes found care-entrusting to be a more emotionally stable approach to navigating a child's critical illness. Attempting to care-captain without much cultural health capital could lead to high levels of frustration, increased anxiety, and conflict. Families who blended or switched between these two approaches throughout the illness and treatment process bring the emotional and medical advantages of each into clearer view. I introduce these families in the chapter ahead.

5

Blending and Switching Care Strategies

Finding Emotional Equilibrium

You go into a doctor's office, you know, when you're dealing with something this serious, *everything could scare the
crap out of you.* So, I just have learned that I sit back and I
pay attention. I listen to what they're talking about. What is
it that *they're* watching? What's important about that? . . . but
I don't ask about every single thing they're monitoring. Because they monitor so much . . . It could be a ton of different
things. . . . I still haven't learned it all, and I'm not going to
try to, but, you know . . . if it's like really whacked out, and
then *they* start showing concern? *Then* we worry about it.
—Charlotte Caldwell, mother of seventeen-year-old Brenton

Though many families leaned heavily toward care-captaining or care-
entrusting in conjunction with the cultural health capital they could
bring to the management of a child's life-threatening illness, cases that
were less straightforward reveal more vividly the emotional pushes and
pulls at the root of these strategies. Some families with sufficient cultural health capital did not care-captain as much as they could have,
while those with very little cultural health capital sometimes made significant efforts to care-captain—if less effectively. Shifting attention to
these more complex cases helps bring the emotional nuances of these
strategies into clearer view.[1]

Straddling the Middle Ground

After a long day of chemotherapy at the hospital, ten-year-old Jackson
Klein wasn't feeling well. Back at the Ronald McDonald House, Jackson
lay curled on the couch under a blanket, resting and watching television

while his mom and I chatted at the small circular dining table nearby. The following week, Jackson would be admitted to the hospital for several months for a sibling-donor bone marrow transplant.

This wasn't the first time the Kleins had come to Kelly-Reed in the hopes of ridding Jackson of the leukemia he was diagnosed with sixteen months earlier. His mom, Deirdre, a white forty-nine-year-old mother of five with chin-length auburn hair shot with streaks of gray, spoke warmly and gently as she guided me through Jackson's illness—which was tightly intertwined with her own. In September of 2011, Deirdre was diagnosed with stage-IV (metastatic) breast cancer. Because her cancer had spread to her stomach and intestines, her local doctor sent her immediately to Kelly-Reed—about three hours from her home, bypassing a regional university research hospital in between. He believed Kelly-Reed would be best equipped to manage her complicated situation. Deirdre and her husband Rick had been separated for five years, but when Deirdre was diagnosed, Rick took over primary care of the children. Two months later, when Jackson began to feel ill, ran a low-grade fever, and wasn't getting better, Deirdre skipped the pediatrician and took him to see the doctor who diagnosed her, because he was "known to run several tests on things." Jackson's white blood cell count was exceptionally high, signaling leukemia. He was transported to Kelly-Reed by ambulance the same day. Deirdre was too ill to accompany him, so Rick went with Jackson, and they asked their college-aged son to come home for a semester and help care for Deirdre and for Jackson's other siblings.

Both Deirdre and Jackson seemed to make "miraculous" recoveries, and Jackson's leukemia was successfully kept at bay for many months with ongoing treatment. But just before Christmas the following year, it came back. Ever since, Jackson and Deirdre had been at the Ronald McDonald House, where he was receiving different and more intense chemotherapies to reduce the cancer enough so that he could undergo transplantation.

Throughout the process, Deirdre engaged in minimal care-captaining despite having reasonable amounts of cultural health capital both from her own experience with breast cancer and the class-based skills and resources she acquired as a college-educated elementary school teacher (and wife of an occupational therapist). Although she care-captained at particular strategic moments, she adopted a primarily care-entrusting approach because of its *emotional* benefits. She explained:

A whole lot of [it is] coming to terms with how much control you really have. And, um, I don't want to make it sound like you become blasé and don't care, or that, you know, there aren't things that you shouldn't be doing, or I shouldn't be doing. But the idea that I can control the situation— once you can finally let that go, there is just a certain amount of peace that passes, or understanding, when you realize you can't control it.

Using her emotions as signposts, Deirdre carefully considered how involved to become in directing her son's treatment. Generally, this drew her toward a care-entrusting strategy. She explained that when Jackson was first diagnosed, she chose not to do the kind of sweeping online research that care-captaining families conduct, because "if the probabilities weren't good, I didn't want to see them at that time." At other times, Deirdre *did* turn to the Internet for information, for instance, to look up a new chemotherapy drug, but did so with caution, only after deliberately assessing her emotional state.[2] She explained: "It depends on where I am. If I'm feeling very secure about things, I will look it up. If I'm not feeling confident, the Internet doesn't give me confidence. It actually tends to undermine [it]." For Deirdre, maintaining confidence was more important than gathering additional information or seeking further treatment possibilities. She became frustrated when others suggested that there might be more she could be doing or other alternatives to explore:

People would say, "Oh, have you checked out [another top-ranked research hospital in a different state]? Have you checked out The Cancer Centers of America?" You know, "Are you sure you want to go to Kelly-Reed?" And then after a point you've just got to say, "Nope, this is the path." . . . I wouldn't say I often showed it, but you know, my mind was going, "You idiot, you have no idea what you're talking about" [when these comments were made in relation to her breast cancer treatment]. . . . But with Jack, I think I recognized, you know, "You might be absolutely right, but this is the road we're choosing and if I look at where you're telling me to go, I can't stay on the road." . . . You can't be that. You have to be focused. And you can't let that [distract you]. . . . You can't second-guess yourself.

Deirdre's blended approach to illness management did not preclude care-captaining, however, when it offered clear and concrete advantages.

Deirdre described several incidents when Jackson was inpatient when they were transported to other parts of the hospital or to nearby clinics for tests or consultations and were kept waiting for long periods of time without a "transport" back to his room. Though she rarely questioned the doctors, she told me, "I am a complainer when things go wrong." In each instance she "went to the patient representative and complained." Once, she explained to me calmly, in her same warm and even-keeled tone, she had taken matters into her own hands: "You know, I've got an inpatient who has very little immune system and you're leaving me here for forty-five minutes. I mean, he shouldn't be sitting in a waiting room for forty-five minutes when he's got a bed upstairs. Actually, with that one I just left. I wasn't supposed to, but I told Jack, I said, 'Jackson, we're gonna go.'" Deirdre left his records behind, and pushed him back to the other end of the hospital herself. She added softly: "You'd think that was a simple thing, but it's kind of, it was definitely an act of rebellion!" She later spoke with the head of transport, who chided her that this was "a safety issue." She told me that she had responded in kind. "'He has a compromised immune system and you're leaving him out there,' I said. 'That's a safety issue.'"

Though Deirdre took a care-entrusting approach (particularly with the physicians she held in especially high esteem), she was able to quickly, comfortably, and successfully step in to address any problems that arose with an interactional ease undergirded by cultural health capital and race and class privilege. In doing so, Deirdre took on a significant role in guiding Jackson's care, but constructed important limits around that role:

> There's a fine line between taking your care in your own hands—and you *are* ultimately the one responsible—and knowing the trust you have with your doctor. . . . You can have a doctor right in front of you who is an expert in his field tell you one thing, and then you'll go online and read something from a source you have no idea [about], and it makes you start to doubt the doctor you're talking to. (Emphasis hers)

Again, Deirdre pointed to the emotional risks of care-captaining—the potential for outside information to raise doubts and shake her confidence. For Deirdre, protecting her emotional state and maintaining hope for her son's recovery were priorities. At the same time, the comfort with which she was able to step in when she was concerned about the quality of her son's care allowed her to feel efficacious. Deirdre's cool composure, which remained consistent across my time with them at the Ronald McDonald House, in the hospital, and in the face of her own declining health several months later, reflected the emotional success of her approach.[3]

Seeking Emotional Safety

While Deirdre's steadfast equanimity stood out as exceptional, she was not alone in finding emotional stability in a blend of care-captaining and care-entrusting. Despite Nora Bialy's regular efforts to care-captain, she too hit a point when care-entrusting sometimes offered her more emotional benefits than care-captaining could. Nora explained that at a recent clinic visit Benjamin's neuro-oncologist at Kelly-Reed had asked her if she would like to view Ben's latest MRI, but she chose not to look at it— "because at this point," she explained, I've looked at a lot of those, and I know what they look like, and I don't need to *make myself crazy* with seeing a spot that I know has something, but it's going away, that's just, 'punch me.' I don't need that, I just need to know that things are working the way they should" (emphasis mine).

Yet for Nora, care-captaining had also offered her important emotional benefits early on in Benjamin's illness by providing an outlet through which to manage her anxieties about her son's health. She recalled that when Benjamin was first diagnosed,

> I remember being in shock, and then at that point, once you know that something has to be done, you just start going through the motions to do it. I felt like I just had to do whatever needed to be done to get him safe, because he wasn't safe. He was at risk of having major problems if we didn't get him treatment, so we were just focused on securing the treatment plan, and moving forward from there. . . . It's almost like a way that you keep yourself safe is to focus on the goal, which was to get through the standard treatment. . . . I was able at a certain point to say, "Okay this is terrible, but we're going to be okay," . . . but I still felt a sense of wanting to control the situation. Like, you want to be in control of it.

Nora's statement about keeping *herself* safe points to her need for emotional safety—to avoid feelings of fear and despair. Upon her son's diagnosis, she needed to take actions that would allow her to produce hope that Benjamin would recover. Mobilizing medical networks, seeking the best possible surgeon, reading medical articles, and other care-captaining efforts allowed her to construct a path forward that she felt would be most likely to lead to the hoped-for outcome. Yet she contrasted her early impulse to intervene and exert as much control as she could with her more recent emotional need to pull back from that intense engagement in all aspects of Ben's care, because after his tumor recurred, "I started to really see things differently. Like, 'Okay, I'm not controlling this. I'm not controlling this, there's no way I'm controlling this.' So, you just kind of . . . recognize that. Put your faith in people who know what they're doing, and that's it."

Being able to blend or switch strategies as needed helped Deirdre and Nora reap the medical advantages and feelings of efficacy they could derive from care-captaining *and* the emotional advantages of care-entrusting. It freed them to relieve themselves of some responsibilities and avoid some of the stress and potential exposure to discouraging information that care-captaining could involve. Importantly, Nora and Deirdre's comfort in care-entrusting some of the time (in Nora's case) or most of the time (in Deirdre's case) remained rooted in the fact that they understood medical hierarchies well enough to view Kelly-Reed—and the other elite hospital where Benjamin had been treated—as top-notch, or "the best."[4] Nora parlayed this hierarchy into both greater hope for her son and a justification for care-entrusting after accessing elite care:

> When you're at a teaching institution, whether it's Kelly-Reed, or [another elite research hospital], you're getting cutting-edge treatment, it's right on the tip of—it's the best information available for that point in time. . . . If you do what they say, if you do things the way you're supposed to do them, they really have the experience. They've worked with so many people. If you think you can do it better than them, usually you're going to be disappointed. I mean, you know, I totally have faith in them.

Deirdre had done a bit of early care-captaining as well, activating medical social network ties to confirm that she was getting the best possible care for her son—which solidified her comfort in care-entrusting from that point forward. She explained that she asked an out-of-state friend who worked as a nurse oncologist to put her in touch with a physician at her hospital whose son had also been through cancer treatment to "give [her] the three best hospitals,' um, for the kind of cancer he has. And he said for the area, Kelly-Reed is definitely [the best]. And I know that's word of mouth, but they know a lot. So, I was just kind of like, you know, we can't go any further, and I don't want to go any closer because this is the best. So I feel very fortunate that we can make it to Kelly-Reed." Because Deirdre understood herself to have gotten her son to the best treatment possible, she felt comfortable turning his care over to Kelly-Reed doctors. This reduced her perceived need to become deeply involved in ongoing decisions about Jackson's medical treatment and offered her a more consistent ability to hope for the best possible outcome. Cultural health capital then was a resource that could facilitate emotional benefits even when not directly tied to regular care-captaining interventions.

Reserving Emotional Energy

Charlotte Caldwell used a strategic blend of care-captaining and care-entrusting to protect herself emotionally and protect her hope for her son's recovery as well. Charlotte's son, Brenton, a biracial (black/white) seventeen-year-old, was undergoing stem-cell transplantation for leukemia at Kelly-Reed when I met them. Charlotte, a white, forty-eight-year-old single mother of three with an associate's degree, whose thick jet black hair spilled over her shoulders as she spoke frankly and casually with me, had also care-captained early on to get her son to Kelly-Reed, having determined it a superior option in comparison to a research hospital in their home state. At age thirteen, Brent had started having what they believed to be sports-related knee pain which led to an exploratory surgery. Charlotte reported that the surgery "revealed gobs of dying tissue"—something the local surgeon told her he had never seen before. Charlotte asked them to "overnight it to Kelly-Reed" so doctors there could examine it. When I asked, "Why Kelly-Reed?" she told me that when her daughter had been diagnosed with an autoimmune disorder she had looked up several different regional and university hospitals. She explained: "There was something that just told me Kelly-Reed would be the best place to go. I had, you know, searched around a little bit and saw that they had a pretty good rheumatology department, so I just brought her here. [So for Brenton] I was like, I can't think of any other better place."

Because Brent's insurance at the time was through their home state's Medicaid program, Charlotte had to get special permission for him to receive treatment out of state. Fortunately, she explained, after Kelly-Reed called to tell her that the tissue exhibited "leukemic qualities," Brent's white blood count was "sky high," and she needed to get him down there first thing the next day, she got out-of-state treatment approved through her home state's Medicaid program. This is something that others may not even consider when confronted with similar bureaucratic hurdles.[5] Charlotte, who had hovered between working- and lower-middle class status throughout her adult life, possessed a solid enough knowledge of both formal and informal norms for navigating institutions—what Lareau calls "the rules of the game"—to be savvy and successful in advocating for her son.[6] This was the first of several times she would have to negotiate with bureaucracies and creatively piece together coverage to keep Brent's treatments paid.

Nonetheless, Charlotte soon deescalated her care-captaining efforts. The emotional risks of remaining intimately involved in directing Brent's medical care were too high, in her estimation. When I asked her what sort of research she had done about his illness and treatment, she pointed explicitly to the risk of becoming alarmed and upset too frequently, which could cause her feelings of hope for her son to falter:

> We did a lot of the online stuff [initially]. But I have learned through [other serious family health problems] that there's no way that you could ever—you're not going to get too much comfort from looking on the Internet because that's going to give you a worst-case scenario. . . . I try not to do that. Even now, with graft versus host [disease], I mean, things that's going on? I don't even go on there to look. Because it could just scare the pants off of you.

Like Deirdre, Charlotte used her emotions as a barometer to determine when and how to involve herself more directly in her child's medical care. If she began to find online medical research too frightening or discouraging, she stepped back from it.

When I asked if she had looked into the records of the physicians treating Brent, as other families in this study had done prior to transplant, she said "not really," though she did read about Dr. Vogel, the head of the program, online. She explained, "It's not something I do regularly because, you know, that's just not, I don't really have the time for it." As a single mom, Charlotte's time was already squeezed. What remaining energy she might have had was taken up with the lengthy and complicated bureaucratic hoops she had to jump through in order to maintain her son's state insurance coverage eligibility—and when that failed, to get him access to dependent coverage with the VA through her ex-husband's status as a disabled veteran. These were time-consuming hassles families with private insurance didn't have to contend with as frequently—and are yet another way that inequality is built into the illness experience.

Charlotte also worked hard to conserve her emotional energy and avoid becoming emotionally drained by limiting the amount of attention she devoted to the large quantity of medical information she could have pored over if she had chosen to care-captain more intensely. She explained how she worked to find a middle ground, particularly in relation to the daily lab reports she received while Brent was in the hospital: she looked to Brent's healthcare providers for cues about what she "really" needed to be concerned about, and let the rest go. She elaborated:

> You pay attention to what's important to the doctors. What are they paying attention to? . . . I just sit back and I watch their reaction. . . . It's just like if you're on an airplane, if you've never flown before, and you know, you hit pockets [of turbulence] and stuff, and you're like oh! [gasps]. You're scared? But if you watch the flight attendants, if they're calm, peaceful, not acting like there's an issue, you're fine. . . . You go into a doctor's office, you know, when you're dealing with something this serious, *everything could scare the crap out of you.* So, I just have learned that I sit back and I pay attention. I listen to what they're talking about. What is it that *they're* watching? What's important about that? That's what I try to find out. What's important about that number? . . . but I don't ask about every single thing they're monitoring. Because they monitor so much. I mean, if I showed you a lab sheet that they do on him every day, it's like,

about thirty things they're looking at. All the way from calcium to phos-
phorous to magnesium to white blood count. You know? It could be a ton
of different things. . . . I still haven't learned it all, and I'm not going to try
to, but, you know . . . if it's like just on the very end of this number or just
on the top side of this number I don't worry about it too much. But if it's
like really whacked out, and then *they* start showing concern? *Then* we
worry about it. And then I learn something. (Emphasis hers)

By winnowing down the number of things she needed to pay attention to, Charlotte could avoid becoming overly worried about a large
swath of relatively minor concerns and conserve her emotional energy
for larger problems. In this way, Charlotte trusted Brent's medical team
to adequately oversee his care and help her make strategic decisions
about where to focus her efforts. Like Deirdre Klein and Nora Bialy,
Charlotte had great faith in Brent's providers. "They have not misled us,
ever," she assured me.

Once Brent was discharged from Unit 27, Charlotte found the level of
direct care she would now need to provide for him to be tremendously
daunting. She explained:

I have to do blood work. I have to draw labs off of his lines. I gotta label
them, I gotta package them. I've got to, uh, give him Solu-Medrol steroid
pushes in his lines, I've got to do that. I have to change caps three days
a week. All three caps on here, which is a process. I have to get all of his
medications together. He takes about twenty-five pills a day.

Charlotte explained how resistant she had been to doing any of these
things when she was being trained in the hospital prior to discharge,
telling her twenty-two-year-old daughter who was visiting: "'*I do not
want to do any of that.*' . . . I hate to even admit it, because I want to do
everything I can for him, but I said, 'I do *not* want to do it.' [My daughter replied], 'But Mom, you're gonna.' I said, 'I don't even, I don't—it's
not that I think I can't do it, I don't *want* to do it,' you know? But, I do it
[now] and I do a good job" (emphasis hers).

When I asked Charlotte what led to her staunch resistance, she explained that some things just felt too risky:

CHARLOTTE: It was really, more so, [I was] just kind of intimidated by it. And afraid that I'm gonna contaminate him. I still won't do [the] dressing, will I Brent?

BRENT: No.

CHARLOTTE: I still won't do the dressings. If you see where his central line goes into his chest? [Brent comes over to show me]. That cover there. When you do that . . . it's like you have to be in full mask and you have to have sterile gloves. It's a, it's a job.

AMANDA: Thank you for modeling!

BRENT: You're welcome.

CHARLOTTE: And he can get an infection in there. I just don't wanna take—any time you open it, you are really taking a chance. So, I'm thinking, I'd rather not even open it. I don't want to touch it. And, you know, I know I could do it. But I don't want to. I'd rather for that to be done in a [sterile] hospital environment. So, whenever we're over there and I know that we're gonna be in clinic and I know the nurses can do it . . . So, I've got it set up to where we just get it done, we go over there, so I don't have to touch that part.

Though Charlotte found changing the dressing on Brent's central line to be too nerve-wracking an undertaking for her to bear, she also felt guilty for not doing it, and feared that her unwillingness might also put her son at risk. She continued:

I should be doing it, because the problem that we had on Monday was like, he's been sweating when he sleeps, and it's part of the medications. [That] makes [the dressing] come loose. And so, he's sitting here, and he's a little nervous because this is wide open at the top. That's not good. And I'm thinking, if I knew how to do it I could just replace it, but I don't want to touch it. So, yes, there are times you can feel really nervous about it. You know? I mean, I just don't want to. And I already, I still feel nervous about opening up the caps because when you take the blue cap off it's a wide open [line] into his heart. It's just an open hole, in a line that goes into his heart. I'm thinking, "Ugh!" [rolls eyes and groans]. So, I just move fast and carefully. Don't touch anything. Don't touch the cap. Don't, just get it in there, close it off, flush it, and put it away. You know, 'cause it's no joke.

This entire process was highly stressful for Charlotte. The current structure of the healthcare system has increasingly shifted care provision from trained healthcare professionals to unpaid family caregivers, sometimes thrusting them into roles that are overwhelming and uncomfortable. A taken-for-granted ideology of family responsibility discourages caregivers from resisting this devolution of care onto their shoulders because "caring for family members is understood as an inherent moral obligation, superior to any other form of care."[7] Yet with her son's medical care placed in her hands, Charlotte worried constantly that she might make a mistake that could harm him. By drawing a line around which care she felt was too risky for her to provide, she worried that she might be abdicating her motherly duties and putting him at greater risk than if she were willing to quickly perform the dressing change herself. For Charlotte, her inability to become more confidently involved in her son's care led to additional emotional difficulty.

Some other families, especially those with exceptionally high cultural health capital, felt so confident in their medical abilities that they were actually *less* stressed when providing medical care themselves so that they could be certain it was done to their standards. But this set of responsibilities was a heavy burden for Charlotte, who had some cultural health capital, but much less than others. She felt unsure about whether she was doing the best she could do for her son whether she engaged in direct nursing tasks or deferred them to medical professionals. When it came to the dressings around Brent's central line, Charlotte's emotional goal of avoiding particularly acute feelings of anxiety drove her to push this care responsibility back to his medical team. For the most part, though, Charlotte's blend of care-captaining and care-entrusting led her to obtain some key medical advantages for Brent (swift access to highly specialized care and seamless coverage for his transplant) while protecting herself from more regular emotional upheaval and maintaining confidence that Brent was receiving the best care available.

Charlotte also advocated for her son's comfort in small ways, which helped her to feel efficacious on a more routine basis:

You know, [I'd say] "He doesn't really want to take this drug or that drug. If it's not that important, do we have to do it?" They're like, "Well we have to do this one, but we don't have to do the other one. How 'bout we just stop doing that one?" And, you know, Brent would be a part of that [decision] and that's what we would do. So, you know, like a Colace pill, which is like a softener type thing. You know, different things that really don't mean anything in the grand scheme of things other than just for his comfort? Um, if he doesn't wanna do it, take it off the list and stop sending it in there. You know, those kinds of things.

Working to influence Brent's care in these small ways helped Charlotte to feel as though she was directly helping her son feel better throughout the treatment experience. Even with limited cultural health capital, Charlotte had enough of it to engage effectively in these ways. For families with little or no cultural health capital, efforts to care-captain even occasionally could lead to regular conflict, frustration, and constant feelings of uncertainty.

The Emotional Turmoil of Care-Captaining without Adequate Cultural Health Capital

Tina Morgan, a white thirty-year-old mother with a high school degree who was currently unemployed, was pregnant with her second child when she learned that her baby would be born with a congenital diaphragmatic hernia. This condition is often fatal, as it leads to organ displacement and poor lung development. Babies born with the condition often go into respiratory distress upon birth. Survival rates are beginning to increase, though, especially when infants can be treated with extracorporeal membrane oxygenation immediately. For this reason, doctors at the regional hospital who had diagnosed the condition told Tina and her fiancé, a machine-shop worker, that she should deliver her baby at Kelly-Reed (several hours away from their home town) so that this treatment would be available if their daughter required it. Physicians at Kelly-Reed also performed the initial surgeries involved in repairing the hernia.

After her daughter was born, Tina felt the emotional impulse to care-captain. But she didn't have much cultural health capital to back up her efforts. A petite, slender woman with angled chin-length dark red hair, Tina was stretched out on the twin bed in her room at the Ronald Mc-Donald House in dark blue jeans and flip flops, as we talked late one night, while four-month old Kassidy was receiving an automated feeding through her G-tube in a crib nearby. Tina had vented to me off and on for several weeks, lamenting the fact that doctors at Kelly-Reed were "always freaking her out." She was especially frustrated on this night, as she had just been told that her daughter had failed a second hearing test and would need to have a third. Infants born with congenital diaphragmatic hernia are thought to be at increased risk for sensorineural hearing loss, and are subject to extra screenings as a result. Tina, however, found this baffling, given that she perceived her daughter to be doing well and responding to her voice:

> The lady, she did some of the hearing [tests] on her, and she said she failed. On everything. When she passed on one ear before, she failed on both ears today. I don't get that, I think it's their equipment for some reason. 'Cause she'll respond to music, she'll respond to talking to her, you know? Different things. But they wanna do further testing, and the further testing has, has to have her asleep, which I think is so weird, I think it's the brain waves, or something, I forget what she said. . . . It was really weird.

To Tina, a lot of the things providers at Kelly-Reed wanted to do for her daughter seemed "weird." She tried to "look things up," but simply Googling without an in-depth understanding of medical hierarchies or an ability to sort and interpret information and recognize which sources would be taken seriously by providers meant that her efforts to intervene fell flat. This fostered deeper divides between Tina and Kassidy's providers and exacerbated her anger and distress.

Like other care-captaining parents, Tina wanted to hold providers accountable for what she deemed to be sub-par care, but she was unable to successfully do so. One morning, for example, she arrived at the hospital while Kassidy was an inpatient to learn that she had fallen out of her bouncy seat and hit her head under a nurse's supervision. Tina was outraged. Yet she never managed to report the nurse whom she viewed as negligent for not preventing or immediately informing her of Kassidy's fall. This was not due to a lack of desire or effort, as she explains: "It was quite aggravating to file, try to get, figure out who [the nurses reported to]. I went to the information desk in the front of the hospital, or on the fourth floor. They don't want to tell you. 'Oh, they're gone, oh, they're on vacation.' It's like you get the run around." This upsetting incident led Tina to try even harder to care-captain, which caused further contention between her and Kassidy's providers. For instance, Tina was eager to participate in the routine care of her new daughter and was frustrated that she could not feed her by bottle [as opposed to the feeding tube] more than once a day for ten minutes. Kassidy's speech therapist was concerned that doing so might cause her to aspirate, but to Tina this was "stupid, 'cause how is she gonna get it if you don't keep trying?" She added, "As long as she wants [the bottle], I felt like I should be able to do it whenever I was there."

The speech therapist was willing to consider increasing Kassidy's bottle feedings, but only if Tina consented to a swallowing test [a barium swallow] to make sure Kassidy's esophagus was functioning properly. Tina adamantly refused. Her denial of the test was in part an extension of her frustration stemming from the bouncy seat incident:

> When [Kassidy] fell out of her bouncy seat, we asked if they were going to do anything to check her head and make sure everything was all right—an MRI, CAT scan, or ultrasound. "No," [they said], because the, um, radiation risk is too high, and they think she was fine. [That] is exactly what they told us. But the speech [therapist], she wanted to do the swallowing test, and it is three minutes of continuous radiation. Three minutes. Which is more than the MRI and everything else. I said absolutely not! You're telling me, "Well, if you don't get it done, then you cannot feed her by a bottle, NO." I said, "Fine. I won't do it then!" Because we did research [online, Googling], and a lot of the risk of that is, um, a leukemia. The kids develop leukemia, and it's really like, the risks were really up there for that, and we're like, "No." You know, we'll figure it out or something.

Here, Tina care-captained: she did her own research, came to her own medical decision, and refused a recommended procedure, thereby exerting influence over her child's medical care. But beyond being suspicious of doctors' recommendations and possible radiation side effects, she was not able to request, or argue a case for, an alternative. Instead she refused the test, abstractly hoping that the situation would get "figured out or something," and put aside her desire to participate more in her daughter's care by bottle-feeding her. By attempting to care-captain with little cultural health capital, which might otherwise have helped her to assess and evaluate online information and then effectively deploy this information in conversation with her daughter's providers, Tina's anxieties were heightened and her efforts to manage her daughter's care became even more stressful and confusing. Since Tina did not fully relinquish control to the doctors and stay on the medical sidelines, an approach that offered other families without much cultural health capital some measure of calm and comfort, she had more contentious interactions with providers, and a far more angst-ridden and maddening experience managing her child's illness

Tina believed that the providers at Kelly-Reed were always looking for something to be wrong even if nothing was wrong—as in the case of the repeated hearing tests. Tina told me that she and her fiancé, who had remained back home to work and care for Tina's older daughter, were eager to get Kassidy back home so they could switch back to the doctors at their local regional hospital. They felt the providers at Kelly-Reed were too directive, and did not give them a chance to offer their input:

> I felt like I had no say-so in it. And that's another reason why I—we want to move [her] out to go to [Regional] or something, somewhere where they ask you, "How do you feel about, doing this?" Instead of, "We're doing this!" [claps hands]. "Right now!" And like the lady today is telling me, "Well we have to do further, you know, testing." No, you don't! *I'm* the parent. I have to sign a release for it. You don't *have* to do it. I have the say. I'm grown. I'm thirty years old! I pushed her out! (Emphasis hers)

Tina felt that she, *as the parent*, should be given the final say in medical matters, and she used her *status as a parent* to intervene in Kassidy's care when she lacked the medical knowledge and vocabulary to make a medical argument. But without more cultural health capital or middle-class status and resources, her assertions of parental authority increased contention with providers who did not view her efforts to intervene as reasonable ones.

While one of the high–cultural health capital care-captaining mothers I observed faced some pushback as well during an attempt to shift her son from a diet of breast milk combined with fortified formula to a blenderized diet (combining breast milk with blended foods such as fruits, vegetables, and hard-boiled eggs), she was able to leverage her cultural health capital and bargain with the nutritionist. She assured her son's provider that she and her husband were keeping careful calorie counts and monitoring his stool for signs of poor digestion. And she presented the nutritionist with the careful charts they kept of every feeding and diaper change. In doing so, these parents gained acquiescence from their son's dietician in ways Tina was not able to with Kassidy's speech therapist.

On another occasion, Tina recalled, Kassidy was asleep when she came for one of her twice-daily visits. Tina became frustrated when the nurse told her not to wake Kassidy to give her a bath: "How [are] you going to tell me don't wake up my child? So I can hold her? If I'm allowed to hold her, you know, once I was allowed [by doctors]. I'm going to change my child's diaper, and pick her up, and give her a bath whenever I want to. As long as *she's* up for it, you know? That's things I can do" (emphasis hers). Tina wanted to provide basic loving care for her daughter. But because she did not fully care-entrust in the medical arena, and because healthcare providers viewed her interventions as ill-informed, her interactions with providers became confrontational, and communication broke down entirely.

Tina worried regularly about medical issues and conducted frenzied web searches, but without the cultural health capital to effectively sort through this information, they caused her only greater alarm. Her anxiety about her daughter's health drove her to care-captain, but doing so increased emotional turmoil because she lacked the cultural health capital to make her efforts to influence her daughter's medical care effective. The emotional upset and amped-up anxiety that could result from the mismatch between a parent's level of cultural health capital and illness management strategy help explain why families with little cultural health capital rarely adopted a care-captaining approach.

Turning It over to God

Cultural health capital was a necessary foundation for blending care-captaining and care-entrusting effectively, both medically and emotionally. At times when families bumped up against the limits of their capacities to influence children's medical trajectories, religious families could use their faith tradition as a more readily available resource for managing feelings of helplessness. Deirdre Klein's faith in God and solid belief in an afterlife in heaven helped her to feel comfortable care-entrusting much of the time. She told me calmly:

> I guess you do kind of come to the conclusion that, if you believe, if you're Christian . . . if I really believe what I say I believe, then this world is temporary. We will not live here forever, and the next step is better. And, you know, with that in mind, I have moments of real sadness for both Jack and I, or, for—you know, my seventeen-year-old could get in a car [accident] and you know, I would not see him again. But the idea that it is better on the other side, and we will recognize each other [when we meet there] . . . that's a real comfort.

Deirdre's religious beliefs assured her that she would not be permanently separated from her children if either she or they died. Taking comfort in this fact, Deirdre could feel better about relinquishing some efforts to control all aspects of her son's medical care.

Jamilla Finley, a thirty-six-year-old black mother of three whose seven-year-old daughter, Teyariah, was being treated for neuroblastoma—a pediatric cancer affecting the sympathetic nervous system—also took a blended approach. Jamilla care-captained to get her daughter to Kelly-Reed and did occasional research into treatment options recommended by fellow parents,[8] but largely care-entrusted outside of these efforts. The possibility of her daughter's death weighed on her heavily, but knowing her daughter would be with God if she died offered Jamilla some real reassurance: "I can't say how I would deal with it, but I would know that I gave her back to God because she was God's before she was mine. So, she's done been baptized—I got her christened—I know where she's going." Religious faith helped parents to construct firm limits around their abilities to do more to remedy their children's illnesses—and accept what they could not accomplish. Sociologist Michelle Wolkomir has similarly found that Christian wives of gay men coped with their situations in part by "giving it up to God," deferring to his wisdom, and accepting that they were "no longer responsible for the master plan."[9] In this way, religion could be a useful resource for emotion management as well—particularly for those with low levels of perceived control over negative life experiences.[10]

Lakira Harris told me adamantly that while she would do "anything in her power" to save her son, Jayden, this was not something that was within her control. After describing a particularly perilous hospitalization following a sickle-cell crisis that threatened Jayden's life before coming to Kelly-Reed, Lakira presented her determination to keep her son alive as both empowered and constrained: "Not in my power. No way. If it was God's will, I can't do anything about that. But if it were my will? NO. I'm not gonna let it happen." Like Deirdre and Jamilla, Lakira felt less anxious about what she should be doing for her child at peak moments of crisis by believing that God had the ultimate power over the outcome of her child's illness. For these three mothers it was comforting to believe that ultimately it was out of their hands.

For Nicholas Henderson, a belief in God also served as an outlet for coping with conflicted feelings and making sense of his son Elijah's illness and recovery. He told me: "I mostly talked to God, to myself, and kept my faith through it all. And every time I'd go to cry, or go to get down, I'd know that I was weak, and He's strong, and that miracles could happen. And I just knew inside that everything was gonna be alright." When Elijah came down with pneumonia, Nicholas told me that the doctors were puzzled at how quickly he recovered and how active he remained during the infection. Nicholas, however, said he'd informed them confidently, "I know what it is, it's God. He's gonna make him alright." Both Nicholas and his wife, Connie, attributed the success of Elijah's liver transplant to God as well; for her part, Connie understood it as evidence that "God listens to everybody, no matter where you're at."

Given that the Hendersons saw Elijah's health as something that was not in their hands but in God's, they could draw on a resource readily available to them—their ability to pray, which they did regularly—to give them something to *do* for Elijah during a time when they otherwise felt helpless. In this way, prayer itself served as a useful emotion management strategy.[11] Jamilla Finley reported that she went straight for her Bible when she was upset or especially worried about Teyariah. Mayyadah Tahir, Nazia Khalid's mother, told me she turned to her Quran. Eva Campos, who activated a massive network of support on behalf of her ten-year-old son, Ignacio, to raise money to bring him to Kelly-Reed from Argentina for a bone marrow transplant with experts in his rare disease (metachromatic leukodystrophy, or MLD), told me that she took great comfort in knowing that people around the world she had never met were praying for her son. Just as care-captaining, care-entrusting, and a blend of both approaches helped families feel that either they and/ or the appropriate experts were "in control" of a child's illness, when families lost a sense of control, religious faith helped some to feel less anxious about that reality.

Managing Illness, Managing Emotions

If you keep track of *every freaking thing that's going on*, you will *lose your mind*! I just go with the flow. As long as my baby ain't having no seizures, and acting, you know, like he's about to [whispers] die? Or something like that? I'm good.
—Lakira Harris, mother of eight-year-old Jayden

Care-captaining and care-entrusting, as general approaches to managing a child's critical illness, exist along a continuum. Some families lean heavily, or *almost* entirely, to one end or the other. But in reality, it is likely that all of my interviewees care-captained and care-entrusted at some point along the way. This chapter highlights families who were regularly inclined to blend or switch strategies, illuminating the emotional pros and cons of each approach and bringing the resources needed to accomplish this successfully into sharper relief.

The families I met who regularly care-captained were often driven by a need to feel they were taking matters into their own hands and doing everything possible to save their children.[12] But if care-captaining parents' efforts did not achieve the desired result—a healthy, cured child—or if the illness continued for longer than they could maintain such an intense approach, *surrendering* control by constructing their child's fate as beyond their influence and turning more of their child's care over to doctors, to God, or to both, made for a more emotionally sustainable approach. Parents who could do so adapted their *illness* management strategies to meet shifting *emotional* needs throughout the illness process.

These efforts helped parents to construct and maintain hope for their child and avoid additional episodes of emotional upset while seeing their children through demanding treatments for an indefinite period of time. It could also help them to mitigate feelings of guilt or inadequacy for not doing more. Sociologists David Karp and Valaya Tanarugsachock, in their study of emotion management among caregivers of loved ones struggling with mental illness, similarly found that once caregivers accepted that they could not control their family member's illness, they could begin "to decrease involvement without guilt."[13]

For families with less cultural health capital to draw on, turning control over to doctors or to God was even more important, and tended to occur early in the process. Attempting to follow and control every detail of their child's treatment plan was not a viable option for those with less medical knowledge to bring to bear on this enormous task. This lack of cultural health capital led families to adopt a primarily care-entrusting philosophy that helped them feel their child would be okay despite their inability to micromanage the multitude of technical medical details involved in their treatment and care. As Lakira Harris put it, "going with the flow" in the absence of obvious signs of deterioration could be the only way to avoid becoming overwhelmed.

Living with and managing a child's critical illness was nerve-wracking even when children's treatment plans were proceeding smoothly. When children were not doing well, parents moved onto even shakier ground. Families were most strongly pulled toward, and torn between, care-captaining and care-entrusting when the medical interventions upon which their hopes were pinned began failing.

PART III

Tangled Up in Hope

6

When Everything Is Not Enough

I never came out and said, . . . 'There's nothing we can do.'
I told them, 'We'll continue to do everything we're doing
that we can, that we know to do. And my expectation is
your child is going to die. And probably, you know, days or
weeks,' . . . but I don't come out with a hammer and say, you
know, 'Your child is going to die.'
—Dr. Fadian

We came here with all expectations. We were not expecting
this.
—Edward Rivera, father of five-month-old Noah

About two weeks after I visited the Rivera-Cruzes on Unit 27 and Noah's
post-transplant engraftment rash had seemed to indicate that things
were progressing smoothly, I stopped by to visit them again but found
the room dark and empty. When I asked a nurse where they were, she
furrowed her brow. Noah had been transferred to the pediatric intensive care unit (PICU). Little Noah, whose immune system was destroyed
with high doses of chemotherapy prior to the transplant (to keep his
body from attacking the donor stem cells) had, despite all precaution,
caught a virus. His new immune system had not yet fully developed, so
he was unable to battle even the simplest infection. Catching a common
cold at this point in the transplant process can be fatal for kids undergoing this potentially life-saving, but high-risk procedure.

I texted his mother, Juliana, to see how they were doing and offer
any help I could provide. She sent me their new room number, and I
visited the PICU a few days later with some peaches and éclairs for her
and her husband, Edward, and chocolate-covered cookies for their four-
year-old daughter, Sophie. After I was buzzed through the foreboding
metal double doors to the unit, I was struck by the much more somber

environment of the PICU in comparison to Unit 27. There was no bright artwork lining the neutral walls, and no children were moving about. The nursing staff were more hushed and reserved in their conversations. The muted tone seemed to finally yield to and underscore the substantially compromised conditions of the children who reached this space.

After I found their private room and waved to Juliana through two panes of glass, I entered an airlock through one set of automatic sliding glass doors.[1] Noah's nurse, sitting at a computer beneath several monitors, instructed me to put on a thin papery yellow gown, a blue facemask, and a pair of latex gloves before I entered Noah's room through a second set of sliding glass doors. She told me, "You can touch him, but just don't move him." I promised to do neither.

I was not prepared to see Noah spread out motionless and sedated on the bed, a half dozen tubes taped to his cheek and running in and out of his small nose and mouth. His face was swollen, his neck bruised. Juliana told me that Sophie caught a simple virus. It was nothing her body's now well-developed, new immune system couldn't handle, but she unwittingly passed it on to Noah before she developed obvious symptoms. Without enough time for his donor cells to grow and his new immune system to take root and fight the virus, Noah's kidneys were failing, so he was placed on dialysis. His lungs were also failing, so he was intubated and placed on a ventilator.[2] Paralytics (medications to induce coma) had to be administered to keep him completely still so that the mechanical ventilation he depended on to breathe would not cause further damage to his lungs.

As I sat by Noah's bedside watching his blood and another amber-colored fluid (the contents of his stomach, Juliana explained) cycle in and out of his swollen body, machines whooshing and humming around him, I was stunned to see the happy baby whose toes I'd tickled in his infant carrier when the family first arrived at the Ronald McDonald House a few months earlier, now in this frozen, helpless state. Juliana, perhaps intuiting my reaction, remarked, "It's so difficult to see him like this." Edward came in soon after so that Juliana could go pump breast milk to keep in reserve. He echoed his wife's sentiment, telling me: "It's really hard on us to see him and not be able to do anything. . . . You just watch the numbers all the time, it's very stressful. . . . I don't like to see any yellow up there," (an indication that Noah's vital signs were out of normal range). Today Noah was stable, but previous days had been "very stress-ful" for Edward and Juliana because alarms sounded regularly, and the doctors were in and out constantly. "Every day is different," he said. "You have to see what each day brings."

Forging Paths through Children's Declines

The harrowing experience of navigating a child's life-threatening illness enters new, even more treacherous territory if treatments begin to fail and children edge closer to death. In these heightened moments of cri-sis, the emotional impetus to care-captain or care-entrust can reach a fever pitch—or fluctuate dramatically. Edward Rivera and Juliana Cruz, for example, continued to care-captain throughout the final weeks of their son's life, though their emotional strategies eventually diverged from one another's. Lakira Harris, in contrast, stepped back even further from Jayden's care when he was transferred to the PICU, and his graft versus host disease (GVHD) spiraled out of control.

Physicians were acutely aware of their role in managing families' ex-pectations for their children's recoveries during these downward spirals. They devised strategies to shepherd parents through such emotional minefields and if necessary eventually begin to dismantle—or from their perspective, redefine—their hopes. So important were these interactions that some physicians intentionally began laying the groundwork for the possibility of a child's death from the beginning of treatment. Parents, in their efforts to maintain confidence that their child would recover, sometimes remained impervious to these efforts.

Close examination of the delicate dance between parents and health-care providers at such intense moments reveals just how powerful emo-tion management strategies may be in shaping the experiences of both parties and their interactions with one another. Even lightly nurturing hope has the potential to smooth difficult social interactions and help families and physicians alike demonstrate the depth of their care. But physicians also believed that they needed to build stepping stones for families to help them begin to understand that their children may not survive. Families' fierce care-captaining or their fervent care-entrusting in an unrelenting effort to maintain hope at this time could pose obsta-cles to these efforts. And as we have seen in previous chapters, differing emotional strategies could also precipitate inequalities between families during the dying process, and in the experience of loss and grief as well.

Looking for Hope around Every Corner

Edward Rivera and Juliana Cruz remained intimately involved in directing their son's care even as his condition worsened. Juliana did much of the carework that nurses might otherwise do, such as keeping Noah clean, suctioning his airways, and closely monitoring his vitals and urine output. Juliana's parents flew in from Puerto Rico to care for Noah's sister, Sophie, back at the Ronald McDonald House, so that both Edward and Juliana could spend full days with Noah in the PICU. Yet as we saw in the previous chapter, even parents who primarily care-captained can be drawn to a care-entrusting approach when doing so is emotionally protective. The powerful pull toward care-captaining or care-entrusting is especially palpable during the most acute moments.

For instance, Edward was visibly torn when two doctors stepped into the airlock while he and I were sitting by Noah's bedside. The doctors waved to us, but continued conferring with one another while looking at the monitors. I asked Edward if he needed to go speak with the doctors, but he shook his head and said, "No." After a moment, he added, "Sometimes you don't want to know too much."

Yet, a few minutes later, when one of the doctors poked his head into the room to ask how we were doing, Edward did go out to speak with the physicians. Despite his earlier inclination to avoid encountering potentially disheartening information, he asked a series of questions about the flow rate on Noah's dialysis, what could be done to avoid the clotting issues that they had confronted the day before without impacting his blood pressure, and the possibility of giving him a shot of white blood cells, which he'd heard about from another family. In doing so, Edward worked to steer these doctors toward potentially reassuring information with which he could maintain some semblance of hope for Noah's recovery.

Edward's efforts were successful. The PICU doctors agreed to retest for the virus to see if progress had been made (despite cautioning Edward that the results would not influence his treatment), and they encouraged Edward to "take one day at a time," warmly reassuring him when he suggested that his hope and faith were wavering. "Keep your hope, keep your faith," one of the doctors told Edward before they left the room, promising they would check back soon.

I visited the Rivera-Cruzes in the PICU again the following week. When I arrived, Noah was being reconnected to dialysis after a short period during which he had been taken off the machine to see how his kidneys were functioning on their own. Noah was now nestled under a sheet of large plastic air-bubbles topped with a multicolored fleece blanket. The nurse explained that this helped to keep him warm, since "all of his fluids" were being cycled through room temperature air, making it difficult for his small body to regulate his temperature. Noah's lips were chapped and swollen around the tubes down his throat. His body vibrated slightly with the oscillation of the ventilator.

Edward was on the phone with his sister when I arrived. When he got off the call, he came in and sat by the bed with me for a few minutes. I asked him about Noah's white blood cell count, and he began to cry. I put my hand on his shoulder and told him I couldn't imagine how painful this must be. He wiped his eyes, but continued crying. Though I didn't understand the Spanish he had been speaking to his sister, it sounded like a difficult call. "Excuse me" he said, and put his head in his hands. "It's very hard," he said, after he stepped away to get a tissue. "Every day you have expectations." He explained that when Sophie went through her transplant, nothing like this had happened. They never thought it would happen to Noah.

Juliana came in a few minutes later. She greeted me cheerfully and was upbeat. Though Edward was losing hope for his son's recovery, Juliana's optimism seemed unwavering.[3] She remarked happily to the nurse that the little bit of urine that had collected in the measuring cup at the foot of Noah's bed was a bit lighter in color than before. The nurse tried to dampen her enthusiasm, reminding her that the volume still wasn't much—"His kidneys just aren't there yet." Juliana didn't engage with this more cautious assessment. When she helped the nurse change Noah's diaper, she also optimistically proposed that it was a good sign his bowels were moving. The nurse agreed that it was, in fact, a good thing. Juliana turned to me to add that his genitals were much less swollen than they had been a few days earlier—though the nurse remarked that because his heart rate had increased while he was changed, he must be sore.

Juliana and I chatted for a bit, and she showed me a video of Sophie at the pool that her parents had texted to her. Before I left, she gave me two photo buttons. One was a picture of the four of them on a blanket at the park; the other one was a close-up of Noah with his big brown eyes gazing straight into the camera, the picture of a healthy baby just before the transplant. It would be several weeks before I could visit again, as I was on the way to Minnesota for my brother's wedding. I promised her that I'd keep all of them close in my thoughts over the coming weeks. I hugged Juliana and silently waved goodbye to Noah, trying hard not to tear up. I was worried that I might not see him again. Edward nodded to me, but continued to sit quietly by the bed, cupping Noah's forehead in his hand. I slowly made my way back through the airlock, through the maze of the PICU, and out to the jarringly bright and bustling world beyond those heavy metal doors.

The Interactional Dynamics of Hope Work

During my interviews with physicians, I shared my observation that parents often latched on to very small "improvements" in their children's health status even under relatively bleak circumstances in an effort to bolster their hopes for recovery. They immediately recognized this impulse. Dr. Fadian told me:

> Let's take adenovirus [for example] . . . but it could be all kinds of things. You know, an adenoviral copy number [ascertained through DNA polymerase chain reactions to measure levels of viral infection] of half a million versus 750,000 is the same number. They're both bad. And then when it goes to a million, it's still bad, and a million and 1.4 million are the same numbers, they're just bad. But parents, you know, if it went from 1.4 million down to one million they'll say, "Oh it's improved!" But it's not . . . it doesn't matter—200,000 is bad. We look at orders of magnitude when it comes to these viral PCRs. But the parents are looking at that as good, you know what I'm saying?

Dr. Fadian viewed parent's interpretations of such "improvements" as misguided. Yet he deliberately tried not to counter them, even when he knew that parents were holding onto slivers of hope that he saw as futile. He explained:

> You can't totally alienate the parents. If they say something is positive, and you totally cut their legs down to "Oh it's worthless," or whatever, after a while they won't listen to you. And *you never want to totally remove all hope*, because you know, we're not infallible. . . . But again, they're focusing on these [viral] copy numbers, you know, 200, goes to 2,000 and 5,000, 4,000. It's not good. The trend is up. And that's going to be a problem. So you have to help them understand what the big picture is. And they'll focus on the little things *because they want positive stuff.* [Let's say that] the creatin went from 1 down to 0.8. Well, you know, that's good. But in the big scheme of things, with the adenoviral copy at 1.4 million, it's clear [to me] what's going to happen. And so again you just have to work with them as a team, educate them and let them know what your experience is. (Emphasis mine)

Dr. Fadian was reluctant to "totally remove all hope" because he found that validating families' hopeful interpretations was important to maintaining a strong relationship with them. He juggled this interpersonal goal with the need to "educate them" and focus their attention on "the big picture" in order to lay the groundwork for clinical decisions (and the potential dismantling of hope) that might need to occur in the near future. In Dr. Fadian's experience, aggressively countering families' efforts to maintain hope might weaken the trust between them and damage his ability to communicate with them effectively at the end of a child's life:

> When you're telling [parents] their child's dying, they don't want to hear it. But if you've built this trust with them, they'll hear it. They don't want to hear it, but they will hear it. And they'll act on it. They will want to latch on to positive things; *let them do it*, because you don't want to take away all their hope. But again, at the same time, *you've got to help pull them back.* And that's what you do a lot of. You know, with [one family] I was spending probably forty-five minutes a day to an hour, for several days, until things really clarified themselves. . . . So I don't come out

and say, "Well, that [small improvement] doesn't mean anything." I'll say, "You're right." Because they *are* right, you know? It is a little better. But clinically, it doesn't change the picture. (Emphasis mine)

Dr. Fadian engaged in hope work strategically when children began to decline following a transplant. Though he sought to "pull families back" from overly optimistic assessments of their children's status, he saw it as equally necessary to validate their efforts to maintain hope. If he did not, he worried that he might lose influence with parents at a critical juncture in their child's illness.

Dr. Coleman also believed it was important to help parents to maintain hope even as children declined. In fact, he tried himself to focus on the positive, or put the negative aside, with the families in his care. He explained:

> I listen to what parents have told me over the years. I had a very young couple, but very mature, and after their child died in the ICU, after a *long* stay there, they actually walked around and they talked with everybody, and kind of gave an exit interview, or an evaluation. And what they told me was, "You're our main doctor. *You have to be our cheerleader every day.* You have to come in and find something to tell us, to help us keep going." That gets hard though, when every, you know, everything is going wrong. And the last couple of days that I came into their daughter's room, I just came in and didn't say anything about anything medical. I asked how they were doing, how they were sleeping. They didn't want to hear anything bad about their child [so] I didn't talk medicine. I just socially engaged with them. But I do hear that mother's words, "You have to be our cheerleader." So I do try to stay very optimistic, as long as possible. And then if something, you know, really makes us see, you know this isn't [turning around], this is very unlikely, *we [still] never say never, you know*? [Because] there are kids who just survive, somehow, and we don't understand how. And there's other kids who die who shouldn't have died. There's never a zero [percent chance]; there's never 100 percent. (Emphasis mine)

Even for physicians, then, the most remote possibilities for a positive outcome tug powerfully enough to justify helping families to sustain hope in the face of a child's deteriorating health.

The fact that physicians may feel an obligation to be their patients' cheerleaders increases the extent to which speaking directly about death feels interactionally risky and threatening to their relationships with patients.[4] Broaching the topic of death inherently suggests that a patient may not "defeat" his or her illness, that a parent may not be able to "save" his or her child. Because illness is so often framed with military symbolism as a "battle" with heroic "survivors" who have refused to succumb to an "invading force" such as cancer by mustering extraordinary strength and courage, opening up the possibility of death can seem like admitting weakness and defeat.[5] To be supportive of someone, in many contexts, is often understood as "believing" in that person's limitless capacity, and it is generally taken for granted within the culture of positive thinking that people are more likely to accomplish that which they "believe" they can. This reasoning alone can encourage physicians to foster hope in patients and creates a situation in which failing to express "belief" in a patient or ill loved one can feel hurtful and unsupportive.[6] As Dr. Coleman implies, anything less than "cheerleading" could seem incompatible with reassuring families he was on their side.

One solution some healthcare providers use to resolve this conflict is to shift conversations about death and the work of managing it to hospital chaplains, as sociologist Wendy Cadge found in her multi-center study of hospital chaplaincy programs.[7] Because the physicians on Unit 27 generally did not outsource this role (though a well-loved chaplain visited many families, both religious and nonreligious, regularly throughout the transplant process[8]), Dr. Coleman struggled with this contradiction, and presented it as both an emotional and an interactional problem:

> When enough organs are injured, when there [are] enough strikes against the kid, then you really do have to start being realistic. So it is, uh, you know, the emotional side for the doctor, the emotional side for the family, is very tough. It's very tricky waters, because you want to keep them optimistic for as long as possible until you've tried all your tricks and done all of the interventions that you think might work. But when it's inevitable and everybody agrees, this path is not gonna turn around, then you do have to sit down with them and help them deal with that and come to terms with that.

Not only is it emotionally difficult for doctors and families to loosen their grip on hope for a child's survival, but keeping parents optimistic can make the practical work doctors need to do—the logistics of "trying all of the interventions you think might work"—easier. It helps to smooth their interactions with families during an exceptionally difficult time and keep them stable enough to continue moving through the medical process.

The effort to balance hope with the likelihood that dreaded outcomes will be realized is an especially delicate form of emotion work. In sociologist Jennifer Lois's study of wilderness search and rescue missions, rescue workers who were assigned to stay with the family members of those who were lost or injured in the wilderness were in a similar position to the physicians in my study.[9] Family members were terribly anxious about the fates of their missing loved ones. Rescue workers had to strike a balance between keeping panicked family members calm through many hours with little or no information, while preparing them for the possibility that an avalanche victim, for instance, may not have survived. Ambiguity is at one level the core problem: that is, it is difficult for those involved in the interaction to define the situation they are confronting. On the other hand, ambiguity can help workers keep family members from becoming entirely "defeated," in the words of one of Lois's interviewees, and falling into emotional states that would make rescue workers' jobs more difficult.

Likewise, interactions between physicians and families of children who are not likely to survive might continue for prolonged periods of time. Keeping families hopeful throughout this time helps physicians feel they are being compassionate, eases interactional awkwardness, and may help families to cope over extended periods. Dr. Ravipati explained:

> When patients are not doing well, parents want hope. That is a very hard time to give them hope. But at the same time *you don't want to take the hope completely away*, um, because then it is *hard for them to go day by day without that hope*. So, when the parents are in that situation, and they see the small, small things, we have to just acknowledge that that's a good thing. But at least I would, at the end of the conversation, tell them that there are still all these issues, you know? And if the parent is very much into trying to get hope, then I just say that we have to go day by day. "Let's

see what happens tomorrow." You know, on the one hand, it's good to not mislead them, that there is no hope. But a lot of times there are situations where we know for months: there's no hope. And we almost know with 100 percent surety the patient is not going to survive [in the] long run. But then the patient struggles for three to six months. Um, so you don't want to every day tell them that your patient is going to die—your son is going to die, your daughter is going to die. Right? That's uh, *rude.* It's just not very compassionate. So we have to strike a balance, you want to tell them, "Yeah, this is good," and you know, explain to them why we are doing what we are doing. And what I tell them is that in order to know that he is really doing better, this is what we need to see, in addition [to the positive fact they are focusing on]. So if their sodium and creatin are a little bit better? Meaning the lung, you know, kidney function is better? I tell them, "Yeah that's good, but we need to see some improvement in the oxygen numbers. And we need to see that he is getting off oxygen. We need—." So we, we focus them on the big picture.

Hope, then—though it often helps to propel families to gain access to the most advanced medical care possible—becomes hazardous terrain for physicians and families alike when the goal of saving a child's life begins to slip out of reach. The physicians I interviewed saw hope as a necessary tonic for families, helping them to endure day to day while making interactions with their healthcare providers less painful.[10] Aggressively dismantling hope can violate these interactional norms—or come across as "rude," as Dr. Ravipati put it. But emboldening families' hopes can become a problem when physicians exhaust remaining medical options and believe that it is time to stop treatment or withdraw life-supporting care. Leaning into ambiguity allows physicians to help parents stay in an emotionally sustainable place in the interim.[11]

Preparing for the Worst

The inherent conflict between being a family's "cheerleader" and helping them let go of a child at the end of life, if it came, was something each of the physicians I spoke with had to regularly juggle. Careful emotion work, strategically deployed—sometimes from the day they first met their patients—could help them, at least partially, to walk this fine line. Dr. Oliver, who pioneered a life-saving tissue transplant for infants born with a fatal chromosomal deletion syndrome, explained that because some patients would not make it through the transplant, she began laying the foundation for loss from the moment she met the babies she transplanted. She did so first by demonstrating to parents her genuine love for, and commitment to, these children. She told me matter-of-factly:

> A quarter of my patients are going to die. I do not want the parents to think that I'm just trying to free up a bed with what I'm doing. I want the parents to feel that I love that baby. And for me, it's easy, because I do. You know? I just look forward to meeting my new baby because I know that I'm going to fall in love with that baby, and this is the most wonderful thing. And the family watches me with their baby and they know I really care about their baby. And so whatever I'm doing, they feel it's with the baby's best interest at heart.

Dr. Oliver made a conscious effort to *perform* this love for families by being as demonstrative as she could with each baby she accepted for transplant. She explained earnestly, "You can do certain things that make the parents feel you love their baby":

> When you have a baby, you pick up the baby, and you go "Goo! Goo, goo, goo!" and, "What a beautiful baby!" and "How wonderful this baby is!" and "Oh, look at you! And you've got your head up, push, push, push, push! Oh, look at that head rising! Oh, that's wonderful!" [Dr. Oliver spoke in a high-pitched enthusiastic tone.] I mean, you know, that's *easy*! It's *easy* to do this. And you just *fuss* over these babies. But it's so much fun. I mean, you know, you're saying, "Push, push, push, push!" you know, "You can do it!" And "Look at your development!" and, oh, it's just wonderful. (Emphasis hers)

Dr. Oliver believed that demonstrating such love was "a teachable thing," but emphasized that it had to be explicitly taught to the residents and fellows she trained, because otherwise, "they won't do it. They won't have any idea." That Dr. Oliver found this skill to be lacking among recent medical school graduates suggests that it is one that physicians develop only as they accrue real-life experience dealing with the difficult emotional dynamics medical practice can involve.

Social expectations related to women's nurturance also likely shaped this interaction. Patients may have expected Dr. Oliver, for example, to be especially effusive and affectionate with the infants in her care, holding her to a higher standard of caring than they might have held a man.[12] But her gender also helped her nurturing performance seem natural, enhancing its effectiveness. By "fussing" over the babies in her care, Dr. Oliver worked to assure parents that she would do everything possible to save their children and to communicate proactively to them that if these efforts failed, it was not due to a lack of commitment to their child.

Dr. Ravipati took a different approach to laying the groundwork to prepare families for the possibility a child's death. He focused his efforts on explicitly and repeatedly outlining the risks and chances of death during initial consultations and the consent to treatment process. He lamented, however, that he still had to work quite hard to keep families from holding onto hope when his patients were dying in the PICU. At these times, he refined the language he used to more directly convey the hopelessness of the situation:

> At every opportunity we have, we try to explain to them if there is any possibility of recovery or not. So in those situations when a patient is in the ICU with multi-organ failure, we usually give them some concrete information. So for example, "If your child does not improve within seven days, then the chances of improvement are unlikely." And then there are some parents who will say, "Unlikely, meaning there's still a one percent chance, right?" So then we say that if the patient is not improved after two weeks, we have *never* seen anyone improve. (Emphasis his)

Such semantics, according to Dr. Ravipati, contributed to some families' beliefs that physicians sometimes offered conflicting opinions about children's prognoses when they were in the PICU. He suggested that if he told a family that their child was "unlikely to survive" while another doctor said "he is not going to survive," parents would mistakenly believe that physicians were not in agreement, when in fact, from his perspective, they were. Here too, he believed, the desire to maintain hope led families to grasp at straws: "'Unlikely to survive' means he's not going to survive. But the family [doesn't] hear that. The family [hears] there is hope. There is a small chance. And all the families in this situation are talking about miracles, and God, and you know, that's where they turn to, which is appropriate completely. But I'm trying to explain [what is] happening."

That families can hang their hopes on the remote possibility of survival that is left open by words like "unlikely" puts physicians in a tough position. As we've seen, physicians believe that removing *all* hope puts parents in a position in which they cannot endure day to day, while also putting too great a strain on their relationship with them. This dynamic may have led Dr. Ravipati to use the language of "unlikely to survive" despite the fact that in his mind the outcome was certain.

Conversely, Dr. Newell and Dr. Coleman attributed parents' difficulties letting go when children were dying not to semantics, but to the untenable emotional position of having to decide, for instance, to take their child off of life support. They developed their own linguistic strategies to take parents out of this position and put themselves in it instead. Dr. Newell offered her view of this dynamic:

> There have been times at the end of life where it doesn't seem like the parents can make those decisions. They're just not in that emotional spot to be able to say [it]. "I can't," you know, "I can't withdraw care of my own child." It's just not something that they can do. And that is where I think it is helpful just to sometimes make, not make the decisions for them, but to take the pressure off of them and say, we really are at a place where we cannot do anything more. We have done everything we can. And not put them in that position where they just can't be.

Dr. Coleman explained similarly that he worked to shift the difficult burden of making end-of-life decisions away from families by telling them: "'This is my recommendation'—and always trying to put it on my shoulders and not on theirs. 'My recommendation is that we take Johnny off the ventilator today.' Um, 'My recommendation is'—you know, 'that we stop transfusing him. We're not, we're prolonging suffering, we're not prolonging his [life], we're not increasing his chances of survival, we're prolonging his dying phase.'" Dr. Coleman found that emotionally resonant moments could help to facilitate this final process. He recalled one family whose child's birthday was coming up and who were struggling with the decision to remove life support. He suggested to them: "You know, 'Maybe what's supposed to happen is that we close the circle on his birthday.' I think, you know, 'My recommendation would be to take him off the ventilator on his birthday.' His birthday was on a weekend. I wasn't on call that weekend. He wasn't there on Monday. They had listened."

Dr. Fadian used yet another emotional strategy to encourage parents to come to terms with a child's impending death and the limitations of medical intervention. He elaborately delineated every possible intervention that could be performed, emphasizing both the suffering it would cause and what would not be accomplished. He shared the story of a family whose child was facing an intractable infection from which he could not possibly recover. Rather than simply informing the parents that there was nothing left that they could do and arguing that they should stop interventions, he brought in a number of consulting doctors who explained the elaborate, painful, and disfiguring interventions they could provide while emphasizing that even these treatments would not change the end result: their child would still die from the infection, which was uncontrollable. Dr. Fadian promised the family that if they did not pursue these options, he would continue to provide antibiotics and other basic care and keep their child as comfortable as possible. He was glad when the family chose not to put their child through those arduous procedures and emphasized that he made a point *not* to tell families there was nothing left that he could do. Instead, he chose his words strategically, telling families, "We're doing everything that we *know* to do." Once again, a little bit of wiggle-room for hope was left open.

Letting go of *all* hope was something that providers were reluctant to do even in talking with me in a private interview. As they experienced firsthand, distant hopes could, at times, be realized. Getting access to Kelly-Reed for stem-cell transplantation or other experimental or even standard treatments can save the lives of children with what are typically terminal diagnoses. Not all children who are transferred to the PICU die. One child in my study survived *two* stints in the PICU. Physicians on Unit 27 realistically had to help families let go of hope, but they themselves presented the possibility of hope as nearly ever-present, pointing to cases in which children surprised them and got through seemingly hopeless setbacks. Dr. Newell explained: "We all have a story, or you know, there's—I can give you a list of patients that I didn't think were going to make it, and 'WOW, he got through.' 'Oh WOW, she got through.' So there are those 'miracles' for lack of a better word." She also pointed out that "because we're dealing with families who have had the one-in-a-million chance happen to them . . . they do know about what it's like, the one-in-a-million chance, because that disease was [also] supposed to be one in a million, and their child has it."

In this context, odds and statistics may become meaningless to families because there is always the possibility of one of these "miracles." Dr. Vogel echoed this sentiment. She told me: "I can say to a family there's a 1 percent risk of this, and they look at me and say, 'Well there was a one in a million chance they could get this disease, so what does 1 percent mean?' Or you can look at a family, you know, you can look at a kid with relapsed cancer, where their chances are 10 percent to get through this, but to that family, 10 percent sounds like a lot."

In this way, even daunting statistics can be transformed into a reason for hope. With something as valuable as a child's life on the line, the most remote chance of survival can be the crack of light families needed to keep hope alive.

Dr. Fadian also presented hope as realistic by explaining that he and the other physicians on Unit 27 tried hard to send kids to the PICU only if there was still a chance that they might recover. He explained that children could decline precipitously during the weeks after transplantation but that if the new stem cells successfully engraft, they could improve relatively quickly as well.

> You [can] get respiratory issues and things like that, but if you can just get past the engraftment period—which they do—it takes about five days to get better. . . . In transplant, almost everything is multi-factorial. It's not one thing that's causing [a] problem. If it is, it makes it easier because you can just deal with that. But pulmonary edema, you know? Chemotherapy causes it, engraftment causes it, infection causes it. And usually they're all going on at the same time. So the expectation is, it'll get better with time, you've just got to get past it.

This view of riding out the downturns with hope of coming out on the other side sometimes led to a clash between the physicians on Unit 27 and the PICU doctors.

The physicians on Unit 27 explained that the PICU doctors, for example, were quicker than they were to believe that children's deaths were a foregone conclusion. Unlike children who might arrive in the PICU with pulmonary edema, organ failure, or other critical conditions requiring life-supporting care due to a tragic accident or sudden illness, children transferred to the PICU from Unit 27 with such problems might still benefit from the donor stem cells, which might begin to grow and engraft if the child is stabilized. Dr. Fadian recalled a situation in which he was in disagreement with the PICU doctors: "The PICU staff were telling the parents there was no way the child was going to survive. And at the time . . . I was thinking, 'Well, that's not true.' Some of the things that were adding to the problems were potentially reversible. [The PICU physicians] were, I mean, in the long term, they were right, but it took about two months to find out. Because things got better, and then things got worse."

Upholding strict professional boundaries around their own domain of expertise can also help physicians justify leaving room for hope where little hope for survival might remain. But when doctors disagree—or seem to disagree—families can feel as though they are receiving mixed messages. As Dr. Ravipati explained,

> As a primary doctor, sometimes you don't want to shock them, so you say that, "Okay, the kidney function is uh, poor, and we have to see if dialysis will help." So the family hears that "dialysis will help." And then the dialysis doctor goes in and says, "No, it's not going to help. Your child has liver and lung and heart dysfunction." So they heard "the dialysis will not help," "dialysis may help" . . . and how can I go and say that dialysis will absolutely not help? I'm not a renal doctor.

Constructing other specialists as the experts for a specific problem leaves room for the possibility that there may be potential for improvement—one that may simply be beyond the scope of a particular physician's expertise. A primary physician may feel a greater responsibility to avoid "shocking" families by keeping the door open for hope even when it is

not likely to be realized. Again, the relationship physicians aim to maintain with families encourages them to help families preserve hope.

Within a broader cultural context in which positivity and cheerfulness are lauded and open expressions of sadness, distress, and grief are
discouraged, it is not surprising that healthcare providers also find it
hard to escape these models for social interaction.[13] And as I will illustrate further in the next chapter, expressing hope can serve as a language
through which physicians and caregivers alike express *care*. If physicians
fear that expressing hopelessness communicates a lack of care for or
commitment to a patient or family, the emotional hurdle for broaching
conversations about death is that much higher.

In the contemporary United States, death and dying are generally kept
as separate from daily life as possible. Because open discussion of death is
deemed impolite, we are left without much practice thinking and speaking
about it, much less helping one another through it when the time comes.
When both parents and physicians avoid engaging the likelihood of death
until (and sometimes even after) it is imminent, they can get tangled up
in linguistic mazes. To the extent that it further discourages frank discussion, hope can impose unrecognized costs and leave room for confusion.
Though Dr. Ravipati proposed that it would be "rude" to continually remind parents whose child may struggle for months before dying that "your
son is going to die, your daughter is going to die," I wonder how things
might be different if we *didn't* feel this way. If we could speak honestly and
directly about impending death, even for months on end, new and more
stable avenues for taking care of one another might open up to us.

Reluctantly Letting Go

When the time came, facilitating peaceful deaths and helping families
embark on the grieving process was something the physicians I spoke
with worked hard to accomplish. The reconstruction of hope was at the
center of this process. Dr. Newell explained that instead of working to
help families let go of hope at the end of children's lives, she could help
them to "change hope" by shifting its focus. She elaborated:

> Somebody told me one time that you never have to lose hope. You never
> have to give up hope. But you change your hope. And I think that has

been a helpful concept for me. We're not giving up hope on your child. We're changing the hope. We're hoping for, instead of a cure, we're hoping for comfort, we're hoping for quality time, we're hoping for, you know, good memories. And I think that concept helps me, in terms of my interactions with families. That you don't have to give up hope. Because that is asking a lot of a parent. To give up hope on their child? It's something that rips your heart right out even thinking about it. But if you can change hope. I think that is a framework that makes it um, easier to, at least for me, in terms of my conversations with families. Um, then they never feel like we're giving up hope. We're just changing hope.

Even when doctors were as certain as they could ever be that a child's life was beyond saving, hope remained seductive and wriggled back into their language in new ways. Dr. Newell's comments suggest that because giving up hope for a child felt especially cruel, changing hope was more humane for everyone involved. By maintaining a discourse of hope even as children were dying, the emotional difficulties of these experiences could be softened—for families and physicians alike. Dr. Coleman adopted a similar approach, explaining: "What works for me is 'I can still do something here.' I can still help them have as peaceful, and as peaceful a memory of the last minutes of their child's life [as possible]. Um, And there are good ways to do that and there are very bad ways."

Sometimes reconstructing hope at the end of life involves getting families to shift hopes that have been tied tightly to medical technologies over to the realm of the spiritual. Dr. Coleman recalled learning how to help families do this. A nurse who was working with a family whose medical team viewed their child as suffering unnecessarily on life-supporting care taught him a lesson he found particularly valuable:

[This] family was struggling with taking their child off the ventilators. And they were talking about miracles. And [the nurse], he finally says simply, you know, "God doesn't need a ventilator to have a miracle." You know, "He doesn't need a dialysis machine to have a miracle. If there's gonna be a miracle," you know, "You don't need the equipment." And that, I've used that occasionally, in the appropriate setting. "If you're waiting for a miracle, that's fine." Haven't seen one yet, but um, "Your child doesn't need that ventilator to have a miracle occur."

Invoking the potential for miracles to occur through intangible, spiritual avenues leaves open the most remote hope conceivable, even as children are taken off of life-supporting care to die. Miracles, too, can be reconstructed; as Dr. Coleman added, "Sometimes, the miracle is that we made it this far."

Hear No Evil, Speak No Evil

Jayden Lacoste didn't get the miracle his mother, Lakira, had been hoping for. When Jayden's first cord-blood transplant failed, she decided to proceed with a second transplant. His own harvested stem cells could have been returned to him instead, but he would have continued to suffer with sickle cell. They "hadn't come this far," Lakira believed, to return home with Jayden still suffering from frequent and potentially life-threatening vasso-occlusive crises. She opted for the riskier treatment in the hopes of a cure. It was not until after I later interviewed Unit 27 physicians that I understood how risky a second transplant really was, with significantly lower chances of success. But Lakira was determined that her son would return home without sickle-cell disease. Unfortunately, after the second transplant, the donor cells again failed to engraft adequately, and Jayden's organs began to fail.

After Jayden was transferred to the PICU, Lakira returned to the Ronald McDonald House, where she spent most of her time. To providers, staff at the house, and other parents, this may have appeared to be an indication of detachment and an alarming lack of concern, but her choice was deliberate. Unlike those who stayed to care-captain even more fervently in the most dire circumstances, Lakira care-entrusted almost entirely. She spent very little time at the hospital. "I'm glad I'm here," Lakira told me at the Ronald McDonald House, "because it gives me time away from being up there and worrying. I try not to worry, but it happens . . . so I try not to stay up there too long." Lakira felt that staying positive for Jayden was the most important thing she could do for him. "I refuse to think anything negative," she told me adamantly. This was an easier task to accomplish if she avoided watching her son suffer for long, and it was the one thing she felt she could completely devote herself to and successfully achieve. Though Lakira admitted that the doctors were urging her to tell her family back home about Jayden's deteriorating condition, Lakira refused to do so. "No," she told me flatly. "I'm not going to tell them anything except that he's fine, because he *is* fine" (emphasis hers). Fiercely holding onto hope for her son's recovery and avoiding information and interactions that might threaten that hope became Lakira's primary goal.

Despite her decision, Lakira still felt the tug-of-war between care-captaining and care-entrusting at times. She felt obligated to walk up to the hospital most mornings at about the time rounds occurred. The physicians encouraged her to be there, and she also had a nagging sense that "I feel like I can't miss even one day, or something won't happen like it's supposed to." But at the same time, she felt that being in the room was bad for Jayden—believing that her presence alone caused his blood pressure to rise. Without the cultural health capital to become more involved, Lakira wasn't able to intervene to influence Jayden's care or communicate effectively with his healthcare providers as Edward and Juliana had. Thus, she was not present to encourage nurses to keep perfect timing with medication schedules, to double-check laboratory work, to suggest possible tests or treatments, or to gather detailed information about Jayden's condition that might increase her cultural health capital and allow her to participate more actively in his care. Maintaining a constant presence without feeling she could do much to comfort her son or improve his condition was simply too painful for her.

Lakira abstractly worried that perhaps she "should've fought harder" when Jayden began having the severe pain that preceded his ultimate decline, but she lacked the cultural health capital needed to research the possible causes of his increasing symptoms or to engage multiple physicians on the unit, as care-captaining parents often did. Jayden's physicians had also initially struggled to determine the problem. Lakira qualified her sense of regret, asking me: "How can you fight when they're doing what they're supposed to do and you're looking at the test yourself and you're like, 'Well, I don't see nothing either?'" To avoid becoming emotionally overwhelmed by the distress of being in such a helpless position, Lakira moved further toward the sidelines in the final weeks of Jayden's life. She remained devoted to her son by praying for him, "refusing to think negative thoughts," and walking up to the hospital most evenings to kiss him goodnight. But that was all she felt she could do.

I drove Lakira to the hospital for one of her evening visits and was again taken aback to see the playful boy I had come to think of as my little buddy lying motionless under a colorful fleece blanket, intubated and swollen. I held his hand lightly and his eyes fluttered open a few times before closing again. Lakira held his other hand, kissed his forehead, and spoke to him softly. We stayed in the room for about ten minutes. On our way out, Lakira told the nurse she would call her later to check on him. "We'll be here!" the nurse replied reassuringly.

Seeing Jayden in the same state I'd seen Noah Rivera-Cruz fail to recover from deeply worried me. Each time I arrived at the Ronald McDonald House over the ensuing weeks, I was relieved to find Lakira's name still on the "census" list. Yet when I talked with her, I was disheartened to hear that there was no change. When I asked about how Jayden was doing, Lakira might initially respond with a tired, somewhat forced optimism, "He's doing good!" Though a note of skepticism crept into her voice, she seemed to genuinely believe that there was still hope for his recovery. Even the last time I spoke with her, she told me that he would need a lot of physical therapy to "get back moving again" once he woke up. She assured me that she had seen him near the brink of death before and that God would see her son through this crisis too.

I couldn't reach Lakira the following week, so I cautiously stopped by the hospital to see if I could find her there. The doors to the PICU were open, but as I walked toward Jayden's room, I saw that the lights were on, and a small crowd of physicians surrounded the bed. I asked at the front desk if Jayden was still in Room 4. "Yes, he is," a nurse behind the counter told me. "Is this an okay time to come by?" I asked hesitantly. He gave the other nurse a quick sideways glance and waved me over to the side of the counter. "Jayden is dying," he told me quietly, but firmly. I nodded. He elaborated a bit about his heart rate over the past few days. I asked if it would happen today. He replied, "Yes. But I thought that yesterday, and he's still hanging in there." He told me that Lakira and her brother (her family had apparently been flown in by a charity organization a few days earlier, something that I'd known was in the works) had stepped out, but Jayden's grandmother was there.

An elderly heavy-set black woman with graying hair sat in a chair just outside Jayden's room. I sat down next to her and introduced myself. She told me Lakira would be back soon. We both sat gazing at Jayden, who still lay motionless, but even more swollen than before. His eyes looked bruised, and unable to open. His skin had taken on an ashen gray hue under the bright fluorescent lights. I worried he might take his final breath while Lakira was away.

"I don't want them to put no more medicine in him," Jayden's grandmother told me after a few minutes had passed. She repeated this a few times. I nodded. "I'm afraid he's not going to make it," she told me. I nodded again, and with a hard lump in my throat, said, "Me too." A nurse came out of the room, and Jayden's grandmother called her over to us. "Don't give him nothing else," she told the nurse emphatically. "No more medicine." The nurse affirmed her, telling her this was a "good thought" but that it was up to his mom to decide. Jayden's grandmother expressed her dismay at what, in her eyes, had "been done" to Jayden by putting him through treatments and the administration of medications that appeared to her to be making her grandson so ill. The nurse explained that Jayden had a lot of infections and that they were treating those infections as well as they could and doing everything they could do for him. Jayden's grandmother was confused about whether or not he'd already had the transplant. The nurse explained that he had, and his grandmother responded, somewhat accusatorily, "Well, maybe that wasn't for him."

A few minutes later, one of the physicians who had been in Jayden's room stepped out and leaned down, taking a knee in front of Jayden's grandmother. He gently explained that he was the "main PICU doctor" and that Jayden was "very sick, he's got a lot of things going on." Jayden's grandmother told him that she had worked in a hospital when she was younger. She then proposed again that it had been wrong for Jayden to have the transplant. The doctor explained that he wasn't one of the transplant doctors, but that the transplant doctors and Jayden's mom had been trying to give Jayden "the best chance" they could. "We know sickle cell is a bad disease," he said. "Transplant isn't perfect either." The doctor then reiterated that everyone involved in the transplant decision had wanted to give Jayden the "best shot" they could and "do the right thing based on what they knew then." "It's really hard to see the future," he told her.

I increasingly sensed that when Lakira returned, these physicians would be confronting her with a conversation about taking Jayden off of the ventilator immediately. I did not want to be in the way or divert her attention at this critical time. I asked for a pen and paper at the nursing station and left a note for Lakira with the nurse to say that I would be holding her and Jayden close in my thoughts. Jayden died the next day.

Feeling Unprepared

Both Jayden and Noah's parents worked hard to hold onto hope for their sons' recoveries even in the final weeks of their lives. That they did so in very different ways led to significant emotional inequalities between them. Edward and Juliana spent the final weeks of their son's life close to him, with a solid understanding of his medical status, and were comfortable taking an active role in the decision to stop interventions. Lakira, on the other hand, spent much of her son's final weeks isolated from him and with a fuzzy understanding of his health status at best. These different experiences throughout the illness and dying process can have consequences for families as they move through the aftermath of grief as well.

I was in the Midwest for my brother's wedding when Juliana texted to tell me that Noah had died and to ask for my address so she could send a photo card they had made for him. They returned to Puerto Rico a few days later. We kept in touch occasionally in the ensuing months, and I visited with them again about nine months after Noah died, when they returned to Kelly-Reed for a regular follow-up for Sophie and to participate in an annual fundraising walk for the program, which included a balloon release ceremony in honor of current patients and in memory of those who died.

During a formal follow-up interview one night back at the Ronald McDonald House, Juliana explained that they had been the ones who urged the doctors to stop treatment. She told me that they had gotten conflicting opinions from the PICU doctors, the kidney doctors, and the transplant doctors. But his kidneys failed to function each time they tried to stop the dialysis. Though they were told that they could put him back on dialysis and keep trying, they reasoned, "He's suffering a lot, we are suffering also." They finally decided that if they didn't see any progress after he was taken off dialysis the next time, they would take him off the ventilator that was keeping him breathing. Juliana could no longer bear to see her baby splayed out alone on the hospital bed. She was relieved when he was off the ventilator and back in her arms. They held him for about twenty-four hours before he died.

Even though their son did not survive, the fact that Edward and Juliana had care-captained from beginning to end offered them some solace. When I asked if there was anything that gave them comfort, Juliana responded without hesitation: "That we tried everything that was in our hands." They were not plagued by the "what if" questions and doubts regarding quality of care that Jayden's grandmother grappled with in the hours before her grandson's death. I was not able to speak with Lakira after Jayden's death because she returned to her home state immediately after he died. I sent flowers to the funeral home and reached out a few months later, but her number had changed (she had already changed phones twice since I met her). I'm fairly certain, however, that she did not feel the same degree of confidence in Jayden's care or in her negotiation of it. Lakira's final weeks with her son were marked by distance and feelings of helplessness. This was not because she cared any less, but because she lacked the cultural health capital that might have encouraged her to participate actively in her son's care and in the excruciating decision to take him off of life-sustaining support.

Research on coping has found that those who are able to engage in "problem-focused coping" (by actively tackling a problem causing distress) feel more efficacious and a greater sense of control over stressful life events than those who use "emotion-focused coping" (by primarily seeking social support or trying to ignore the problem).[14] Here, parents with critically ill children who were able to effectively care-captain, particularly at exceptionally stressful moments, could engage in and reap the benefits of problem-focused coping. However, within the healthcare arena cultural health capital is critical to doing so successfully. Skills and resources are often a prerequisite. Parents without much cultural health capital tended toward emotion-focused coping instead by care-entrusting even more completely when children's health declined. But they were unlikely to feel the same degree of confidence in their child's care or in their own decision-making roles if their children did not survive.

The physicians I interviewed recognized how critical it was for parents to come away from a child's death feeling that they had "done everything they could." Dr. Newell recalled times when "it would have been in the best interest of the child to withdraw [life] support," but she cautioned against pushing too hard against families' emotional readiness to withdraw. She explained: "You're not only considering the child's outcome, the child's comfort, their quality of whatever life that they have remaining, but you also need to balance the family and their need to walk away from this feeling that they did everything that they could for their child. That they were the best possible parents or family members that they could be. They need to have a peace. They need to achieve peace at some point." Even when a child gets to the point that, as Dr. Newell put it, "we are just keeping them alive on machines," physicians feel that parents need to make an emotional transition before making the decision to stop medical interventions—and that last-ditch efforts at care-captaining might be part of that path. As noted previously, Dr. Fadian preferred parental involvement in part because "things don't always work out. . . . If [parents] are involved and they understand, . . . there's more [of] a sense of closure." While Dr. Fadian felt fine about some families' desires "not to know a whole lot" when things were going well, he became concerned if the situation became dire and parents remained on the sidelines. "[If] we're in a very clinically serious scenario, they need to know," he said. "I don't want them coming back and berating themselves, that's important."

Unequal cultural health capital contributed to the diverging illness management strategies that could cause parents to come away from the loss of a child with very different emotional outcomes. Confidence in a child's medical team and one's own interventions did offer comfort in the aftermath of loss. Without this confidence, families were less likely to move into grief with a sturdy emotional foundation for confronting such immense heartbreak.

Regardless of the level of cultural health capital available to families, however, hope remained highly compelling for all actors involved. The ferocity with which hope could be cultivated until and through the very end of a child's life underscores what a powerful force it can be in shaping illness experiences. Without hope in some form, physicians believed, families could not have gotten through the day-to-day experience of navigating a child's serious illness. Physicians wove hope through their interactions with families both to reduce the emotional weight of these frequent encounters on an ongoing basis and to demonstrate that they were genuinely rooting for them. Helping parents to maintain hope was one way that physicians could show families they *cared*.

The critical interactional role that hope work could play in helping patients, families, and physicians to communicate the depth of their caring and commitment to one another revealed itself most clearly to me after I found myself standing in similar shoes. When my father was diagnosed with terminal brain cancer, I had the unwelcome opportunity to intimately experience the myriad ripple effects facilitated by both care-captaining and care-entrusting over the full course of the illness, treatment, and dying process. For us, too, hope paved a clear way forward—until it took us to a place with no more road, without the tools we needed to build a different one.

7

The Fragility and Tenacity of Hope

By the end of September 2012, I had been doing fieldwork at the Ronald McDonald House for almost a year. I had met the Bialys, the Marins, and the Rivera-Cruzes and was beginning to better understand the process of care-captaining and the advantages it could deliver. I drove back to my home state of Minnesota for my brother's wedding in July, and it was around this time that my healthy, active, sixty-one-year-old father started having what he called "episodes." He'd briefly feel anxious and a bit dizzy. Then a "sinking" feeling would wash over him. He thought it must be related to the stress of helping plan such a large event. He was one of ten children, and many of his siblings and their families would all be traveling at the same time. He said he felt worried that something might happen to someone. His anxiety was out of character, but I too chalked it up to stress. One week before the wedding, my stoic father had such severe abdominal pain that he agreed to go to the hospital. He was rushed into surgery and his appendix was removed just before it might have burst. By the end of the week, my father was back on his feet, beaming and greeting friends and family, even bowling a bit after the rehearsal dinner.

But during August and September, he was often asleep when I called, and generally feeling unwell. He'd been having headaches apparently, but I didn't realize how severe they had become until I got a call from my mother a few weeks later. She said that the pain—in his head this time— had again become severe enough that he was willing to go to the emergency room, where a magnetic resonance image (MRI) was ordered. The MRI revealed a five-centimeter mass in the right frontal lobe of his brain.

My father was immediately admitted to the local, urban general hospital where the MRI had been performed. He was assigned to a neurosurgeon who practiced there and who would perform surgery to remove the tumor a few days later. Despite the fact that I was midway through my fieldwork for this book and getting a sense of the advantages care-captaining to steer the course of a family member's medical treatment could produce, it somehow did not occur to me to suggest that we try to find the "best" possible surgeon, or have the surgery done at a nearby university research hospital. We did not receive a diagnosis based on the MRI. The surgeon told us that he had a suspicion of what the mass might be, but it would be more accurate to wait for the pathology results after surgery and gave us no indication as to his hunch. We didn't press the issue. We hoped it would be benign.

Those hopes were quickly dashed. Two days after surgery we learned that my father had one of the most fatal and aggressive primary brain tumors—a glioblastoma, the same brain cancer that struck both Ted Kennedy and John McCain. We were given a life expectancy of twelve to fourteen months. It was a Friday afternoon. After much deliberation, I had decided not to fly back to Minnesota to be present for the surgery itself, but to wait to see what would come next. Hundreds of miles away, I felt shattered and helpless. There was nothing I could do—but try to make this terrible prognosis somehow not be true.

It was in that moment of distraught panic that the impulse to care-captain seized me. I recalled what the families I met over the previous year had done when presented with terrifying diagnoses. Is anyone doing stem-cell transplants for glioblastoma, I wondered? I began searching and learned the answer: Yes. I emailed a physician at the University of Washington who had a clinical trial underway and some preliminary results published. I continued doing PubMed searches throughout the rest of the weekend, asking a friend who worked at a university with a medical school to pull articles I couldn't access through my own. As Juliana Cruz had described in recalling her frantic searches after her daughter's initial diagnosis, the act of research itself kept me at least partly "calm." It was also, I later came to realize, the best way I knew to communicate to my father that I would do anything I could to find some way *not to let this happen* to him.

On Monday, the local hospital called us with an appointment for the next day with an oncologist in a nearby suburb, whose practice was an affiliate of theirs. At this point, I started pushing my parents to get a second opinion at a research hospital—the University of Minnesota— where, fortuitously, one of my father's sisters worked as a nurse manager. Activating her social capital within the hospital, my aunt asked around and heard "great things" about a new neuro-oncologist who had been hired a few weeks earlier. We were able to get an appointment with him on Tuesday afternoon as well, so I booked the first direct flight to Minneapolis the next morning in the hopes of helping my father obtain access to newly developing treatments, just as I'd seen many of the families in my study do so successfully.

The suburban oncologist was friendly and laidback during our appointment. He was also honest. He gave us basic information on the odds of survival: only 5 percent of patients with this tumor live two to three years, and five-year survival rates were closer to 1 or 2 percent. "Okay, what do we need to do to be in that five percent?" I thought.[1] I asked him about some of the clinical trials and recent research I'd been reading about, but he wasn't familiar with most of these studies. This made me uncomfortable. I didn't like the idea that I could know things after one weekend of research that my father's oncologist didn't.[2] He recommended the standard-of-care treatment of radiation and a chemotherapy called Temozolomide. He suggested that if we wanted to, we could explore additional options at the Mayo Clinic (about eighty miles south of the Twin Cities) *after* the standard treatment failed. He warned us, however, that because my father had previously been treated for thyroid cancer (successfully, with surgery and radioactive iodine), he would not be eligible to participate in clinical trials.[3] Therefore, he saw no benefit to seeking care there or elsewhere for initial treatment.

We thanked him for his time and drove across town to the University of Minnesota hospital. Dr. G, a young neuro-oncologist who up until a few weeks earlier had been an assistant professor of medicine at an elite private university research hospital a few states away, was warm, compassionate, and—most notable to me—familiar with and able to engage in discussion about the studies I had looked into. He hoped to get a research program of his own up and running. While he could not yet offer us Avastin—an anti-angiogenic drug that was in more advanced phases of clinical trial for glioblastoma patients at the time—he hoped it would soon be available to patients in his care. He, too, recommended the standard-of-care protocol (radiation and Temozolomide), and didn't encourage us to seek clinical trials for the same reason the suburban oncologist gave: my father would be disqualified due to his previous thyroid cancer.

We all took an immediate liking to Dr. G. He was warm, affable, and clearly "knew his stuff" in my father's words. I knew that even if we sought care elsewhere, my father would still need a local primary physician. I had already attempted to contact Kelly-Reed, remembering the immunotherapy vaccine trial Nora Bialy had told me about during my first interview, which she hoped would be the breakthrough that saved her son from a pediatric brain tumor. My aunt was also hearing from her networks at the University of Minnesota hospital that Kelly-Reed was one of the "best" places to go for this type of tumor. I felt comfortable that Dr. G would be familiar with and able to help coordinate local care with the more "cutting-edge" treatments we might seek elsewhere. At the end of the visit, he gave us each his business card and wrote his email address on the back of it. "You're our man," my father told him. I agreed.

Because we needed to wait for the incision to heal for a week or so before my father could begin radiation, I continued exploring other treatment possibilities—newer, better options that were demonstrating longer survival outcomes. When I finally got a call back from a world-renowned physician at Kelly-Reed whose name had come up through both my and my aunt's medical networks, he told me—contrary to the opinions we had received thus far—that my father's prior thyroid cancer would *not* exclude him from their clinical trials. Even if there wasn't a current trial that we qualified for, they could offer him treatment beyond current standard of care (including Avastin). The only requirement was that he could not have already started treatment, and they would need his imaging results and the tumor tissue slides from the surgery to be sent before we could schedule an appointment.

Arranging to have these materials transferred to Kelly-Reed required a great deal of legwork. I ultimately had to go to the records division of the local hospital that performed the surgery to pick-up a DVD with the pre- and post-surgical MRI images and mail it to the brain tumor center at Kelly-Reed myself. Getting the tissue slides transferred required at least half a dozen lengthy phone calls. By the time I had accomplished all of this, the University of Minnesota had given us a schedule for radiation. My father would have been able to be seen at Kelly-Reed a few days later—but if he began radiation beforehand, we could not be seen until it was complete. I pleaded with my father that it was more important to get the *best* possible treatment than to get the *fastest* possible treatment. My father agreed in theory—but he was nervous.

In the end, my father decided that given the "aggressiveness" of the tumor, and his affinity for the people he met at the University of Minnesota, he wanted to hit the tumor "hard and fast." Though Dr. G was supportive of us exploring options at Kelly-Reed and told my father that a few days of delay would not make a significant difference to his treatment, my father still decided not to wait. He was going to begin treatment on the date scheduled, no matter what. "My gut is telling me," he told me firmly, "to go for it."

I was crushed. Standard-of-care treatment didn't give me much to hang my hopes on. My strong-willed father, who wasn't reading the medical studies I was, didn't need quite as much evidence as I did to firmly anchor his hopes. He adamantly believed that with the standard treatment protocol and the doctors who inspired his confidence leading the way, he was going to "beat this thing." "Let's kill it," he repeatedly told his radiologist, a woman he'd also taken an immediate liking to and joked easily with during each visit. "Kill it dead." My father wasn't thinking about how to get the three years of survival I was desperately working toward. Despite the staggering evidence to the contrary, he intended to live for *twenty* more years.

But Kelly-Reed would be our "Plan B," my father assured me. Though he felt no need to conduct medical research on his diagnosis or treatment options—and would not have done any of this himself even if I had not taken on this role—he was pleased that I was doing this work and finding additional treatment options. He often brought up the possibilities I had uncovered in conversations with friends and family members, boasting about our "Plan B." My efforts not only communicated caring to him, but allowed him to show others how much he was cared *for*. They helped both of us keep a firm grasp on hope, and to tangibly demonstrate that we would fight tooth and nail to accomplish what we hoped for.

A Hold on Hope

I began this research as an "outsider" to the experience of negotiating a family member's life-threatening illness. But I soon found myself living what I had been studying, in some upside-down version of "going native" gone terribly wrong. I share my father's story here not because it is at all equivalent to that of negotiating a child's life threatening illness, but because it became, quite unfortunately, another comparison case—one to which I had the most intimate access at every point along the way. My father's illness became a revealing (albeit quite unwanted) testing ground for the theories I was developing in my research. This was particularly true as I directly witnessed the particularly stark advantages that my care-captaining sometimes produced, and that care-entrusting would have caused us to miss out on.

The most striking instance of this was my effort to have my father's tumor tested for a particular mutation known as "EGFRviii." This mutation is present in about 30 percent of glioblastoma tumors. It was not routinely tested for because no FDA-approved (and insurance-covered) treatment was yet available for people with this particular mutation. However, clinical trials examining the potential for a mass-produced immunotherapy vaccine that teaches the immune system to target this particular mutation (thereby attacking the tumor cells) were in progress. Some preliminary results reported participants who were doubling their overall survival time, from an average of a little over one year post-diagnosis to two years. Over a quarter of the 65 participants receiving one particular vaccine survived three years or more. The chances that my father would survive for even two years with the standard treatment alone were only about 5 percent. We did not know if he had the mutation, but I was determined to find out if he did, and could benefit from this promising treatment.

The University of Minnesota was not participating in any of the relevant trials, and thus could not test for the mutation. When I inquired about it, Dr. G was not optimistic that we would be able to obtain the vaccine outside of a trial (a practice known as "compassionate use") even if my father had the mutation. I didn't care. If there was a drug out there that could double or triple my father's life-expectancy—perhaps giving him the chance to live long enough to meet a grandchild or two—I was dead set on fighting for it. Dr. G warned us that insurance wouldn't cover the $500 test since it technically had no impact on nonexperimental treatment options. We agreed to pay out of pocket. Dr. G arranged for tissue to be sent to a West Coast medical research center for testing.

Weeks went by and we received no results. A patient coordinator told us that the tissue had indeed been sent, but when Dr. G looked into it several weeks later (after I inquired again about the result), it turned out it never had been sent. By this time, my father's six weeks of radiation ended, and I arranged for him to be seen at Kelly-Reed. During our initial visit, we were again assured that my father would not be excluded from *any* of their trials due to his prior history of thyroid cancer. Kelly-Reed *was* participating in the multicenter trial exploring the efficacy of this particular immunotherapy vaccine. We immediately enrolled my father in it—meaning his tumor would be tested for the EGFRviii mutation at no cost to us. Unfortunately, he was not positive for the EGFRviii mutation. This meant the vaccine would be of no benefit to him, and we were back to less promising treatment options.

My persistent care-captaining did not ultimately result in a concrete survival advantage for my father in this instance. But if he had been one of the approximately 30 percent of glioblastoma patients who are EGFRviii positive, the outcome might have been different. If I had not known to request this testing or seek care for him elsewhere, he could have—statistically speaking—missed out on additional months, or even years, of potentially high-quality life. Even though there was no direct health benefit for him in the end, the emotional benefit for me was substantial: the reassurance of knowing that he was not missing out on a simple, hypothetically life-extending treatment due to a lack of knowledge, effort, or arbitrary bureaucratic rules—was one less injustice for me to absorb.

My understanding was that this particular treatment had the potential to offer considerable benefit with minimal side effects had my father been an appropriate candidate. As such, obtaining it—through persistent hope-seeking and care-captaining—could have bestowed a clear-cut medical advantage.[4] At the same time, it is important to note that life-extension alone, at the expense of quality of life, is a significant consequence of medicine's increasing ability to offer grueling and toxic treatments that sometimes lead to very little benefit.[5] Later, at the very end of my father's life, he underwent an unpleasant treatment with very little prospect of slowing the tumor in any meaningful way. At that point, the need to continue pursuing hope at all costs (and a physician's willingness to encourage it) led to additional discomfort and drained his energy just weeks before he died. Sometimes these distinctions are clear;

other times they are murkier. Decision-making about what treatments offer real benefit in these circumstances can be especially hit or miss, and especially susceptible to the rhetoric of hope and the interactional demand to maintain it no matter what.

The compulsion to maintain hope is especially powerful when it takes on significant symbolic meanings. My care-captaining based efforts to pry open every crack of hope I could find in an effort to extend my father's life also provided my father and me with a *language* through which we could communicate. My dogged pursuit, even of dead ends, helped me to "tell" my father that I was deeply distressed by the prospect of losing him, without having to speak treacly words that were not characteristic of either of us or consistent with of the emotional culture of our family. Similarly, by embracing my hope-seeking and forcefully expressing his desire to "beat this thing," my father communicated that he was strong, a "fighter," and committed to sticking around for us as well. In the classic "show, don't tell" adage, voicing hope and actively seeking it provided a conduit through which we could give and receive from one another.

Unfortunately, the fact that hope is a language that expresses care also makes it difficult for people to prepare for outcomes they *don't* hope for. It is interactionally risky to acknowledge the possibility that hopes might not be realized, particularly if such possibilities have the connotation of "giving up" or failing to be wholly devoted to the fight to preserve one's own or a patient or loved one's life. Sociologist Gayle Sulik's critique of the war metaphors that surround cancer is apt here.[6] Patients are encouraged to think of themselves as being in battle with their own bodies—to fight to overcome the "enemy" at all costs. Though my father readily embraced this masculine rhetoric, it placed impossible expectations on him, and the fact that the tumor's progression could be interpreted as a measure of "defeat" made it even more impossible to talk about the realities we were soon facing.

A Thing with Feathers

My father seemed to be doing exceptionally well for several months. I assumed that he was on track to exceed the gloomy twelve- to fourteen-month prognosis. The tumor had not progressed for ten months following the initial surgery and radiation treatment. But Dr. G left the University of Minnesota that spring, and my father was assigned to an oncologist whose primary specialty was gastrointestinal cancers, not neuro-oncology. I was not happy about this, but told myself that it didn't matter much. If and when his tumor recurred, the university would have no further options for him anyway, and he was continuing to be followed at Kelly-Reed every four months as well. When the tumor recurred, I expected we would quickly enroll in a trial there and swiftly gain access to the latest treatment options, which genuinely seemed to be rapidly advancing. I did *not* expect that the tumor would recur, and we would not be clearly informed about it.

But at the end of July, my father's newly assigned oncologist told my parents that the latest MRI was "equivocal." My parents did not pass this information on to me at first, not wanting to "worry me." It was a week before I would be defending my dissertation, the final hurdle I had to clear to complete the requirements for my doctoral degree. When I asked about the MRI, they were vague. Though under normal circumstances I might have probed further, I was in fact overwhelmed with finishing my PhD and moving to start a new faculty position. Besides, I told myself, everything had been going so well, maybe it really was just an unclear image or a discrepancy too small to measure. Perhaps the following month the results would be clear and indicate no growth. Instead of interrogating my parents further, or taking up the care-captaining reigns, I stepped back and "hoped" for the best.

Our collective desires to see my father as "doing well" led us to care-entrust at a risky moment. After the next MRI, performed the following month at the end of August, my father called me with bad news. The oncologist had informed him the tumor was growing. His cancer had recurred.

The demands involved in beginning a new job as an assistant professor of sociology were immediately overshadowed by my even higher-stakes "job" coordinating my father's medical care. My first task was to get him an appointment at Kelly-Reed for the following week. They offered us a slot on September 4, which I eagerly accepted. My father was initially glad to hear this, but then hesitated because he had yet to have his post-MRI appointment with the local oncologist, who had scheduled him for September 6. I gently tried to convince him that it was not worth waiting for the local appointment and that we should take this immediate opening at Kelly-Reed. At first he agreed, but then hesitated, telling me he thought it was more respectful not to usurp the local doctor before that appointment, if possible. This struck me as pointless, but I reluctantly—and in hindsight too easily—capitulated. I had his appointment at Kelly-Reed pushed back to September 11.

For another full week, we did nothing but wait for an appointment with the local oncologist who, as I expected, had no options to offer. My parents left that appointment deeply disappointed that the local oncologist was unable to answer their questions, and offered little beyond a vague recommendation to "explore options elsewhere." By the time that full additional week had slipped by, my father's symptoms returned. He was beginning to have the same sensory seizures he experienced leading up to his initial diagnosis, and noticed his balance faltering. My "tough-guy" father again became anxious and panicky. He told us he could "feel" the tumor growing. He proposed to my mother that they drive to Kelly-Reed through the night and try to get into surgery with the highly lauded neurosurgeon who practiced there immediately. But this was now impractical on multiple levels. We waited for their scheduled flight and the postponed appointment while five more long anxiety-ridden days went by.

Finally, the appointment date arrived. As we sat in the exam room with much anticipation, I hoped my father would enroll in the same individualized immunotherapy trial that Nora Bialy had told me about in describing her son's treatment. But when my father read the information I sent him, he thought it sounded "grueling." When the doctor came in, she opened with the suggestion that my dad would probably prefer to remain in Minnesota for treatment. He perked up, and quickly agreed. When we discussed the pros and cons of staying at Kelly-Reed to participate in the immunotherapy trial, confusion set in. The doctor explained that the trial would most likely add at least another four months of progression-free survival on top of the average four months already anticipated with the Avastin treatment. But my father understood that to mean that the trial would *not* offer more time than he could expect from the Avastin infusions (which he could receive closer to home, at the Mayo Clinic).[7] We all agreed that the newest, most promising, and innovative trial at Kelly-Reed—a modified virus injected directly into the tumor to kill cancerous cells—was the vastly superior and unquestionably worthwhile treatment option. Unfortunately, FDA rules prohibited intracranial injections less than one centimeter from the ventricles (cavities in the brain that produce cerebrospinal fluid), and the location of his tumor was within that margin. The doctor told us that though they had lobbied the FDA to make an exception for some very young patients, given the excellent initial results they were finding, they had not had success in getting around this prohibition. We had come so far, I thought, only to be excluded from this potentially life-extending treatment based on a bureaucratic technicality.

There was one more avenue, however, that I had already arranged for us to explore after we left Kelly-Reed. Months earlier, I had scheduled a trip home to coincide with one of my father's regular follow-up appointments with Dr. G, our original doctor at the University of Minnesota. Though the standard-of-care treatment was still working effectively at that time, I knew at some point this would change. So I took the opportunity to deploy one more strategy I'd observed among the care-captaining families I studied in my research. Time and again, they told me that in order to make difficult decisions or access the best possible care for their child, they asked the doctors: "What would you do if this was your kid?"

In asking this question this way, families sought to heighten the emotional stakes involved. They asked doctors to stand in their emotional shoes and more deliberately adopt their perspective. One mother adamantly assured me that asking both what *they* should do and what *the doctor would do if it was their child* was important because "those are two different answers." Dr. G was roughly my age. So I asked him pointedly, "What would you do if this was your dad?" Though up until this point our conversations had centered only on the treatments available locally, Dr G. answered without hesitation. He named a top-ranked medical center in another region of the country, and one senior physician in particular. I tucked this information away. When, after we found ourselves facing tumor recurrence, I told my father that I got him an appointment with "the guy Dr. G recommended" (another "big name" in glioblastoma research), he was delighted. "Excellent," he said emphatically, with pride in his voice. Our joint commitment to hope-seeking, along with my efforts to care-captain, helped us again to communicate our care for and appreciation of one another.

This third medical center required us to hand carry all of my father's medical records and imaging results to the consultation. As we sat in the waiting room, I opened the thick packet and began reading through his records. I was devastated when I came to the radiology report based on that late-July MRI—the one my parents were told was "equivocal." The radiologist was not equivocal at all. He wrote in conclusion: "*Increased size* of two enhancing foci along the medial resection margin and along the medial aspect of the right parahippocampal gyrus as described above, *suggesting tumor recurrence*" (emphasis mine). This statement stood in stark contrast to the previous months' radiology reports, which concluded with statements like "stable findings," "unchanged," and "no evidence of progression of tumor." Had I requested the report or seen the clinic notes, I would have immediately started the process of pursuing a new line of treatment at Kelly-Reed or elsewhere. I would not have acquiesced to doing nothing but yet another month of treatment with Temozolomide, a drug his tumor was clearly already resistant to.

In the local oncologist's note about the results, he explained that he considered the findings "equivocal" because official guidelines define recurrence as an increase of greater than 25 percent. In his view, the increased size was approximately 25 percent. I was furious. The difference between an approximately 25 percent increase in tumor size compared to an increase just over that threshold is close enough to warrant further investigation and discussion with the patient and his caregivers, especially when dealing with aggressive cancers that have bad prognoses. That we had not been informed of a 25 percent increase and given the chance to make our own judgment about how to proceed shocked me. Not only did we lose that extra week while we were waiting for a follow-up visit after the "unequivocal" MRI in late August, but we could have started addressing the recurrence an entire month earlier and working on a new treatment plan before the tumor had grown so significantly that my father was losing his balance and having dizzy spells in addition to increasingly frequent sensory seizures. But it was September 15 by then, and those six weeks were gone.

Starting a new drug sooner might have kept the tumor at bay a few months longer, granting my father the opportunity to more fully enjoy one last autumn in Minnesota—his favorite time of year—harvesting late-season squash from his large vegetable garden and tinkering in his shop. Or it might have given us all some time to live with a bit *less* hope—and a bit more reality, allowing us to engage more frankly in important conversations about end-of-life comfort care and perhaps have minimized the disagreements we wound up having about how much sedation and morphine he would have wanted during his final days. Perhaps we could have recorded his memories, baked and frozen a few more batches of his famous oatmeal raisin cookies, or asked him how he wanted to pass on his belongings after he was gone. Such planning did not come into focus for us until it was too late. We were working too hard to hold onto hope—which we used to express our confidence in and commitment to one another—to speak matter-of-factly about what lay ahead.

Instead, within a few weeks of those two cross-country medical center visits, my father declined rapidly. The "big name" neuro-oncologist at the second medical center proposed the off-label use of a chemotherapy drug, which, in combination with Avastin, was showing six to nine months "overall survival" rates for recurrent glioblastoma. This was according to a presentation at the American Society of Clinical Oncology (ASCO) meetings a few months earlier. We called Dr. G, the former University of Minnesota oncologist my father most trusted, at his new hospital as soon as we returned from that consultation. Dr. G confirmed that this is what he would recommend as well, in the absence of any other new options. I googled the study presented at ASCO and read the abstract myself. I was sold, feeling confident this treatment would buy us another six months.

Within days my father was receiving both the recommended chemotherapy and Avastin through the Mayo Clinic. But his symptoms were increasing. Two weeks later he told me over the phone that he was having some trouble lifting his left pinky finger when he typed. A week after that, in mid-October, I flew back to Minnesota over the fall break. By then, he was beginning to have weakness in his left leg and developed a limp. He fell several times at home that weekend and once while we were at a restaurant. It was a struggle to get him up again. We immediately called the doctor now overseeing my father's care at the Mayo Clinic, who suggested that he have a CAT scan at a local emergency room to make sure the Avastin had not caused any bleeding (a potential side effect). It had not—but that possibility too was a grasping-at-straws kind of hope. His increasing symptoms meant that the new treatment wasn't working; the tumor was continuing to grow.

By the time I left Minnesota just a week later, on October 16, my father was nearly wheelchair bound. He was put on a high dose of steroids in the hopes that he might regain some movement, at least for a few weeks. He did not. By the first week of November he could no longer walk even a few steps or move from the wheelchair to his bed on his own. My father no longer had the energy to speak on the phone for more than a few minutes. I arranged to have colleagues cover my courses and to fly back again within a few days. He was not scheduled for another MRI for a full month and was still scheduled to receive another Avastin infusion the following week. I told my mother to insist on an immediate MRI to see how quickly the tumor was growing. My father's decline was so rapid that it made no sense to me to continue with the current treatment plan. We needed to reevaluate *now*.

The MRI was scheduled for the morning of my flight. My mother called while I was changing planes. It showed significant growth, and the tumor had spread to the other side of his brain. There was no point to further treatment; at least we could spare him that. We met with hospice the next day, and my father died two weeks later.

The Dark Side of Hope

Regrets pile up, I learned, when time is short, and the quest for hope has eclipsed taking steps that might have helped one prepare for the very real possibility of death. Had we connected with hospice sooner, we might have been better able to take advantage of the services they offer and engaged in more deliberate end-of-life planning. When I first tried to raise the possibility of working with hospice weeks earlier, my mother insisted that we weren't to that point yet—that to raise such a proposition to my father when he was still fighting to live would upset him. I acquiesced. I only fully realized how ill prepared we were during our intake visit with the hospice social worker two weeks before my father died. My father could barely participate. As he sat, his head propped in his right hand with his eyes closed (the tumor had by then seriously damaged his vision), I remarked:

"Dad, you look worried."

"I am worried," he replied.

"What are you worried about?" I asked.

"Everything you can imagine," he answered.

His response pained me. The social worker probed him to give us an example. "I'm wondering what to do with all of my shit," he told her. She affirmed his concern and suggested that we start making a list of who he would want to have certain things. She also suggested that I help him to write a letter to my mother, and for my mother to help him write letters to my brother and me. My father nodded half-heartedly at her suggestions, but had no energy for such things anymore. Before the appointment ended, he was asleep. The time for making lists and writing letters had passed.

None of us had been oblivious to what was coming. We had talked loosely about my father's memorial service, and knew where he wanted it to be held. We knew he wanted to be cremated, and he'd named four specific locations where he hoped to have some of his ashes scattered. One evening during my October visit my father and I sat in the dark, gazing out the large picture window that overlooked his sprawling vegetable garden and watching the moonlight sparkle on the edges of the swirling scrap-metal sculptures he had hung from a high, sturdy branch. We were listening to an instrumental album by his favorite guitarist, Sonny Landreth, and picked out a few tracks that might be appropriate to play during his service.

Though we were somehow able to talk tentatively about these details, we did so delicately, framing them in terms of "just in case." It was harder to talk about things that might suggest his time was imminently short, as if it meant we were "giving up" hope, or not invested in holding on fiercely enough. If I hinted at a shorter timeframe, implying, for instance, that he might not meet his grandchildren, my father would tell me, even in the days after he began struggling to walk, that he was planning on being around for ten or twenty more years. How could I do anything but let him know that's what I hoped for, too?

In hindsight, I can better imagine ways of helping us both devote a bit more attention to the sorts of conversations and proactive tasks that might have lessened our collective sense of regret during the final weeks of his life. I might simply have stated as much, plainly, and framed the conversations I wanted to have as another "just in case" scenario. But in those immediate moments, my sense was that my job was to remain hopeful, too, not to cast any shred of doubt on his conviction or his ability to "overcome the odds."

My own exclusive focus on pursuing the next most promising medical treatment was a stumbling block as well. I paid no attention to the appointments my father had with a palliative care physician and social worker when things had been going smoothly. I understood these to be "medication management" appointments, ensuring his anxiety medication dosing was adequate or that he had other outlets to help him cope— things that didn't require my care-captaining attention. I went through that paperwork when I returned to Minnesota for what became my father's final two weeks. I then discovered that at these appointments my parents had been given information on preparing for the end of life and ideas about things to do before time became too short. Record an oral history. Write letters, as the hospice social worker suggested. Make plans for passing on special belongings. These tasks had slipped beneath my radar. The tenacity of hope prevented all of us from shifting our focus in this direction and putting the time we had left to use in ways that could have helped us to feel more prepared and less anxious as my father's life drew to a close.

In the months after my father died, I was haunted by missed opportunities. I agonized over the suffering that characterized his final days. We did not all agree on how best to care for him after he was unable to communicate with us anymore. The process of "active dying"—the choking, hallucinations, and seizures—caught my brother and me entirely off guard. Despite my asking, we'd never been told concretely what to expect. Each of these problems could have been lessened with more direct conversations about the end of his life before we found ourselves suddenly immersed in it. Had we been able to shift beyond the mandate to remain positive and hopeful sooner, his final days might have included less pain and contention, and a bit more peace and calm.

It was only after my father's death started to settle in my mind after long months of grief that I came to understand how profoundly the relentless pursuit of hope and the difficulty of relinquishing it had shaped every step we took along the way. When I returned to my research data, the role of hope in propelling the families I met at the Ronald McDonald House through their children's illnesses took even clearer shape. Though my father died many years before we would have otherwise expected him to, for a child to bury a parent is the expected "order" of things. For parents to lose children defies our life course expectations—and of course when children's lives are cut so profoundly short, they are deprived of much of the life their parents' had dreamed for them.

Another important difference between my role managing my father's illness and the position of the parents of the children I studied was that my father had full agency in his own care. I could care-captain, ask questions, present him with options he would not have sought out on his own, and prod his providers to connect us to resources beyond those immediately available—and he was enthusiastic about these efforts. But he also made decisions that sometimes diverged from those I encouraged. As disappointing as this could be when I was worried those decisions would hinder his access to the best possible care and outcome, I alone did not carry full and final responsibility for my father's trajectory through the medical system. Those helping to manage the illness of an adult family member capable of consent don't bear the same level of responsibility borne by parents coordinating care for their minor child. This even heavier burden carries the potential for even greater guilt and regret.

The nuts and bolts of care-captaining and care-entrusting, the benefits and consequences of both, and the emotional quicksand involved in managing life-threatening illness were nonetheless borne out in my experience managing my father's terminal illness in ways that were remarkably parallel to those of the families I studied. That my experience was in many ways a shadow of the one facing the parents who participated in my research only underscores the import of paying close attention to these dynamics. Serious and sustained interrogation of these complexities can better equip us to work toward reducing avoidable suffering and addressing the deep-seated inequalities involved in the illness, help-seeking, and, sometimes, dying experience.

8

Emotionally Perilous Paths

Illness Management, Emotion Management, and the
Production of Healthcare Inequalities

I met Blaine and Kara Hilyard about a year after I concluded my fieldwork at the Ronald McDonald House. I was back in town to interview
physicians, and that particular afternoon I was scheduled to interview
Dr. Oliver. The Hilyards, a white couple in their early forties whose
eight-year-old son, Archie, was born with the same rare chromosomal deletion syndrome that Kaelyn Moore suffered, had traveled
to Kelly-Reed from Australia over seven years earlier to obtain the
groundbreaking treatment Dr. Oliver had developed to restore immune
function in infants born with this disorder. The Hilyards were in town
for a follow-up visit (a voyage they made every other year), and met Dr.
Oliver for dinner the night before. She invited them to come see her
research lab the next day, and since they arrived during our interview,
I tagged along for the tour.

Kara told me bits and pieces of her son's story as we wound our way
through the maze of laboratory spaces following Dr. Oliver. Archie's and
his younger brother, Levi's, eyes lit up in awe of the impressive equipment around them. Dr. Oliver, a spry, slender white woman in her early
sixties, whose long, wavy, mostly gray hair was twisted back in a loose
knot, took obvious pleasure in the boys' delight, and in teaching them
the basics of her work. She showed them a sample of the donor tissue
she used in her treatment, explained the role of T-cells in the immune
system in child-friendly terms, and let them watch the cells wriggle
around under a powerful microscope. Archie pointed and beamed when
he noticed a research poster on the wall displaying a photo of his smiling
three-year-old face taken during his first two-year follow-up visit. He
was a literal "poster child" for the life-saving potential of this treatment.
The Hilyards were interested in my research and offered to talk to me

further. I readily accepted, and Dr. Oliver let us slip into a small conference room for an impromptu interview.

From a methodological perspective, my unplanned interview with the Hilyards was strong confirmation of the "theoretical saturation" I had achieved among the case study families I had followed during my fieldwork.[1] Their story tracked the familiar care-captaining trajectory. Blaine's account of the quick and efficient path they followed to Kelly-Reed was a familiar one: "We contacted [Dr. Oliver] before they'd even [officially] diagnosed him because we knew [we needed to], just from all the information that we'd gathered and the study that we'd done and because [our immunologist at home], she said, you know, contact Dr. Oliver at Kelly-Reed University. [So] we contacted her and then we got consent forms from our government to get [his US treatment costs covered through Australia's] overseas medical treatment program." As I had found among the many other care-captaining families I met, the Hilyards took an active role in propelling their son to the highest quality care available for his particular life-threatening condition. Other than the immunologist who alerted them to Dr. Oliver's work, the rest of their local doctors had simply suggested—based on the existing options within their home country—that Archie undergo standard stem-cell transplantation even though it is significantly less effective in treating this condition. The Hilyards forged ahead in pursuing the newest technology and most specialized treatment possible for their son's condition, even though it would require herculean efforts on their part. The treatment Dr. Oliver pioneered offered their son the highest odds of survival, so they uprooted their lives and relocated to the United States for the nearly year-long treatment and recovery period.

The Hilyards' care-captaining may well have saved their son's life. It also highlights the most significant inequality that can exist between families who are able to effectively care-captain and those whose particular constellation of cultural health capital, material resources, and emotional goals lead them to exclusively care-entrust. Observing Archie's sweet demeanor and polite, smart interactions with the adults around him, I found it disturbing to imagine that this bright charming little boy might not have obtained the treatment that allowed him to live a full and healthy life now.

But the Hilyards had a few other advantages US families did not. Australia provides universal health-care to its citizens—including the "overseas medical treatment program" Blaine mentioned, which can cover the costs of obtaining life-saving care that is available only abroad. As a result, the Hilyards did not have to worry about how they would pay for the steep costs of their son's treatment. Other international families had to raise enormous sums of money to get their children access to care at Kelly-Reed. Even the Moores, a case-study family who happened to live not only in the United States, but fortuitously *in-state*, and who had Medicaid insurance for their daughter, had to fundraise extensively to help cover the costs of this same groundbreaking treatment.

Absent this enormous stress, the Hilyards were able to make the decision to seek highly specialized care for their son in another country with relative ease. Negotiating their son's illness of course remained practically and emotionally challenging. But they were able to focus the significant time and energy other families had to devote to the task of fundraising, pressuring insurance companies to provide coverage, or dealing with repeated petitions and appeals to caring for their son and preparing for the journey ahead of them.

Another factor that simplified the decision-making process was the year-long parental leave the Hilyards, like all Australians, were entitled to. Though only partially paid, this national policy protected Blaine and Kara from job loss in ways the United States' Family and Medical Leave Act—which provides at most twelve weeks of unpaid leave—does not protect US families in their position. I will return to this issue later in this chapter, as I consider what more could be done to support families like those in my study.

Yet on top of the benefits the Hilyards' derived from these far more generous and supportive national policies, they brought their own resources to bear on augmenting their son's care, in order to seek the highest possible quality of life for him. After they completed treatment at Kelly-Reed and returned home, the Hilyards care-captained to get Archie the swift access to physical, speech, and occupational therapies that would help him overcome the developmental delays that can accompany this condition. To do so, Blaine and Kara bought themselves out of the public system. Kara explained: "There is an early intervention program through [Australia's] Department of Human Services at home, but they've got all the gatekeepers on, you know. Oh, you have to [take certain steps before obtaining treatment, or] you're on a twelve-month waiting list. Well, you can't wait that long. It's critical you get in early. So we just went private anyway . . . [and] we paid for all of that ourselves."

The Hilyards' investment in private therapies seemed to yield the results they hoped for. Though Archie struggled at first to catch up with his peers—due to the cognitive effects of this condition, spending his first year of life in a less than ideally stimulating hospital environment, or both—his cognitive, social, and intellectual skills at age eight were impressive. Dr. Oliver repeatedly introduced him to researchers in the lab as "our rock star" and announced that they had all viewed a video the Hilyards had emailed to her in which Archie plays the violin. Archie blushed shyly but grinned as she bragged. Kara told me that Archie had googled Dr. Oliver and read her online Kelly-Reed profile in the car on the way there. I visibly dropped my jaw and told Archie, "Wow, you are an advanced reader!" "He is," Kara agreed. "He read the whole Harry Potter series in one week," Blaine added proudly.

A total and unflinching pursuit of hope—backed by a sturdy foundation of material resources and cultural health capital—carried the Hilyards around the world and back again, delivering them safely into the future they had most hoped for. But not all families get the chance to pursue such opportunities or have the support available to them to negotiate this path as smoothly. Even among those who do make it to the top of the US healthcare system, extraordinary efforts and promising new interventions do not always translate seamlessly into the outcomes families seek. For care-captaining and care-entrusting families alike, the mismatch between expectations—ramped up by institutional rhetoric and carefully constructed emotional cultures—and the actual results of even the most advanced medical treatments can be shattering for those who bet everything and lose. In this final chapter, I work to begin untangling this paradox, and point to a few ways forward.

"I Would Have Gone to the Moon to Save Him": The Communicative Powers of Hope

That the pursuit of hope can offer significant advantages while simultaneously tripping us up so that we miss out on others is the quandary at the core of this book. Clearly, working to generate hope for children's recoveries can lead to concrete medical advantages under the right circumstances. Maintaining hope can also help families negotiating critical illness to minimize emotional upset and preserve enough physical and emotional stamina to endure the long road ahead. But hope is also a *language* through which people communicate love, commitment, appreciation, and need for those they care about when their loved ones' lives are threatened.

Given this communicative power, hope does some serious heavy lifting in the social arena. Our collective agreement to remain hopeful in the face of life-threatening illness smooths social interactions in both institutional contexts and within families. Because death and grief are splintered off and largely separated from daily life in contemporary US society, our linguistic strategies for engaging them when we must often involve euphemism and quickly changing the subject. This refusal to engage their potential, their likelihood, or their inevitability allows us to avoid awkward interactions for which we lack solid and readily available blueprints.

Working to produce and maintain as much hope as possible at every juncture also helps us to perform identity work.[2] In other words, it helps us present ourselves to others as we'd like them to see us—as a good daughter, for instance, or a deeply devoted mother or father.[3] Remaining steadfastly hopeful and describing extensive efforts to fight for their children's lives at all costs allows families to explicitly demonstrate their dedication as parents. For care-captaining parents, lengthy and detailed descriptions of tireless advocacy efforts and their unwillingness to accept anything but superior care for their children becomes a way to communicate their inexhaustible love for their child.

For instance, Argentinean mom Eva Campos, whose ten-year-old son, Ignacio Maldonado, was diagnosed with metachromatic leukodystrophy (MLD, a devastating progressive neurological disease), explained that she did extensive medical research and looked across three continents in seeking life-saving care for him. Researchers she contacted who were leading a clinical trial in Italy referred her to Dr. Vogel at Kelly-Reed, where "Iggy" underwent a sibling-donor bone marrow transplant under the care of a physician with experience transplanting children with MLD (something physicians in her home country were not willing to do). When I asked her if it had been difficult to decide to travel so far to obtain treatment—which had at this point already kept her away from

her home, job, husband, and two other children who visited intermittently, for over a year—she told me flatly, "*No. Me Hubiera ido a la luna*
[I would have gone to the moon]" to save him.

The image of a mother traveling to the moon if that's what it takes to
save her child is a powerful one. Eva had the educational background
and professional experience as a high-school principal to develop cultural health capital and care-captain extensively throughout her son's
illness. Her statement overtly connected her myriad care-captaining actions to her deep motherly devotion. Not all families could regale me
with lengthy descriptions of sophisticated medical research and negotia-
tions with providers the way that Eva and other care-captaining parents
did. Poor and working-class families who primarily care-entrusted had
to lean more heavily on broad emotional proclamations to communicate their dedication to their children. For instance, Lakira Harris told
me, "It's been a fight, you know. I fight a lot. I stand up for my child."
Jeanetta Moore similarly assured me that she would do anything to help
heal her daughter: "We're gonna do what we gotta do. That's how I honestly felt. . . . If it was, if I could've gave her something out of myself?
I would've done it. If it was my arm that would've made her better, I
would've done it." Lakira and Jeanetta also pointed to their "choices" to
give up jobs (which, in truth, they were pushed out of due to absences
related to their children's illnesses and hospitalizations and the afore-
mentioned absence of policies to protect them) in order to devote more
time to caring for their ill children and cement their total commitment
to them.[4] The pride with which care-entrusting parents like Mary Shaw
and Tariq Khalid emphasized their efforts to follow doctors' instructions
"to a T" similarly reveals their desire to establish themselves as good
parents *because of* their dutiful obedience to medical experts.

Both approaches to signifying one's goodness and devotion as a parent require the maintenance of unshakeable confidence that their child
will survive. Refusing to consider the possibility that a loved one can die
becomes the strongest, brightest signal of the depth of their love, care,
and commitment. Vivian Patterson was adamant that her son would be
okay, even after Shawn's brain tumor recurred. She found others' willingness to consider the possibility of anything less than his full recovery
appalling: "When they hear the cancer has come back . . . they already
think, 'Oh my gosh, what does that mean for you?' I was like, [firmly] 'It

means *nothing* different for us.' . . . So [I was] trying to make sure they understood that nothing's changed for us . . . we're still on Plan A. . . . Our goal is that he will be delivered from this. So [there is] no plan B." Vivian's unyielding hope and refusal to speak of anything other than a positive outcome were reminiscent of similar stances I observed among other families. She also worked to get others around her to cooperate with this construction of reality. She chose Kelly-Reed, in fact, not only because she understood it to be "more specialized" than a university research hospital in their home state, but also because she recalled Shawn's Kelly-Reed physician (and head of the brain tumor center's pediatric program) telling her: "We work on 100 percent so we're just going for it. . . . We're going to get this resolved."

But if patients, families, and healthcare providers remain exclusively committed to maintaining hope under any and all circumstances, where are they left if life-saving efforts fail? If we believe that speaking of a patient or loved one's potential death signifies an openness to it that betrays a *lack* of total care and commitment, families are stuck holding tightly to hope long after it can help them. It is in these ways that hope limits social support and shuts down opportunities for families to more thoughtfully consider how they would like to navigate not only illness, but shortened lives and the dying process.

The Pitfalls and Possibilities of Hope

Both care-captaining and care-entrusting helps families produce and maintain hope in different ways. For families with reasonable amounts of cultural health capital, care-captaining can garner concrete medical advantages for children that in turn bolster their hopes for recovery. For families with less cultural health capital, care-entrusting can help them protect themselves from becoming overwhelmed by feelings of helplessness and inefficacy and to preserve a (potentially more fragile) sense of hope. But care-entrusting can lead to delays in access to appropriate care, less than optimal treatment experiences, and less effective communication with providers. Care-captaining can be taken too far and burn families out. Both can lead families to prolong treatment attempts beyond the point at which they can offer much benefit and leave families unprepared for the end of children's lives if treatment fails. Although families may blend and switch illness management strategies to help them more flexibly facilitate both medical and emotional advantages, this is a difficult balance to strike.

Significant and sometimes rapid advances in medicine provide families with reason to increasingly believe that almost any condition can be successfully treated and that hope for children's recoveries is always around the corner. There are many success stories that point to the seeming inevitability of technologically driven life extension. When anthropologist Myra Bluebond-Langner conducted her study of children living with a sibling's fatal illness (cystic fibrosis), life expectancy was approximately nineteen years of age. By the time she published a book on her work a decade later, it had grown to twenty-nine years.[5] Today, children with cystic fibrosis can expect to live close to forty years, and there is reason to believe life expectancy will continue to rise.[6]

Prenatal genetic testing and newborn screenings also tantalizingly promise to help identify and potentially treat rare conditions sooner and more effectively than ever before by helping more children gain access to treatment immediately and thus get a head start against even tough odds.[7] As sociologist Stefan Timmermans and anthropologist Mara Buchbinder demonstrate, however, such universal screening comes with its own set of risks, as it can raise red flags or lead to false positives that generate an enormous amount of angst for parents—angst that is sometimes unnecessary. Stress itself—as manifested through increased cortisol levels in pregnant mothers—has well-documented damaging effects on developing fetuses, not unlike those of smoking or excessive-drinking. Simply waiting for the results of prenatal screening tests can cause increased stress for many women.[8] Still, early identification that can allow families to pursue advanced medical technologies swiftly has real benefit in some cases. The routinization of such testing itself conveys the message that with swift and proactive medical intervention, previously devastating conditions might be successfully and relatively easily resolved.

For a number of families in my study, novel and experimental treatments indeed offered enormous benefit. But at times, pursuing the newest medical technologies could be more like chasing a mirage. Even treatments with promising and proven success in others can fail.[9] Yet because narratives of hope and inevitable progress are so alluring, it is hard for patients, physicians, and researchers alike to resist them.[10] Unfortunately, it is difficult to hold steadfastly to hope and reap the benefits it can offer, while at the same time considering and preparing for outcomes we do not hope for.

The families I introduce in this book found themselves navigating tricky terrain: they confronted the acute crisis of a child in grave danger and lived this crisis over an extended period of time. They had to integrate this dramatic new reality into their daily lives, while logistically negotiating lengthy treatments and everyday care responsibilities. Hope helped families avoid the emotional drain of despair and kept them from becoming paralyzed and unable to complete the myriad practical tasks required of them each day. Hope could make social interactions with friends, family members, and physicians easier to move through. It could take the edge off the unknown future that loomed menacingly on the horizon. It could help physicians shepherd families through the most precarious points of the treatment process, seeing them through to resolutions that sometimes saw children's lives saved, but could not always stave off children's deaths. Along the way, hope functioned as a language that parents, physicians, friends, and family members could use to signify their love, caring, and depth of commitment to their children, patients, or loved ones.

Perhaps it should be unsurprising then that "hope" is packaged and sold in the modern healthcare system more aggressively than ever before. Sociologist Alan Petersen, who has examined the discourse of hope as it pertains to a variety of biotechnological advancements, shows how hope has been "symbolically mobilized" to sell everything from cord-blood banking to fly-by-night stem-cell injections in unregulated settings. Technologies and scientific research more broadly, he argues, "are both the subject of hopeful expectations and the means by which 'hope' is mediated and marketed."[11] High financial stakes can be at the root of efforts to sell hope to as many patients in as many ways as possible. Echoing Nancy Berns' analysis of how emotional "closure" is sold to those grieving the loss of a loved one, Petersen shows how hope and its accompanying good feelings are increasingly commodified, especially when illness and death are the outcomes the hope-seeker is promised he or she can escape.[12]

Indeed, the rhetoric of hope is omnipresent in contemporary healthcare. In his 2005 best-selling book *The Anatomy of Hope*, Jerome

Groopman, a hematologist-oncologist, argues that hope can be "as important as any medication I might prescribe or any procedure I might perform."[13] He shares stories of patients whose lack of hope prevented them from pursuing treatments with "real" promise, and others whose relentless pursuit of treatments no one imagined would help led them to survive years longer than anticipated. He warns against "ignorance is bliss" hope, in which a patient is not fully informed of the true status of his or her condition or the potential for treatments to fail. But he cautions against presenting too bleak or grim a prognosis, which he argues may prevent patients from enjoying the time they have.

In Groopman's celebratory conceptualization, hope "helps us overcome hurdles that we otherwise could not scale, and it moves us forward to a place where healing can occur."[14] He recognizes that many treatments will eventually fail and patients will die. But the book presents hope as a powerful healing force *in itself*, and a valorous path for patients and families to embark on. That hopefulness is so universally lauded reflects, at least in part, an entrenched social phobia around death and does nothing to challenge those fears. While it may indeed have the benefits Groopman proposes at times—and my data show without question that adamantly pursuing hope can net patients and families benefits of many kinds—it can prevent people from making clear-eyed choices about the time they have available to them or engaging in end-of-life planning that might shorten or ease the dying process if and when it arrives.

Atul Gawande, another physician whose popular writing has repeatedly landed him on the bestseller list, paints a somewhat different picture in his 2014 book *Being Mortal*. Gawande laments the tendency for physicians who are treating patients with life-threatening conditions to offer increasingly futile treatment options until the final days of their lives. Doing so, he argues, can prolong and exacerbate suffering and stand in the way of patients' abilities to wring the most possible remaining enjoyment out of life. Shifting focus away from medical interventions when treatments are failing and talking openly about death help to facilitate better decision-making, decrease suffering, and offer terminally ill patients and their families a pathway that allows them to live more fully in the time they have left.

There is no easy solution in medicine to this paradox of hope. When my father was critically ill, our inability to relinquish hope led him to undergo an unpleasant and invasive treatment just three weeks before he died, at a time when moving from one room to another was already a grueling undertaking. But pursuing hope through care-captaining got us very close to two much more promising treatments—which under different circumstances might have meaningfully extended and improved his life. Exploring every possible avenue we could find, at some of the "best" medical centers in the country, also offered us the critical reassurance that we had done "everything possible" to save him.[15]

Sophie Rivera-Cruz, Kaelyn Moore, and Aaron Shaw could join Archie Hilyard as poster children for what access to cutting-edge medical care can sometimes accomplish for children with otherwise fatal conditions. Sophie and Kaelyn are both likely to live long, healthy, and high-functioning lives despite being born with fatal neurological or immunological conditions, respectively. Aaron Shaw's long-term life expectancy is less certain, but with the enzyme replacement infusions and physical and other therapies he receives weekly at Kelly-Reed, he is still attending school, playing video games, and maintaining reasonable mobility far beyond that observed previously in children with his disease. Without access to new technologies and physicians with experience treating their extremely rare conditions at Kelly-Reed, these children would almost certainly not be alive today.

Though Jayden Lacoste died due to complications from the stem-cell transplant his mother so desperately hoped would cure his sickle-cell disease, a teenage girl who spent many months at the Ronald McDonald House during my fieldwork recovering from the same treatment for the same condition returned to high school entirely cured of her disease, went on to spearhead a successful fundraising effort to benefit other families at the Ronald McDonald House, and is now attending college. Medical and technological advancements *have* made vast strides, and for the lives they save, the great lengths families went to in order to obtain them paid off. Yet not all families are able to go to such lengths. Among those who are, these efforts do not always result in the miracles families and healthcare providers hope for. As medical research continues to provide more successful treatments for a rapidly multiplying array of conditions, those who bump up against the limits of biomedicine are caught increasingly unprepared. Whether families are best emotionally served by care-captaining, care-entrusting, or a combination of both can have real consequences for their end-of-life experiences. Ultimately, families need much more support in both pursuing hope *and* stepping away from it. I offer some suggestions along these lines in the section below.

Illness, Inequality, and Emotions Revisited: Implications for Change

Sociologists rightly focus much attention on how access to resources can set people onto vastly different paths through life and shape the contours of one's life chances overall. But emotions play a bigger role in the reproduction of inequality than is usually recognized. For the families I studied, who, in addition to the everyday exigencies of raising young children, confronted the challenge of managing a child's life-threatening illness, resources were certainly key. Abundant cultural health capital and access to material resources and social support facilitated care-captaining and yielded the concrete medical advantages many of the families I met were able to obtain. But powerful emotions—and efforts to change them—also propelled families down paths of care-captaining or care-entrusting, or prompted them to jump tracks.

To keep the most difficult emotions at bay, the families I studied managed their children's serious illnesses in ways that helped them maintain as much hope and minimize as much fear and anxiety as possible. In this way, the emotion work at the core of these illness management strategies also substantially drove the diverging experiences between them. Efforts to manage emotions can thus become the foundation for the production and maintenance of inequalities.[16] Failing to recognize the emotional impetus behind the illness management strategies explicated here would limit our understanding of what is at stake for families, as well as what would be required to reduce the inequalities between them. Because material resources and emotional goals were tightly bound up with one another in pushing families to care-captain or care-entrust, both must be taken seriously in order to offer families living through medical nightmares like these the support they sorely need.

Some solutions are straightforward, at least conceptually. Improved—*and paid*—family leave policies would go a long way toward lessening the brutal financial impact a child's illness has on all families, but especially poor and working-class families who are the least likely to have jobs that might voluntarily provide continuity in medical benefits or hold positions for those who need to attend to caregiving responsibilities. That families lose jobs and income that may be more desperately needed than ever when children become sick is a problem that does not require new breakthroughs in medicine, good genetic fortune, or a "war on cancer" to solve. Such policies could dramatically reduce the financial stresses and anxieties that pile up on top of those inherent in the illness and treatment process.

Unfortunately, efforts to improve and extend US family and medical leave policies have largely fallen flat. Ideologies of individual and family responsibility do little to encourage political mobilization around unmet social welfare needs, and a climate of economic fear and political apathy has made the work of those mobilizing for change even more difficult.[17] It should go without saying that separating children's access to needed medical care from a family's ability to pay, negotiate with private insurance or state Medicaid programs, or obtain financial assistance from friends and family members would remove a significant barrier between precariously ill children and the experts and treatments that might save their lives. Yet efforts to reform the US healthcare system—most recently in the form of the Affordable Care Act—remain not only hotly contested, but in significant peril. Even these hard-fought reforms do not make affordable and high-quality healthcare available to all. Though no perfect health system exists, less inequality in other systems offer important "lessons for the U.S."[18] Reconceptualizing access to quality healthcare as a human right is one approach those working for continued progress have taken.[19] The appetite for more universal healthcare options in the United States is growing, particularly among younger generations, and would go a long way to addressing the most basic issues of access that many still face.[20]

Additional support for parents and other family members who find themselves providing long-term care for dying or chronically ill loved ones is also long overdue. Though there are many benefits to caring for patients at home rather than in hospitals or other institutions (particularly at the end of life), the burden on unpaid family caregivers is substantial. The high physical, economic, and psychological strain can push caregivers to the brink. In-home nursing and other respite care are often not covered by insurance, and it is financially out of reach for many. Efforts to provide greater funding for these services at both state and national levels have not gotten far or come anywhere close to meeting the needs of families in these exhausting positions. Sensible models exist for how caregivers could be better supported, and campaigns to meet this need have also been mounted, but have likewise repeatedly collapsed politically.[21] This is another area ripe for mobilization, and a space for local support agencies to step into in the interim.

It must also be noted that even in a dramatically altered policy landscape, some inequalities in access to high quality-care would remain. As the Hilyards' story illustrates, even in contexts where access to healthcare is substantially more equal for all than it is in the United States, well-resourced families are often able to secure additional medical and emotional benefits for themselves and their children. At an even deeper level, then, across the board improvements to families' economic security—higher minimum wages and more uniform and perhaps guaranteed access to basic resources such as food, housing, and childcare—would also do much to even an unequal medical playing field.

Addressing these large-scale inequalities is critical, but no easy task, particularly in this highly contentious political moment. Other interventions may be more immediately implemented at local and institutional levels. None of the families in this study started out at Kelly-Reed. They got there by climbing, or being referred and shuttled, up the healthcare ladder. To promote better access to new treatments and specialized expertise for rare diseases or serious illnesses, a pan-institutional healthcare liaison who could help families locate those experts and treatments might be beneficial. Medical social workers traditionally help families meet basic needs and obtain local resources—for instance, housing at the Ronald McDonald House, transportation, cafeteria vouchers, or referrals to agencies like the Make-A-Wish foundation. Alternatively, a healthcare access liaison could help families negotiate the healthcare system itself, including helping families better understand how to go about seeking, assessing, and obtaining coverage for less widely available treatment options for rare or particularly difficult to treat conditions. This could also help to shift a portion of the burden of unpaid care work away from parents who are already overburdened by an all-encompassing and deeply distressing crisis. Building cross-institutional infrastructures that can quickly and efficiently move serious cases up the ladder with less mystification could be especially useful for those with less cultural health capital.

Of course, this strategy would require thoughtful implementation and a sensitivity to the fact that *not all families will be interested in taking a more directly care-captaining approach*, even with greater assistance. Another late fieldwork moment when I felt the reassuring repetition of "theoretical saturation" came during my second-to-last shift at the Ronald McDonald House. It was a bright, sunny afternoon, and I was baking cupcakes in the large communal kitchen with the mother of a teenage brain-tumor patient. In chatting casually about her son's care at Kelly-Reed, I asked her if she'd had to make difficult treatment decisions. She assured me that she did not: she left such decisions to the experts and quipped, "The doctors and nurses know better than I do anyway." Parents who lean strongly toward a care-entrusting approach may not appreciate being pushed, even with well-intentioned and sensitive support, to take the helm of the ship and assume the role of active directors and coordinators of their children's care. Such an initiative would therefore need to be deeply cognizant of the complex emotional dynamics beneath families' illness management strategies.

Physicians, nurses, and other healthcare providers would benefit from more education in this regard as well. Incorporating a focus on the emotional dynamics of hope- and help-seeking into medical, nursing, and other healthcare-training curricula could be one concrete way to facilitate this. Over time, those designing these curricula have gradually recognized the importance of teaching the social side of medicine, particularly around cultural difference and social inequalities. The recent addition of a behavioral and social science section to the revised 2015 Medical College Admission Exam (MCAT) is further evidence of this shift—and in turn has increased pre-health students' awareness of and enrollment in social science courses that cover these issues in depth. But the next shift needed may be more explicit training and mentorship around emotion work that emphasizes the role healthcare providers can play in shifting emotional cultures in medicine and helping patients and families navigate a fundamentally emotional social experience.

While it is unrealistic to expect all providers to become the equivalent of therapists or palliative care counselors, a solid understanding of the emotional goals driving families' illness management strategies would better equip physicians and others working with patients and families to reduce healthcare inequalities by helping them more effectively navigate both the medical and the emotional mazes they face. Such training could also discourage practitioners from drawing conclusions about a family caregivers' level of commitment to their loved ones based on snap judgments about their illness management strategies. Direct and comprehensive training in how to most effectively care for patients and their families as the end of life nears remains patchy at best.[22] Making this a routine part of professional preparation across the board could lead to real improvements in the quality of care and guidance provided to those struggling with end-of-life decision-making and help prepare caregivers for the aftermath of loss.

Hope Reconsidered

As optimistic as some of the policy changes and interventions proposed above may seem in the current political climate, that such changes would benefit families is obvious. The problem of hope itself—and how to balance hope against the possibility of unhoped-for outcomes—is less clear. While hope can be a balm and a beacon that genuinely benefits some patients and caregivers, it can be a stumbling block at key moments as well. It is also important to recognize that on a larger scale, hope can be one component of "a much wider effort to engender [obligatory] optimism and happiness in populations."[23] Within this context it is imperative to question the assumption "that a 'hopeful' approach in heath and healthcare . . . [must] always be positively valued."[24] Though it is entirely understandable that families faced with the prospect of the potential loss of a loved one will look for and hold on to hope wherever possible—sometimes to great success—a more expansive emotional culture would make room for the wider variety of emotional experiences patients and their families may have over the course of a life-threatening illness, and beyond.

Some patients have already pushed against the boundaries of the restrictive emotional culture around illness and death. Women with breast cancer have worked to "deflate the culture of optimism" by sitting for photographs that put mastectomy scars, hair loss, and other visible signs of illness on full display.[25] For decades, AIDS patients, caregivers, and advocates have fought to bring greater attention and resources to the disease by mobilizing in ways that make space for, and instrumental use of, many "negative" emotions, including anger and outrage.[26]

Widening the emotional culture around illness and death could allow patients and families to speak more openly about, more effectively prepare for, and be more fully supported in suffering and grief. In her study of an inpatient hospice care center in England, anthropologist Julia Lawton found that despite the increasing desire of patients to die at home, deaths marked by significant bodily deterioration were the ones most likely to be "sequestered" in such institutionalized spaces.[27] She argues that this practice, in combination with the sanitized images of "gentle death" often depicted in film and television and the promise that hospice and palliative-care providers can manage or even eliminate end-of-life pain, masks the reality that death often still involves other forms of suffering and loss of dignity and that these can be devastating for patients and families. A culture that is willing and able to look directly at these stark realities would help all of its members be better prepared for, make more clear-eyed decisions about, and better support one another in these pivotal moments. Such honest discussion could also usefully inform policy debates around the rights those who are dying should have to exert agency over their own deaths.

Loosening our grip on the rhetoric of hope can feel like an unmooring, and when hope serves as a language to express caring, doing so poses social and interactional risks. But symbolic interactionists, who have long recognized that meanings are constructed through our interactions with one another, point to the agentic role social actors constantly play in this ongoing meaning-making process.[28] We routinely collectively engage with, resist, and modify the meanings attached to behaviors and identities.[29] The meanings attached to hope are no different. This raises the possibility of *reconstructing* the meanings attached to hope—and to the meanings associated with stepping back from it.[30] Though the language of hope can serve as an easy and fluid way to communicate care and commitment, its pervasiveness makes it harder to communicate effectively about outcomes we *don't* hope for. These are the conversations that must be reevaluated, redefined, and practiced.

Rather than feeling that we are calling our "good"-ness as family members into question or expressing a willingness to lose or "abandon" those we care about, conversations about death and dying could be reconceived as an expression of *greater* care. Family members', friends', and healthcare providers' willingness to delve into painful territory openly, honestly, and consistently could be understood as a gift that provides a foundation for a smoother way forward if "hope" fails to conquer all. Rather than "giving up" hope—or even "changing hope" while still sticking to its positive mandates—conversations about those things we do not hope for, and a willingness to make space for raw sadness and suffering, could be reconstructed as loving acts, rooted in deep care for and devotion to one another.

This is something akin to what former palliative-care program director Stephen Jenkinson proposes in his 2015 book, *Die Wise*. Jenkinson warns that when we "don't let dying change how [we] live together . . . the consequence is missed last chances for authentic talk . . . for shared sorrow . . . [and for] learning how to live as if what is happening is happening."[31] He argues that being unable to carry the reality of death—our own and those of the people close to us—with us consistently over the whole course of our lives is to fail to understand life as it is, fully, from beginning to end. If our culture were more open to and adept at grieving, we could all more intentionally carry with us those who have died before us after they are gone, and help others living with loss to do the same. Our relationships with those we have lost might even extend and expand. As a result, Jenkinson suggests, we might all find less reason to feel anxious as we anticipate and ultimately approach our own mortality.

During a grief support group I attended in the months after my father's death, I met a young woman in her twenties who had lost her mother to breast cancer. Though she died in July, her mother had recognized the likelihood that she would soon die and had selected and wrapped Christmas gifts for her husband and daughter to open in her absence during the holidays. This small act allowed her to reach out to and communicate with her family, connect with, and provide love and comfort to them months after she died. These are the kinds of things that we can offer to one another when we openly acknowledge and engage with death and give it space to breathe.

Illness and loss are some of the most unsettling experiences humans face. At the core of individual and collective responses to illness are powerful efforts to manage emotions—our own and those of others. These responses undergird inequalities in healthcare by shaping how we interact with the institutions that provide our care and how those providing our care and other needed resources interact with us. Bringing greater clarity to the social-emotional motivations at the root of illness management strategies—and what they both offer us and take away—can help us to begin untangling these complex dynamics and to take steps toward reducing the inequalities they engender.

It is worth reiterating here that hope can do much good, and this book is not intended to discourage those who are ill or caring for someone who is seriously ill from pursuing it in many forms. But by performing hope—through what we do and don't do, say and don't say—we collectively weave the social and cultural fabric of illness and medicine. To the extent that this fabric can at times become more of a straitjacket, we might consider how we can weave it less tightly, add more metaphorical threads and colors, and continuously examine the ways in which it serves us *and* how it does not.

In her critical analysis of the cultural mandate that those grieving loss seek "closure," resolve upsetting emotions, and "move on" as quickly as possible, sociologist Nancy Berns reminds us that it is possible to "carry complicated combinations of emotions," like grief and joy, both at the same time.[32] Constructing a broader, more flexible emotional culture around illness and death—one that is expansive enough to accommodate both hope and fear, determination and fatigue, perseverance and rest, lightness and profound sorrow, existing solidly, side-by-side—could allow us to more collectively shoulder the heavy load critically ill patients and those caring for them must carry. Reducing inequalities in the illness experience will require substantial change at both micro- and macro- levels, change in policy, and change in everyday, habitual interactions. Paying careful attention to the complicated role emotion work plays in driving these inequalities, and the power of hope to distract us from their consequences, is an important step in that direction.

ACKNOWLEDGMENTS

As I reflect on the wealth of people who made this book possible, I recognize that I am standing on the backs of many turtles—and it truly is "turtles all the way down." Impossible as it is to determine quite where to stop, I have no doubt about where to begin.

That any of the families whose stories fill these pages made time and space in their lives for me is astonishing. I am not often speechless. But there simply are not words to adequately thank them. I am honored and profoundly grateful. I can only hope to have done some small justice to their experiences, and that their trust in me was not misplaced. In addition to my father, this book is dedicated to them, and especially to the memories of Benjamin, Noah, Brent, Jayden, and Shawn.

The project itself was initially incubated and nurtured by my graduate school mentors, who provided me with a formidable web of support that saw me through the most arduous portions of data collection and analysis. Peter Conrad's complete and total confidence and trust in me from the beginning is what prompted me to pursue this leap into an entirely unplanned topic of inquiry. His vast knowledge on all matters medical sociology (and well beyond) and astute observations nudged me in important directions as the project developed, and his unparalleled generosity of spirit makes every occasion for interaction a happy one. Karen Hansen and Ana Villalobos's expert methodological guidance and enthusiasm for this project helped propel me forward, particularly in the early months when the path was unclear. I thank them both for their steadfast faith in me, for their glowing and effusive praise when I was far from convinced it was warranted, and for their ongoing friendship and multifaceted support. Wendy Cadge and David Cunningham also provided thoughtful and savvy advice on any number of matters personal and professional during graduate school and beyond, and I am grateful for their insights and encouragement.

I owe my deepest and longest-standing mentorship debt to Michael Schwalbe for introducing me to the craft of ethnography, training me to do it well, and helping me discover the kind of sociologist and scholar I wanted to be. His high standards, honest appraisals, and incisive eye drove me to continuously sharpen my work and hone the skills needed to do it well. Without this apprenticeship, it is unlikely that I would have found my way as a researcher or a writer, and it is impossible now to imagine my life any other way. Thank you, Michael, for bringing me into the fold.

I may never have found my way into the profession at all were it not for the truly exceptional educational opportunities afforded me by Steve Kantrowitz, Tim Tyson, and Craig Werner as an undergraduate at the University of Wisconsin, and equally fortuitous opportunities to work on issues of institutional inequity with Rodney Horikawa and Seema Kapani while I completed my master's degree in social work. Allan Johnson, Paula Rothenberg, and Tim Wise also shaped and supported me in vital ways during this formative period. I hope they all know that their influence continues to permeate my thinking and my intellectual and pedagogical commitments to this day.

At Wake Forest, my colleagues in the sociology department have been extraordinarily supportive from day one. I am especially grateful to Ana Wahl and Steve Gunkel, who have provided assistance and sustenance in many forms, time and time (and time) again, from the moment I arrived. Joining a department that came with their friendship was an incredible stroke of luck. Hana Brown and David Yamane also deserve special note for their generous support, camaraderie, and invaluable practical guidance on negotiating the tenure track. I also thank my colleagues across the university, especially members of the 2014–2016 Medicine Across the Disciplines humanities seminar and the 2015 Women's Center summer writing group, who offered accountability and early feedback on drafts of two of the chapters contained here. Nick Albertson, Elizabeth Clendinning, Simone Caron, Kristina Gupta, Stephanie Koscak, Scott Mehl, and Mir Yarfitz provided good company, fresh meals, emergency childcare, and moral support during both the writing process *and* my transition to parenthood. I thank you all for truly having my back through the ups and downs of both.

I am particularly indebted to Stephanie Koscak in this regard, whose abundant provisioning of all of the above has been absolutely indispensable. During the final leg of this journey Karin Friedrich, Amanda Griffith, Anna Keller, Kevin Keller, Angela Mazaris, Katie Payne, David Payne, and Erika Zimmerman have helped me navigate the trials and triumphs involved in our collective efforts to juggle work, life, and raising small children, and I am so glad to be sharing that endeavor with you all.

I received important financial support from a variety of sources, including the National Science Foundation, the Andrew Mellon Foundation, and a Wake Forest University Summer Research Award. The writing was additionally supported in part by a Junior Research Sabbatical at Wake Forest University. I thank Kate Smalley for her diligent and meticulous transcription services, and Casey Clevenger for expert editorial assistance with the full manuscript as the final deadline loomed.

Janet Shim embraced this project from our first meeting at the American Sociological Association Meetings years ago, and I feel so fortunate to be engaged with the work of such a whole-heartedly generous scholar and advocate. I thank her for excellent practical advice and abundant good cheer in equal measure at multiple points along the way. Gayle Sulik's careful, tender, and critical eye on the entire first draft of this manuscript is a gift I can only hope to pay forward one day. Without her holistic care for this book and its author, it may well not have come to fruition. Jennifer Lois provided insightful and sincerely encouraging feedback on early drafts of several chapters, inspiring me to keep writing and pushing ahead when the finish line seemed terribly far away. Her comments on the entire final manuscript as that line eventually neared offered precisely the reassurance and final tweaks needed to cross it.

Jennifer Reich's sharp and thoughtful comments at the midpoint helped me further boost the quality of this manuscript. My editor, Ilene Kalish, has championed this project from the moment I shared it with her, and I am deeply grateful for both her enthusiasm and her commitment to seeing it through each step of the process swiftly and surely. The reviews she commissioned were also instrumental in shaping the development of the final product, and I thank those reviewers profusely for investing their time in my work, helping me pinpoint areas needing more attention, and their kind words about the value of this endeavor. Sonia Tsuruoka and Alexia Traganas helped make the production process as seamless and painless as possible, which was an invaluable kindness to me.

The kinship, support, and solidarity offered by many others in my extended academic family—at Brandeis, North Carolina State, and beyond—buoyed me at various points throughout the research and writing process, and I feel so fortunate to have had each one of them with me at some point over the course of this long road. I'm especially looking at you, Sarah Epplen, Matt Ezzell, Nicky Fox, Clare Hammonds, Kendra Jason, Ken Kolb, Becca Loya, Tom Mackie, Marya Mtshali, Kylie Parotta, Emily Sigalow, and Miranda Waggoner. My deep, heartfelt thanks to you all.

During the most personally difficult and emotionally challenging parts of this journey I leaned most heavily on Casey Clevenger and Steve Hitlin. From the death of my father to the birth of my son, they have borne witness to the most sorrowful and most joyful moments of my life, in raw form. The heaviest burdens of the human experience simply cannot be shouldered alone, and the most awe-inspiring and deeply fulfilling ones are richest when shared. Thank you both for your shoulders, and your celebrations. And maybe just a few conversations about sociology and this book here and there as well . . .

At the same time that I embarked on the final stages of writing this book, I became a mom. Nothing could possibly have prepared me for the ferocious, heart-bursting love I would feel for this tiny person. Watching him grow and learn and discover how to engage with the puzzling and exhilarating wonders of this world has been magical. Matthew's sweet smile, gleeful laugh, and kind, gentle heart enchant me each and every day. I love you forever and always, my little bug.

Last but not least (or even last, to continue the turtle metaphor), because my father died during the course of the research for this book, I'm especially attuned to the seeds he planted that helped prepare me to see such a project from start to finish.

My father was the one who quit his job and stayed home to care for me after I was born. I remember sitting at his feet on his leather Red Wing boots, watching *Sesame Street* or *Mr. Rogers* while he patiently combed through the tangles in my long, fine hair—one section at a time, so it wouldn't hurt as much—before I went school.

Under his tutelage, my kindergarten science project outlined the process of metamorphosis, complete with an elaborate poster depicting each stage in the cycle, accompanied by a dried cocoon and a perfectly preserved monarch butterfly carefully pinned in a plastic display case. I remember feeling awfully proud of myself as I basked in the praise we received—not fully appreciating, of course, the extent to which his curiosity about the natural world and passion for teaching even abstract scientific concepts to others were laying the ground work that would encourage me to ask questions about the world around me for years to come.

During late night drives to visit my grandparents when I was older, we speculated about the vastness of space, the boundaries of the universe, and the nature of "nothingness" (which he assured me was most definitely *not* nothing) as we flew down the dark two-lane country roads of southwestern Minnesota. He quizzed me on the tapes he popped into the cassette player, making sure that I could immediately recognize the distinctive voices of Tom Petty, Elvis, Roy Orbison, and David Bowie or the signature guitar riffs of Jimi Hendrix and Carlos Santana.

In my early twenties he took apart and reassembled my first fifty-dollar Dirt Devil vacuum, keeping it going years longer than it had any right to. He could effortlessly sketch the inner workings of atomic structure or explain the complex process of photosynthesis to a first-grader. "All energy comes from the sun," he liked to remind people, whenever a relevant moment arose.

One morning while he was in town for a medical appointment of his own, I left him in the lobby of the Kelly-Reed children's hospital while I observed a follow-up visit with a family in my study. When I returned, I found him performing "magic" for the children nearby. He'd discovered that one of the fish in the large aquarium was attracted to the red color of his shirt and would swim swiftly back and forth to follow him as he walked past. "See? Magic," he told them with a sly grin.

When he taught me to ride a bike he refused to give me the "crutch" of training wheels. Instead, he strapped a long sturdy broom handle to the seat with duct tape, and ran along beside me during my first shaky pedals as I begged him not to let go. He held me up until I was steady and had enough momentum, then let go anyway to prove his point: I didn't need training wheels; I could ride on my own.

I didn't always love lessons like those. But I don't know whether I would have had the drive, patience, tendency toward perfectionism, or perseverance required to tackle a doctoral degree, this book, or single motherhood for that matter, had I not had such a stubborn, smart, and endlessly inquisitive role model in whose footsteps to follow.

Thanks, Dad.

Doing Fieldwork in Emotionally Fraught Settings

A Brief Reflection

About a week before he was admitted to the hospital for transplant, Jayden, Lakira, and I roamed the wide brightly lit aisles of a nearby Walmart to stock up on some of the basics Jayden would need during his months-long stay. Armed with a list of needed items and gift cards from the patient assistance program, we browsed long rows of children's slippers and dug through bins of six-pack superhero underwear. We rifled through racks of pajamas searching unsuccessfully for the button-down style the hospital recommended in order to keep the central line that would be implanted in Jayden's chest easily accessible. As we filled the cart, Jayden's eye was caught by countless enticing items on neighboring shelves.

"Can I have this?" Jayden implored his mother, holding up a brightly colored trinket.

"No!" Lakira gently scolded him. "We're not here for that stuff."

When he told us he was hungry, I pulled a strawberry fruit strip from my bag to distract him for a bit. By the time we neared the checkout line, Jayden had deemed his mother a lost cause, so he turned to me.

"Will you buy me a toy?" he asked, flashing me his signature impish grin.

"I'm not going to buy you a toy!" I replied, hands on my hips, with a show of artificial indignation. But my heartstrings had been effectively tugged.

"Can I have some gum?" He tried, hopefully.

"I'll tell you what," I conceded. "I'll bring you some gum when I visit you in the hospital next week."

"Yay, gum!" Jayden cheered.

When I got home that night, I felt guilty for denying Jayden's requests. What if, like little Noah Rivera-Cruz, Jayden never got out of the hospital? What if this had been one of his few remaining nights out in the world at large and a spontaneous splurge could have made it an extra-joyful one? I had been raised in a frugal family and steeped in the Lake Wobegan–esque hard-scrabble Minnesotan ethic that children's whims should not be indulged lightly. To the contrary, children should learn they *can't* always get everything they want, or they will quickly become spoiled. But was this the time for that lesson, I wondered? What if there was no long game for Jayden, and making the most of every remaining hour was all that mattered? The question gnawed at me.

I of course wanted to believe—and *felt compelled to act in ways that demonstrated my confident expectation*—that Jayden was going to come out healthy and cured on the other side of the transplant, as another sickle-cell patient at the Ronald McDonald House recently had. When he did not, I could not help but think back on this seemingly mundane moment, and wish that I had caved.

Because Jayden was one of the children I ultimately interacted with the most—given his age, the fact that I met them as soon as they arrived, and that I sometimes stayed with him on Unit 27 for a few hours at a time to give his single mother, who was far from friends and family, a break—I became particularly attached to Jayden. Unlike some of the other children in my study, his condition was not neurological. If the transplant had been successful, he had a long and vibrant life ahead of him. The "what if's" tied to the possibility of how a different set of circumstances might have led to a different outcome have stayed with me in the years since his death. The alternatives are of course unknowable. What I do know is that an unrelenting pursuit of hope for a cure did not succeed. And I wish it had been easier for everyone involved to talk about, and genuinely imagine, the possibility of his death. I wonder how doing so might have contributed to a different outcome.

I did bring an oversized pack of spearmint gum with me the first time I visited Jayden on Unit 27—which he proceeded to chew all of, and swallow, in less than an hour, much to his mother's chagrin. I told him no more gum from then on, but usually brought a small token (a candy bar, perhaps, or Angry Birds trading cards) with me on visits, and gave him a Teenage Mutant Ninja Turtle for his birthday two months later. But it didn't feel quite the same as helping brighten one of his final nonhospitalized days with the small, unexpected thrill of spontaneous childhood consumption.

When people ask me how I managed the emotional challenges of doing fieldwork with seriously ill and sometimes dying children, these are probably not the moments they are thinking of. Yet that snap decision that kept me from bringing just a few more hours of unsullied joy into Jayden's short life is one that haunts me still.

* * *

Sociologists Carol Heimer and Lisa Staffen wrote about how they, too, were personally affected by their research with critically ill children in a neonatal intensive care unit.[1] They reported that they "both had some nightmares" during the course of the research and were "left with vivid memories of babies who died what looked like agonizing deaths, of distraught parents, and of extremely premature or disfigured infants."[2] Myra Bluebond-Langner, whose seminal work *The Private Worlds of Dying Children* laid the groundwork for an understanding of children's awareness contexts and feelings about their own impending deaths, grappled with similar emotional challenges during her fieldwork.[3] "At the end of the day I was always afraid to leave them," she wrote. "I might miss something. They might not be there when I got back."[4]

Because my point of contact was the families rather than the institution, and because my involvement with many families was sustained and spanned both medical and social settings, the relationships I developed with them heightened my emotional investment. When Noah Rivera-Cruz was first transferred to the pediatric intensive care unit (PICU), I was not particularly alarmed. I had heard another family recount tales of their son's frightening stints in the PICU, but he pulled through, and they had taken him home with them. I imagined that I would watch this same process play out for the Rivera-Cruzes, in real time. But as the weeks wore on, I grew increasingly concerned. When Noah died, even though I had by then come to see that as a very real possibility, it hit me hard. I was particularly struck by the contrast between his and his sister's outcomes. Sophie stood as living proof of what stem-cell transplantation could offer families of children with MPS, and the life her brother was missing out on. I had imagined that life for him, right alongside his parents.

Edward and Juliana returned to Puerto Rico within a few days to hold a funeral service for him. Because I had driven across the country for a family wedding just before Noah died, I was not there to offer a shoulder, help them pack, or care for Sophie while they wrapped their heads around this unparalleled loss. From afar, I felt even more unsure of how to communicate my sadness or offer support. Though I am not religious and was not raised in the church, I decided to go to my grandmother's Catholic church to light a candle for him.

This small ritual was a way that I could feel that I was "doing something" to show Edward and Juliana my symbolic support, to communicate my grieving, and to honor Noah. Edward and Juliana were both Catholic, and Edward had asked me during a text exchange after Noah was first transferred to the PICU to "keep praying for my baby." Though I shied away from the language of prayer myself, I replied that I would, even if my own version of "praying" was a more secular one. When Noah died, lighting a candle in a church that had a history in my family felt like a bridge I could build between myself and his parents—one that held significance for us both.

Though I was logistically unable to attend Noah or Jayden's memorial services, I felt strongly about attending those that I could after wrestling with my rationale for doing so. One of my mentors' mantras that "everything is data" echoed in my head. I felt deeply uncomfortable with this idea as applied to children's memorial services. But I ultimately felt that above all else, being one more face in the crowd was a way to, in a very traditional sense, "pay my respects." I saw my presence at the service as a way to indicate that these children and their families were important enough to me to set everything else aside and devote time to remembering and honoring the child's life.

Yet it could not *not* be a kind of data, as well. When I drove with another staff member from the Ronald McDonald House to a neighboring state to attend Brent's memorial service, I learned more about him and his life before he was ill, and got a small glimpse into how medical professionals respond to children's deaths. Brent and Charlotte were members of a large nondenominational community church that held weekly services in a high school auditorium. On the day of Brent's "life celebration," videos his classmates had made sharing their favorite times with him were projected on a large screen, family members came on stage to share stories, and one of Brent's Kelly-Reed oncologists attended and spoke. Observing this led me to ask the physicians I later interviewed how they engaged with families after children died, and how they made their own decisions about funeral attendance.

When Shawn Patterson, another teenager in my study, died, he had been back home for over a year. I had limited time with Shawn and his parents at Kelly-Reed, as my own father's illness took me away shortly after their arrival and our initial interview. But I had continued to follow Shawn's health on Facebook and in time saw that Shawn was receiving home hospice care. When he died, I traveled to attend his funeral, in part because even the complete strangers who had attended my father's service had meant something to me—the number of people who'd bothered at least to show up felt like validation of the influence he'd had on so many. I knew there was nothing of real comfort I could say to Shawn's parents, Vivian and Terrance, and that my presence would not actually matter significantly. But I felt compelled to be one more person in the pews, honoring his life. In the end, I recognized that my attendance had most to do with my own efforts to manage my feelings of gratitude and indebtedness—and that familiar need to do "something" to mark the significance of a life lost.

In contrast to Brent's celebratory memorial, Shawn's formal Catholic service was small. I was glad to be there to help fill out the seats. The priest's account of delivering the sacrament and "anointing" him a few weeks earlier was comforting. Shawn was an extraordinarily mature eighteen-year-old when I met him, and as the only "child" whom I formally interviewed, his poise and measured, thoughtful responses had left a lasting impression on me. I was not surprised, then, when the priest reported that he had asked Shawn during a final visit if he was afraid of dying, and Shawn had responded calmly, "No. I just wish I knew when it would happen." I was reassured to know that Shawn's final weeks had not been exceedingly anxious ones. While the priest silently swung his thurible—a small metal cage on a gold chain containing burning incense—methodically to each corner of the closed coffin, I found this ritualistic motion comforting as well. Though I had no knowledge of the meaning of this tradition, its quiet, formal execution felt like the reverent send-off Shawn deserved. After the service I handed Vivian a card with a short note about how much I admired her son. As I wound my way through the mountains and back across the state line, I realized that once again I had gained much more than I'd given in this small effort to recognize the gift these children and their families had given me by inviting me into even a fraction of their short lives.

* * *

Though I was not able to attend Noah's service, I was able to spend time with the Rivera-Cruzes again a few months after he died. They had returned to Kelly-Reed for a follow-up visit for Sophie and to attend a fundraising walk and balloon release ceremony in honor and in memory of current and former patients. When I met them at the hospital, we reunited with hugs and smiles, but Juliana soon remarked on how difficult it was to be back here again, "with so many memories." While we hung out in one of the clinic rooms waiting for Sophie to be revaccinated with a half-dozen childhood vaccines, Juliana showed me photos from Noah's final hours and from the funeral service they held for him in their hometown. I had many questions for her about how Noah's last days had unfolded, but in the moment deemed it best just to listen to the stories she offered. I was nervous about when, how, and if, I should ask more.

A few nights later, at the Ronald McDonald House, it seemed like the right time. With the tape recorder back on, I revisited some of our initial interview questions and asked about how they had made some of those difficult end-of-life decisions. Though we began with matter-of-fact questions and answers about where they looked for information online and how much they wanted to know, one of the questions I posed shifted the mood markedly. When I asked if they had requested the doctors do anything differently than they were recommending, Juliana sighed heavily. "Well with Noah, we decided to stop the dialysis . . . because we don't want him, you know, to get more suffering." This was the first I understood that Edward and Juliana had been the ones to suggest that "enough was enough" and to stop treatment. She went on to tell me about the difficulties and disappointments they had with different physicians and the conflicting prognoses they were offered during their son's final days.

When I asked more specifically how and when they had decided to withdraw ventilation, Juliana began to tear up, and her answers became more succinct. I wondered if I should move to a different topic and was inclined to pull back. But Juliana dabbed her eyes and continued, explaining how important their faith in God had been to them during this time. A few minutes later, I was the one tearing up as I told her how much Noah's short life had affected me, and how unsure I'd felt about how to communicate my caring and gratitude to them at that time. The distinction between research interaction and friendship interaction was not always easily separated, particularly in moments like these.

Social scientists Petya Fitzpatrick and Rebecca Olson similarly grappled with how best to manage their own emotional reactions in their respective research interviews with patients and caregivers managing critical conditions. Both had strong emotional responses to their interviewees and found moments when emotions bubbled up during interviews to be more challenging than they had expected. Fitzpatrick recalled an interview she conducted during which, she said, "I wanted to encourage her to keep talking, but I didn't want to ignore her tears. . . . I worried that my questions would make her feel sadder, but I was also wary of inadvertently shutting her down."[5] Another "source of anxiety," according to Fitzpatrick and Olson, was the "uncertainty about the extent to which our own emotions [are] 'permitted.'"[6] They tried to hold back their own tears and in time, found that they came to emotionally distance themselves from interviewees, which they experienced as an involuntary "callusing."

In my setting, negotiating this rolling emotional terrain felt more natural. I did not experience an emotional distancing as time wore on; in fact, my experience was the opposite, given the sustained involvement I had with the families in my study as the treatment process progressed. Though I felt it was important to ensure that my own emotional responses and sadness for their children did not become an undue burden on them, to entirely conceal these feelings would have felt equally inappropriate. I certainly regularly engaged in emotion work—for instance, by blinking back tears when I said goodbye to Noah the last time I visited the Rivera-Cruzes in the PICU—in hindsight, because I did not want to appear to have given up hope for his recovery. But I did not feel an obligation to put on a "display of detached concern" as Fitzpatrick and Olson had.[7] Because my role in the field fluctuated between researcher, volunteer, and at times that of someone closer to a friend, a larger variety of emotional roles were both available to and required of me. This called for an emotional fluidity, rather than a clear emotional boundary, between myself and my research participants.

This is not to say that research in settings like these calls for a laissez-faire emotional approach in which the researcher's emotions spill everywhere. I strove to make the best decisions I could about when expressing my own emotions was appropriate and constructive and when it might be burdensome or unnerving for families—as when I avoided conveying my own fear for their children's lives. Emotional expressions can have chain reactions, quickly amplifying the emotions of others.[8] And emotions can either deepen or interrupt interactions in instrumental ways.[9] Either way, they cannot be kept out of fieldwork of any kind.

It is vital, then, that fieldworkers be conscious of and reflect on their own emotions and the emotional challenges they may confront during the course of their fieldwork before entering the field. Sherryl Kleinman and Martha Copp offer a helpful set of questions for researchers to ask themselves at the outset of any project to facilitate just this.[10] But as in everyday life, many of these challenges cannot be wholly prepared for in advance.[11] The best a fieldworker can ultimately strive to do is to hone a finely tuned emotional radar and remain emotionally agile in the moment.

I certainly did not begin this project expecting that I would remain unaffected by the difficult circumstances the families I studied found themselves in. But I also did not fully anticipate the variety and scope of emotionally complex moments I would encounter, such as my interaction with Jayden at Walmart that cold, mid-January night. The best lesson I can offer to other researchers doing fieldwork in similarly emotionally fraught settings is to expect that you will become emotional participants in the lives of those you study. The challenge then is to figure out how best to juggle our own and others' emotions as these interactions unfold. This is likely to be an ad-hoc and haphazard process. But remaining a flexible and responsive presence is one of the more meaningful roles we can play for those who do us the honor of letting us in to their emotional worlds, particularly during moments of profound crisis. And it is part and parcel of the incomparable adventure that is collecting data among real people living out unpredictable lives.

* * *

The day after Juliana and I had both cried during the late-night interview described above, Juliana, Edward, Sophie, and I attended an annual fundraising walk and balloon release ceremony wearing team t-shirts for Noah and carrying two homemade tag-board displays Juliana had decorated with photos of her son. The brightly colored balloons, posters of smiling children from current and previous years' cohorts on Unit 27, children's games, and activities contributed to a festive atmosphere. Much of the morning was filled with hugs and happy conversation as the Rivera-Cruzes, their usual gregarious selves, reconnected with other families, doctors, nurses, and social workers from Unit 27. We laughed and chatted while we walked several laps around the track, and Edward and I both took photos with the cameras slung across our shoulders.

When it came time to release the balloons, we wrote short messages to Noah on several of them with a black magic marker. As Israel Kamakawiwoʻole's "Over the Rainbow" played, the crowd released their balloons in unison, and we all gazed up at the bright blue sky as hundreds of colorful dots floated away in a comforting ritualistic ceremony. When I looked down, I saw that Juliana had collapsed in Edward's arms, sobbing. Sophie, blissfully unaware of her mother's anguish, was unsuccessfully blowing on a pinwheel she had picked up at an activity booth. After a split second in which I felt awkward and useless, I knelt to help Sophie spin the aluminum flower, hoping I might feed her fascination and keep her attention diverted long enough to allow her parents an extended and more private moment to grieve.

Though we are virtually guaranteed to face moments of uncertainty about how we handle our own and others' emotional reactions in the field when we do research in emotionally fraught settings, an openness to a variety of emotional possibilities, patience, and close attention to subtle interactional cues can help us inhabit a least-disruptive position at such moments. Remaining emotionally agile can help us respond sensitively to the unpredictable and shifting realities our research participants may confront. Within healthcare contexts, it might also help to add a few more bricks to a new pathway through illness, one that doesn't shunt death, grief, and loss entirely to the side. Ultimately, fieldwork in settings like these requires us to proceed *with care*—both for ourselves and our participants—in every sense of that word.

APPENDIX B

Family and Physician Demographics

TABLE A.1: Case-Study Family Demographics

Family	Primary Caregiver(s) Interviewed	Child's Name/ Age at First Interview	Diagnosis	Treatment at Kelly-Reed	Race/Ethnicity	Parent/ Guardian Occupations	Region or Country of Origin
The Bialys	Nora (m)	Benjamin, 16 years	Brain tumor	Dendritic cell immunotherapy	White	Dietician/child psychiatrist	Northeast
The Brady-Fischers	Simone Brady-Fischer (m)	Max Fischer, 11 years	Congenital Malformation, Pseudotumor	Neurological assessment, Lumbar punctures	White	Program administrator/gov't official	Canada
The Caldwells	Charlotte (s)	Brenton, 17 years	Leukemia	Stem cell transplant (donor peripheral blood)	Charlotte: White Brenton: Black/White	SSI recipient enrolled in online BA program	Neighboring state
The Campos-Maldonados	Eva Campos (m)	Ignacio Maldonado, 11 years	Metachromatic Leukodystrophy (MLD)	Stem cell transplant (sibling bone marrow)	Latinx	High school principal/small business owner	Argentina
The Donnoly-Santoses	Pauline Donnoly (s, custodial grandmother)	Isabelle Santos, 7 years	Kidney tumor	Standard of care chemotherapy/radiation	Pauline: White Isabelle: White/Latinx	Retired hair-dresser	In-state
The Finleys	Jamilla (m)	Teyariah, 7 years	Neuroblastoma	Stem cell transplant (autologous bone marrow), Antibody trial	Black	Security guard enrolled in online MA program/factory supervisor	In-state
The Harris-Lacostes	Lakira Harris (s)	Jayden Lacoste, 8 years	Sickle cell disease	Stem cell transplant (donor cord blood)	Black	Security guard	Southeast

TABLE A.1: (cont.)

Family	Primary Caregiver(s) Interviewed	Child's Name/ Age at First Interview	Diagnosis	Treatment at Kelly-Reed	Race/ Ethnicity	Parent/ Guardian Occupations	Region or Country of Origin
The Hendersons	Nicholas and Connie (m)	Elijah, 4 years	Liver tumor	Liver transplant	White	Seasonal asphalt crewmember/ SSI recipient	Neighboring state
The Khalid-Tahirs	Tariq Khalid and Mayyadah Tahir (m)	Nazia Khalid, 16 years	Aplastic Anemia	Stem cell transplant (donor cord blood)	South Asian	Computer science/ stay-at-home mother	Mid-Atlantic
The Kleins	Deirdre (d)	Jackson, 10	Leukemia	Stem cell transplant, (sibling bone marrow)	White	School teacher/occupational therapist	Neighboring state
The Marins	Todd and Savannah (m)	Jacob, 18 months	Tay-Sachs	Stem cell transplant (donor cord blood)	White	Contractor/ registered nurse	West Coast
The Moores	Jeanetta (m)	Kaelyn, 5 years	Chromosomal deletion syndrome	Organ-tissue transplant	Black	Hospital reception/ maintenance	In-state
The Morgan-Russells	Tina Morgan (m)	Kassidy Russell, infant	Congenital Diaphragmatic Hernia	Extracorporeal membrane oxygenation, surgery	White	Unemployed/machine shop worker	In-state
The Parkers	Trinette (m)	Zarielle, infant	Severely preterm birth	Incubation, ventilation	Black	Social Security Administration (both)	In-state
The Pattersons	Vivian (d)	Shawn, 18 years	Brain tumor	Dendritic cell immunotherapy	Black	Corporate sales (both)	Neighboring state
The Rivera-Cruzes	Edward Rivera and Juliana Cruz (m)	Sophie, 4 years Noah, infant	Mucopolysaccharidosis (MPS)	Stem cell transplant (donor cord blood)	Latinx	Restaurant owner/ pharmaceutical lab technician	Puerto Rico
The Rowlands	Chanise (s)	Anaya, infant	Congenital heart defect	Surgery	Black	SSI recipient	In-state

TABLE A.1: (*cont.*)

Family	Primary Caregiver(s) Interviewed	Child's Name/ Age at First Interview	Diagnosis	Treatment at Kelly-Reed	Race/ Ethnicity	Parent/ Guardian Occupations	Region or Country of Origin
The Shaws	Mary (m, custodial grand-mother)	Aaron, 7 years	Glycogen storage disease	Enzyme re-placement therapy	White	Retired grocery dept man-ager/ re-tired truck driver	In-state

Note: (m) indicates that primary caregiver(s) were married or partnered, (s) indicates that they were single and the only parent involved in the child's care, and (d) indicates that they were divorced or separated but the former spouse was involved in child's care. If only one parent/guardian was present/interviewed, the occupation of that individual is listed first, and the occupation of the parent/guardian who was not present/interviewed is listed second.

TABLE A.2: Physician Demographics

Physician	Race/Ethnicity	Gender	Age
Dr. Coleman	White	M	Early fifties
Dr. Fadian	White	M	Early fifties
Dr. Newell	White	F	Late thirties
Dr. Oliver	White	F	Early sixties
Dr. Ravipati	Indian	M	Early fifties
Dr. Vogel	White	F	Early sixties

NOTES

CHAPTER 1. HOPE IS A THING WITH FEATHERS

1 A pseudonym, as are all names used throughout.

2 Bury 1982.

3 Allison et al. 2000.

4 Lutfey and Freese 2005.

5 Lutfey and Feese's argument grows out of the "fundamental cause" perspective put forth by Bruce Link and Jo Phelan (1995), which argues that unequal social conditions are the underlying cause of health disparities between groups. See also Phelan and Link (2005); Phelan, Link, and Tehranifar (2010).

6 See Chang and Lauderdale (2009); Goldman and Lakdawalla (2005).

7 See Clark, Potter, and McKinlay (1991); Gengler and Jarrell (2015); Johnson et al., (2004); Saha, Arbelaez, and Cooper (2003); van Ryn and Burke (2000); van Ryn et al. 2011).

8 Boyer and Lutfey 2010; Prior 2003. Prior (2003) notes that this culture of lay expertise can be problematic, as patients often lack the knowledge or training needed to be truly effective in this role.

9 Lutfey and Freese 2005.

10 Shim 2010.

11 As Shamus Khan (2011) has shown, an ease with a wide variety of cultural symbols and an ability to demonstrate comfort in two diverging cultural worlds such as these can be a signal of especially elite cultural competence.

12 Rios 2011.

13 Shim 2010:1, 3.

14 Bourdieu 1977.

15 Using a similar framework, Sabrina Chase (2011) studied poor and working-class Puerto Rican women who were living with HIV/AIDs and found that those who had more flexible cultural health capital were able to wrangle higher quality care out of the healthcare system than their peers, despite their shared status as Medicaid patients.

16 Dubbin, Chang, and Shim 2013.

17 Gage-Bouchard 2017.

18 Hochschild 1983.

19 Ehrenreich 2009.

20 Ehrenreich 2009:17.

21 Sulik 2011.
22 Sulik 2011:231.
23 Groopman 2005.
24 Gengler 2015.
25 Moller 2004:158. Moller finds that such isolation is even more acute for those already marginalized by race or poverty.
26 Peräkylä 1991.
27 Lazarus 1999: 655.
28 Mattingly 2010:3.
29 Mattingly 2010:4.
30 Petersen and Wilkinson 2015:115.
31 Desroche 1979.
32 These highly demanding approaches to parenting have gone by many terms, including "intensive mothering" (Hays 1996) and "parenting out of control" (Nelson 2010).
33 Lareau 2003.
34 Pugh 2015.
35 Nelson 2010.
36 Cooper 2014:64
37 Nelson 2010; Elliott 2012.
38 Cooper 2014.
39 Lois 2013.
40 Villalobos 2014.
41 See also Norah Mackendrick (2014) for a discussion of the environmental health risks mothers are expected to ameliorate for their children.
42 Reich 2016.
43 Francis 2015:3.
44 Blum 2015. Poor mothers and mothers of color are judged even more harshly, and with greater consequence, for perceived failure to "appropriately" advocate for their children (see also Elliott and Reid 2019).

CHAPTER 2. STUDYING FAMILIES OF CRITICALLY ILL CHILDREN

1 For Myra Bluebond-Langner, who studied children with cystic fibrosis in the 1970s, the fact that she "had never experienced the death of a close friend or relative . . . had never even attended a funeral" (1978:237) led her to embark on her study with an "innocence" that she viewed as fundamental to her approach and what she was able to accomplish.
2 Though the McDonald's corporation and local franchises donate to the Ronald McDonald House Charity as its "largest corporate partner," the charity itself is a separate nonprofit 501(c)(3) organization, with the majority of its financial support coming from individual and organizational donors. The house affiliated with Kelly-Reed occasionally distributed coupons for a free McDonald's coffee or milkshake to families and volunteers, and a local franchise

owner served on the board—but this was the extent of the connection, in my experience.

3 IRB approval was also obtained for the study.

4 Small 2009.

5 Small 2009:25. This is very similar to a grounded theory approach (Glaser and Strauss 1967), but with greater emphasis on thinking about interviews or participants as "cases."

6 Becker 1998.

7 I often checked with staff before approaching a family about the study or visiting the room of a case-study family, so that I could be aware if they had recently gotten bad news or their child had experienced a setback. Depending on my relationship with them, I either reached out or stepped back during these times.

8 One family who had been staying at the Ronald McDonald House for many months moved to a nearby apartment just before I interviewed them. I conducted two interviews with them in this location. Physician interviews occurred either at the hospital or in their nearby offices.

9 Though all case-study families spoke English, Eva Campos preferred to conduct our formal interview in Spanish. In this case, her older daughter served as our translator. This interview was transcribed in both languages by a professional transcriptionist with Spanish fluency so Eva's words in Spanish were translated both informally in the moment by her daughter and more precisely on the professional transcript.

10 Glaser and Strauss 1967.

11 Mattingly 2010:96.

12 Mattingly 2010:96.

13 Patricia Hill Collins describes controlling images of black women as ranging "from the mammies, jezebels, and breeder women of slavery to the smiling Aunt Jemimas on pancake boxes, ubiquitous Black prostitutes, and ever-present welfare mothers of contemporary popular culture" (1991:5). She argues that such "negative stereotypes applied to African-American women have been fundamental to Black women's oppression" (1991:5). More recently, Dawn Dow (2015) has examined how black mothers continue to negotiate and resist such controlling images.

14 Blum 2015:8.

15 Zelizer 1985:24.

16 Scheper-Hughes 1992.

17 Stevenson 2014.

18 Ofri 2013. See also Fadiman (1997).

19 Gawande 2014.

20 Kleinman and Kolb 2011.

21 Kleinman and Copp 1993.

22 McQueeney and Lavelle 2015.

23 Gengler 2015. See also Register (1999) and Robinson (1993).

24 Kleinman and Copp 1993:42.

25 See also Joanna Kempner, whose research on migraines, which she conducted while suffering from them herself, was similarly deepened by what she called "embodied knowledge" (2014:xiii).

26 Reinharz 2011.

27 Kaufman 2005. See also Erickson (2013).

28 Reinharz 1992.

CHAPTER 3. CARE-CAPTAINING

1 Shim 2010:1.

2 Graft versus host disease, or GVHD, is very common after transplant. It occurs when the newly transplanted cells interpret the transplant patient's body as "foreign" and attack the patient's own cells. This is more likely to happen when the transplant is received from an unrelated donor, as is the case with most cord blood transplants, but is less likely, or less severe, depending on how close a match the donor is.

3 Reich 2016:16.

4 Gengler 2014.

5 See Calarco (2011).

6 This instinctive awareness could be understood as part of Simone's "habitus" (Bourdieu 1977).

7 Even though Simone may not have ultimately pursued this course of action outside of the heat of the moment, that she felt this was a path available to her is a result of the resources she could devote to the task if she chose to, and even imagining taking it helped her feel she could maintain control of the situation and obtain justice for her son.

8 Clark 2005.

9 Desroche 1979.

10 A central thoracic line, or central venous catheter, is a bundle of three short catheters semi-permanently connected to a patient's chest, permitting regular blood draws and administration of intravenous medications.

11 If the Rivera-Cruzes' home doctor had not directed them to Kelly-Reed—as, for instance, the Marin's home doctor did not—this research also would have led them to discover this option themselves.

12 Heimer and Staffen 1988.

13 Heimer and Staffen 1988:232. See also Renee Anspach (1993), who examined conflict between parents and healthcare providers around life and death decision-making in the neonatal intensive care units she studied.

14 Gage-Bouchard 2017:157.

15 Reich 2015:87.

16 Garey 1999.

17 The Marins' concerns were not unfounded. It is true that it can be very difficult to get children off of mechanical ventilation once they've gone on it. Of the families

I met after them, none of the children who were transferred to the PICU and placed on life support like mechanical ventilation survived.

CHAPTER 4. CARE-ENTRUSTING

1 Lakira's confidence that her son would be cured was bolstered by the fact that at the Ronald McDonald House she had become close friends with another family whose teenage daughter had been successfully transplanted for sickle cell and was by then outpatient and doing well.

2 See also Gage-Bouchard (2017).

3 Fortunately, the Shaw's home is within ninety miles of Kelly-Reed, making access to weekly treatments and therapies feasible for the retired Shaws, who lived on a fixed-income.

4 Sixteen-year-old Nazia, on the other hand, told me that *she* did Google things, because "I want to know."

5 I never met Isabelle's biological mother and cannot speak to her style of interacting with the healthcare system or quality of care for her daughter at this time. It seems probable, however, that her lack of class privilege at least increased the speed with which Isabelle was taken into state custody. See Reich (2005).

6 A PET (positron emission tomography) scan is a sophisticated imaging test, similar to an MRI, which ideally can uncover cancer cells that an MRI might not detect.

7 Dr. Oliver later told me that this amount was only a fraction of the cost of the treatment. She has since managed to get most state Medicaid programs to cover the transplant for families like the Moores.

8 Though a broad literature on compliance suggests that adherence to medical regimens can be problematic and may be influenced by race, class, and gender, Conrad (1985) argues that compliance is dependent on the *meaning* any given medication or regimen has for the patient. Whether epileptics, for instance, understand their medication as a "ticket to normality," or they understand going off of it to be a sign they are "getting better" will influence their compliance. Here, doing everything the doctors told them to do helped parents feel they were doing everything they could to keep their children safe and help them get better. The meaning compliance held for them encouraged it.

9 See Carol Stack (1974) and Karen Hansen (2005) for discussion of the interpersonal dynamics involved in negotiating for care and resources from social networks.

10 A number of scholars have documented class differences in child-rearing and their consequences for service-providers' assessments of one's "goodness" as a parent—especially mothers—and race compounds these divides. See Appell (1998), Cancian (2002), Lareau (2003), and Gengler (2011).

11 Collins 1991; Fraser and Gordon 1994.

12 Gage-Bouchard 2017.

13 Lutfey and Freese 2005.

14 Though mothers have shouldered the greater burden of childcare for generations, ideologies about mothers' obligations toward their children have intensified in recent decades despite some shifts toward greater participation by fathers. Sharon Hays (1996) terms this ramped up set of expectations "intensive mothering": accordingly, mothers are expected to devote themselves entirely to the care, nurturance, and development of their children, to the potential exclusion of almost all else. Mothers judged not to meet this standard of care face significant social consequences. See for instance Ladd-Taylor and Umansky (1998), Kukla (2005), and Wolf (2007).

15 Litt 2000.

16 A "port" is a small device implanted in the upper chest, which allows intravenous (IV) medications to be delivered or blood to be drawn without continual IV placement. Unlike a central venous catheter, in which tubes protrude from the chest at all times, a port is implanted entirely beneath the skin.

CHAPTER 5. BLENDING AND SWITCHING CARE STRATEGIES

1 In Howard Becker's terms (1998), we might think of these as "negative" cases—as those that don't perfectly fit the initial pattern identified, but that shed additional light on the broader, overarching patterns shaping one's object of study.

2 Elizabeth Gage and Christina Panagakis (2012) found that parents avoided online research during a child's cancer diagnosis because they found it frightening and untrustworthy or because doctors told them not to do it. The families in my study, in contrast, articulated a complex relationship to online information-seeking. For some it was indispensable, helping them feel a sense of control over their child's illness and reassuring them that they were doing everything possible. For others it was a source of fear that might be best avoided entirely. Parents' efforts to manage their own emotions drove them toward or away from online information-seeking.

3 Sadly, Deirdre's cancer recurred, and she died about a year after Jackson returned home following his successful transplant.

4 Kelly-Reed was consistently ranked among the *US News and World Report*'s top hospitals. The symbolic meanings attached to hierarchical ranking systems like these (see Sauder [2005]) could foster feelings of confidence among those who were cognizant of the status associated with them.

5 Recall that Pauline Donnoly did not attempt to convince her new state's Medicaid program to cover Isabelle's treatment at the hospital in the neighboring state that had overseen her initial treatment for her cancer. She simply switched to the in-state hospital with a bed available for her, which happened to be Kelly-Reed.

6 Lareau 2015.

7 Levitsky 2014.

8 See Gage (2013).

9 Wolkomir 2004:748.

10 See Sharp (2010) and Sharp, Carr, and Panger (2016).

11 Shane Sharp (2010) identified this phenomenon in his study of victims of intimate partner violence who used God as an outlet to whom they could safely express their anger.

12 Similarly, in Jennifer Lois's (2001) study of wilderness search and rescue expeditions, the loved ones of those who were lost and injured often found it too emotionally difficult to stand idly by, and felt compelled to actively join search and rescue missions.

13 Karp and Tanarugsachock 2000:6.

CHAPTER 6. WHEN EVERYTHING IS NOT ENOUGH

1 An airlock is a space between two sets of sliding glass doors that creates a buffer between the hallway and the patient's room to reduce contamination.

2 "Intubation" is short hand for the insertion of a tube into the trachea to maintain an airway for mechanical ventilation.

3 Situated in the family context, emotion-management strategies might take on the added work of maintaining some degree of equilibrium. Juliana may have felt an extra need to remain as optimistic as possible to balance out her husband's increasing feelings of despair in an effort to protect them both from this emotional threat. It may be useful, then, to conceptualize families as a sort of emotion-management team, whose strategies are responsive to one another throughout an illness.

4 See also Good et al. (1990).

5 Sulik 2011.

6 Groopman 2005.

7 Cadge 2012. In another ethnographic study of a hospital, Dan Chambliss found that more generally "responsibility for handling of dying patients is often diffused across a variety of people" (1996: 150).

8 To my knowledge, neither this chaplain nor any of the physicians or nursing staff on Unit 27 was specifically trained in palliative-care medicine. Dr. Coleman also lamented that there was no longer a specialized pediatric hospice provider in the area.

9 Lois 2001.

10 It is important to note, however, that those who are approaching the end of life themselves (even children) have sometimes come to terms with this reality and are much more comfortable speaking about it than friends and family members are (Bluebond-Langner 1978; Loe 2011).

11 Medical sociologists have long analyzed a vast array of forms and types of ambiguity and uncertainty in the practice of medicine and the strategies physicians use to manage it (Fox 2000). The rise of evidence-based medicine is seen by some as being largely rooted in the goal of helping both patients and physicians manage uncertainty in medical decision-making, although Timmermans and Angell (2001) found that sorting through and evaluating medical evidence could

introduce additional uncertainty, particularly for early-career physicians. More experienced physicians may become more comfortable with uncertainty over time, and more inclined to use their previous experience as a basis for decision-making, as I observed among the senior physicians on Unit 27.

12 Cancian and Oliker 2000.

13 Ehrenreich 2009.

14 Lazarus and Folkman 1984. Viktor Gecas and Michael Schwalbe (1983) have argued that the ability to feel that one's actions are efficacious is central to one's ability to feel good about oneself. Parents' especially strong desires to feel good about themselves as parents (an identity Ara Francis calls a "social psychological linchpin" [2012:374]) made the ability to feel efficacious particularly critical in this context.

CHAPTER 7. THE FRAGILITY AND TENACITY OF HOPE

1 My reaction—that we must find a way to get into that "5 percent"—came instantly to mind when, two years later, Dr. Vogel told me during my interview with her that "10 percent sounds like a lot" to some families facing terrible odds.

2 Had I thought about it more pragmatically, I might have admitted that not every doctor can be familiar with every article or trial out there, but my reaction was an emotional one—I wanted to feel the same kind of confidence Nora Bialy had insisted on feeling when she scolded the provider who was unable to answer her questions.

3 We later learned that this was not the case for all clinical trials. Some clinical trials, however, will not enroll those with any history of cancer in order to demonstrate their success in the most straightforward cases and with the best possible results.

4 I have followed the development of this treatment in the years since. Though it continued to perform equivalently in future trials, the control group in a larger trial, quite unexpectedly, performed far better than is typically the case for patients receiving standard treatment. As a result, the trial was concluded, as the company deemed that it could not continue "incurring substantial additional costs" in their effort to develop this drug. The treatment continued to be provided to the patients receiving it through the trial or through compassionate use, as it was still suspected to be benefiting these patients (Celldex Press Release, March 7 2016).

5 Gawande 2014.

6 Sulik 2011.

7 It is difficult to know if this treatment would have allowed him to genuinely enjoy more time, or have extended his life minimally at the expense of being away from the comforts of home and farther from friends and family.

CHAPTER 8. EMOTIONALLY PERILOUS PATHS

1 Glaser and Strauss 1967.

2 Snow and Anderson 1987.

3 Goffman 1959. This is a fundamentally social and interactional process (Schwalbe and Mason-Schrock 1996), and one that mothers often take special pains to execute as flawlessly as possible (Collett 2005).

4 These experiences point to the pressing need to offer families of critically ill children paid leave and job security that goes far beyond the United States' very limited Family and Medical Leave Act (FMLA) protections.

5 Bluebond-Langner 1996:xii.

6 Cystic Fibrosis Foundation, www.cff.org.

7 Timmermans and Buchbinder 2012.

8 Reed 2012.

9 Gawande 2014.

10 Good et al. 1990.

11 Petersen 2015:18.

12 Berns 2011.

13 Groopman 2005: xiv.

14 Groopman 2005:177.

15 Our sense that it was possible and appropriate for us to do so was also a direct expression of race- and class-based privilege, as it was for the well-resourced families introduced previously.

16 Schwalbe (1996), Lively (2000), Ezzell (2009), and Lois (2013) have also pointed to the role of emotions in reproducing social inequalities in a variety of other contexts.

17 Levitsky 2014.

18 See Brown (2002) and Light (2002).

19 Yamin 2005.

20 Pew Research Center 2017.

21 Levitsky 2014.

22 Gawande 2014.

23 Petersen 2015:46. See also Ehrenreich (2009).

24 Petersen 2015:46.

25 DeShazer 2013.

26 Gould 2009.

27 Lawton 2000.

28 Blumer 1969.

29 See for instance Thorne (1993). See also Beard (2016), for analysis both of how the meanings attached to aging and forgetfulness have been medicalized, and how those diagnosed with Alzheimer's resist definitions of "incompetence."

30 For example, rather than viewing caring for dying patients as especially difficult, many of the hospice and other long-term care workers Karla Erickson interviewed conceptualized "accompanying others through death [as] a privilege" (2013:134).

31 Jenkinson 2015:373.

32 Berns 2011:172.

APPENDIX A.

1 Heimer and Staffen 1998.
2 Heimer and Staffen 1998: 378.
3 Bluebond-Langner 1978.
4 Bluebond-Langer 1978:255.
5 Fitzpatrick and Olson 2015:51.
6 Fitzpatrick and Olson 2015:52.
7 Fitzpatrick and Olson 2015:52.
8 Hallett 2003.
9 Goffman 1967.
10 Kleinman and Copp 1993. See also McQueeney and Lavelle (2015).
11 Steven Vanderstaay (2005) offers a compelling example of this in his article "One Hundred Dollars and a Dead Man." Vanderstaay recounts how after he provided $100 to a research subject's grandmother to help her pay an energy bill, his subject stole the money to purchase drugs and subsequently committed homicide. Vanderstaay felt immense pain at his small role in this sequence of events, and calls for greater preparation and attention to these ethical quandaries before researchers enter the field, while at the same time illustrating the extent to which one can never prepare for all possible scenarios.

REFERENCES

Allison, Jeroan J., Catarina I. Kiefe, Norman W. Weissman, Sharina D. Person, Matthew Rousculp, John G. Canto, Sejong Bae, O. Dale Williams, Robert Farmer, and Robert M. Centor. 2000. "Relationship of Hospital Teaching Status with Quality of Care and Mortality for Medicare Patients with Acute MI." *Journal of the American Medical Association* 284(10):1256–62.

Anspach, Renee R. 1993. *Deciding Who Lives*. Berkeley: University of California Press.

Appell, Annette R. 1998. "On Fixing 'Bad' Mothers and Saving Their Children." Pp. 356–80 in *"Bad" Mothers: The Politics of Blame in Twentieth Century America*, edited by M. Ladd-Taylor and L. Umansky. New York: New York University Press.

Beard, Renée L. 2016. *Living with Alzheimer's: Managing Memory Loss, Identity, and Illness*. New York: New York University Press.

Becker, Howard S. 1998. *Tricks of the Trade*. Chicago: University of Chicago Press.

Berns, Nancy. 2011. *Closure: The Rush to End Grief and What It Costs Us*. Philadelphia: Temple University Press.

Bluebond-Langner, Myra. 1996. *In the Shadow of Illness*. Princeton, NJ: Princeton University Press.

Bluebond-Langner, Myra. 1978. *The Private Worlds of Dying Children*. Princeton, NJ: Princeton University Press.

Blum, Linda M. 2015. *Raising Generation Rx: Mothering Kids with Invisible Disabilities in an Age of Inequality*. New York: New York University Press.

Blumer, Herbert. 1969. *Symbolic Interactionism: Perspective and Method*. Englewood Cliffs, NJ: Prentice-Hall.

Bourdieu, Pierre. 1977. *Outline of a Theory of Practice*. Cambridge, UK: Cambridge University Press.

Boyer, Carol A., and Karen E. Lutfey. 2010. "Examining Critical Health Policy Issues within and beyond the Clinical Encounter: Patient-Provider Relationships and Help-Seeking Behaviors." *Journal of Health and Social Behavior* 51(S):S80–S93.

Bury, Michael. 1982. "Chronic Illness as Biographical Disruption." *Sociology of Health & Illness* 4(2):167–82.

Brown, Lawrence D. 2002. "Comparing Health Systems in Four Countries: Lessons for the United States." *American Journal of Public Health* 93(1):52–56.

Cadge, Wendy. 2012. *Paging God: Religion in the Halls of Medicine*. Chicago: University of Chicago Press.

Calarco, Jessica McCrory. 2011. "'I Need Help!' Social Class and Children's Help-Seeking in Elementary School." *American Sociological Review* 76(6):862–82.

Cancian, Francesca M. 2002. "Defining 'Good' Child Care: Hegemonic and Democratic Standards." Pp. 65–78 in *Child Care and Inequality*, edited by F. M. Cancian, D. Kurz, A. S. London, R. Reviere, and M. C. Touminen. New York: Routledge.

Cancian, Francesca M., and Stacey J. Oliker. 2000. *Caring and Gender*. Lanham, MD: Rowman & Littlefield.

Celldex Press Release. 2016. "Data Safety and Monitoring Board Recommends Celldex's Phase 3 Study of RINTEGA® (rindopepimut) in Newly Diagnosed Glioblastoma be Discontinued as It iS Unlikely to Meet Primary Overall Survival Endpoint in Patients with Minimal Residual Disease." March 7. https://ir.celldex.com/news-releases/news-release-details/data-safety-and-monitoring-board-recommends-celldexs-phase-3.

Chambliss, Dan. 1996. *Beyond Caring: Hospitals, Nurses, and the Social Organization of Ethics*. Chicago: University of Chicago Press.

Chang, Virginia W., and Diane S. Lauderdale. 2009. "Fundamental Cause Theory, Technical Innovation, and Health Disparities: The Case of Cholesterol in the Era of Statins." *Journal of Health and Social Behavior* 50(3):245–60.

Chase, Sabrina. 2011. *Surviving HIV/AIDS in the Inner City: How Resourceful Latinas Beat the Odds*. New Brunswick, NJ: Rutgers University Press.

Clark, Jack A., Deborah A. Potter, and John B. McKinlay. 1991. "Bringing Social Structure Back into Clinical Decision Making." *Social Science & Medicine* 32(8):853–66.

Clark, Jacqueline. 2005. "Constructing Expertise: Inequality and the Consequences of Information-Seeking by Breast Cancer Patients." *Illness, Crisis, and Loss* 13(2):169–85.

Collett, Jessica L. 2005. "What Kind of Mother Am I? Impession Management and the Social Construction of Motherhood." *Symbolic Interaction* 28(3):327–47.

Collins, Patricia Hill. 1991. *Black Feminist Thought: Knowledge, Consciousness, and the Politics of Empowerment*. New York: Routledge.

Conrad, Peter. 1985. "The Meaning of Medications: Another Look at Compliance." *Social Science & Medicine* 20(1):29–37.

Cooper, Marianne. 2014. *Cut Adrift: Families in Insecure Times*. Berkeley: University of California Press.

DeShazer, Mary K. 2013. *Mammographies: The Cultural Discourses of Breast Cancer Narratives*. Ann Arbor: University of Michigan Press.

Desroche, Henri. 1979. *The Sociology of Hope*. London: Routledge & Kegan Paul.

Dow, Dawn Marie. 2015. "Negotiating 'The Welfare Queen' and 'The Strong Black Woman': African American Middle-Class Mothers' Work and Family Perspectives." *Sociological Perspectives* 58(1):36–55.Dubbin, Leslie A., Jami Suki Chang, and Janet K. Shim. 2013. "Cultural Health Capital and the Interactional Dynamics of Patient-Centered Care." *Social Science & Medicine* 93:113–20.

Ehrenreich, Barbara. 2009. *Bright-Sided: How the Relentless Promotion of Positive Thinking Has Undermined America*. New York: Metropolitan Books.

Elliott, Sinikka. 2012. *Not My Kid: What Parents Believe about the Sex Lives of Their Teenagers*. New York: New York University Press.

Elliott, Sinikka, and Megan Reid. 2019. "Low-Income Black Mothers Parenting Adolescents in the Mass Incarceration Era: The Long Reach of Criminalization." *American Sociological Review* 84(2):197–219.

Erickson, Karla. 2013. *How We Die Now: Intimacy and the Work of Dying*. Philadelphia: Temple University Press.

Ezzell, Mathew B. 2009. "'Barbie Dolls' on the Pitch: Identity Work, Defensive Othering, and Inequality in Women's Rugby." *Social Problems* 56(1):111–31.

Fadiman, Anne. 1997. *The Spirit Catches You and You Fall Down: A Hmong Child, Her American Doctors, and the Collision of Two Cultures*. New York: Farrar, Straus, and Giroux.

Fitzpatrick, Petya, and Rebecca E. Olson. 2015. "A Rough Road Map to Reflexivity in Qualitative Research into Emotions." *Emotion Review* 7(1):49–54.

Fox, Renee C. 2000. "Medical Uncertainty Revisited." Pp. 409-425 in *Handbook of Social Studies in Health and Medicine*, edited by G. L. Albrecht, R. Fitzpatrick, and S. C. Scrimshaw. Thousand Oaks, CA: Sage.

Francis, Ara. 2015. *Family Trouble: Middle-Class Parents, Children's Problems, and the Disruption of Everyday Life*. New Brunswick, NJ: Rutgers University Press.

Francis, Ara. 2012. "The Dynamics of Family Trouble: Middle-Class Parents Whose Children Have Problems." *Journal of Contemporary Ethnography* 41(4):371–401.

Fraser, Nancy, and Linda Gordon. 1994. "A Genealogy of Dependency: Tracing a Keyword of the U.S. Welfare State." *Signs* 19(2):309–36.

Gage, Elizabeth A. 2013. "Social Networks of Experientially Similar Others: Formation, Activation, and Consequences of Network Ties on the Health Care Experience." *Social Science & Medicine* 95:43–51.

Gage, Elizabeth A., and Christina Panagakis. 2012. "The Devil You Know: Parents Seeking Information Online for Paediatric Cancer." *Sociology of Health & Illness* 34(3):444–58.

Gage-Bouchard, Elizabeth A. 2017. "Culture, Styles of Institutional Interactions, and Inequalities in Healthcare Experiences." *Journal of Health and Social Behavior* 58(2):147–65.

Garey, Anita Ilta. 1999. *Weaving Work and Motherhood*. Philadelphia: Temple University Press.

Gawande, Atul. 2014. *Being Mortal: Medicine and What Matters in the End*. New York: Metropolitan Books.

Gecas, Viktor, and Michael L. Schwalbe. 1983. "Beyond the Looking-Glass Self: Social Structure and Efficacy-Based Self-Esteem." *Social Psychology Quarterly* 46(2):77–88.

Gengler, Amanda M. 2015. "'He's Doing Fine:' Hope Work and Emotional Threat Management among Families of Seriously Ill Children." *Symbolic Interaction* 38(4):611–30.

Gengler, Amanda M. 2014. "'I Want You to Save My Kid!': Illness Management Strategies, Access, and Inequality at an Elite University Research Hospital." *Journal of Health and Social Behavior* 55(3):342–59.

Gengler, Amanda Marie. 2011. "Mothering under Others' Gaze: Policing Motherhood in a Battered Women's Shelter." *International Journal of Sociology of the Family* 37(1):131–52.

Gengler, Amanda M., and Megan V. Jarrell. 2015. "What Difference Does Difference Make? The Persistence of Inequalities in Healthcare Delivery." *Sociology Compass* 9(8):718–30.

Glaser, Barney G., and Anselm L. Strauss. 1967. *The Discovery of Grounded Theory.* Chicago: Aldine.

Goffman, Erving. 1967. *Interaction Ritual: Essays in Face-to-Face Behavior.* Chicago: Aldine.

Goffman, Erving. 1959. *The Presentation of Self in Everyday Life.* Garden City: Doubleday.

Goldman, Dana P., and Darius Lakdawalla. 2005. "A Theory of Health Disparities and Medical Technology." *Contributions to Economic Analysis and Policy* 4(1):1–30.

Good, Mary-Jo DelVecchio, Byron J. Good, Cynthia Schaffer, and Stuart E. Lind. 1990. "American Oncology and the Discourse on Hope." *Culture, Medicine and Psychiatry* 14(1):59–79.

Gould, Deborah B. 2009. *Moving Politics: Emotion and ACT UP's Fight against AIDS.* Chicago: University of Chicago Press.

Groopman, Jerome. 2008. *How Doctors Think.* Boston: Houghton Mifflin Harcourt.

Groopman, Jerome. 2005. *The Anatomy of Hope: How People Prevail in the Face of Illness.* New York: Random House.Hallett, Tim. 2003. "Emotional Feedback and Amplification in Social Interaction." *Sociological Quarterly* 44(4):705–26.

Hansen, Karen V. 2005. *Not-So-Nuclear Families: Class, Gender and Networks of Care.* New Brunswick, NJ: Rutgers University Press.

Hays, Sharon. 1996. *The Cultural Contradictions of Motherhood.* New Haven, CT: Yale University Press.

Heimer, Carol A., and Lisa R. Staffen. 1998. *For the Sake of the Children: The Social Organization of Responsibility in the Hospital and the Home.* Chicago: University of Chicago Press.

Hochschild, Arlie. 1983. *The Managed Heart.* Berkeley: University of California Press.

Jenkinson, Stephen. 2015. *Die Wise: A Manifesto for Sanity and Soul.* Berkeley, CA: North Atlantic Books.

Johnson, Rachel L., Debra Roter, Neil R. Powe, and Lisa A. Cooper. 2004. "Patient Race/Ethnicity and Quality of Patient-Physician Communication during Medical Visits." *American Journal of Public Health* 94(12):2084–90.

Karp, David A., and Valaya Tanarugsachock. 2000. "Mental Illness, Caregiving, and Emotion Management." *Qualitative Health Research* 10(6):6–25.

Kaufman, Sharon. 2005. *And a Time to Die: How American Hospitals Shape the End of Life.* Chicago: University of Chicago Press.

Kempner, Joanna. 2014. *Not Tonight: Migraine and the Politics of Gender and Health.* Chicago: University of Chicago Press.

Khan, Shamus Rahman. 2011. *Privilege: The Making of an Adolescent Elite at St. Paul's School.* Princeton, NJ: Princeton University Press.

Kleinman, Sherryl, and Martha A. Copp. 1993. *Emotions and Fieldwork*. Newbury Park: Sage.

Kleinman, Sherryl, and Kenneth H. Kolb. 2011. "Traps on the Path of Analysis." *Symbolic Interaction* 34(4):425–46.

Kukla, Rebecca. 2005. *Mass Hysteria: Medicine, Culture, and Mothers' Bodies*. Lanham, MD: Rowman & Littlefield.

Ladd-Taylor, Molly, and Lauri Umansky, eds. 1998. *"Bad" Mothers: The Politics of Blame in Twentieth-Century America*. New York: New York University Press.

Lareau, Annette. 2015. "Cultural Knowledge and Social Inequality." *American Sociological Review* 80(1):1–27.

Lareau, Annette. 2003. *Unequal Childhoods: Class, Race, and Family Life*. Berkeley: University of California Press.Lawton, Julia. 2000. *The Dying Process: Patients' Experiences of Palliative Care*. London: Routledge.

Lazarus, Richard S., and Susan Folkman. 1984. *Stress, Appraisal, and Coping*. New York: Springer.

Levitsky, Sandra R. 2014. *Caring for Our Own: Why There Is No Political Demand for New American Social Welfare Rights*. New York: Oxford University Press.

Light, Donald W. 2002. "Universal Health Care: Lessons from the British Experience." *American Journal of Public Health* 93(1):25–30.

Link, Bruce G., and Jo Phelan. 1995. "Social Conditions as Fundamental Causes of Disease." *Journal of Health and Social Behavior* 36:80–94.

Litt, Jacquelyn S. 2000. *Medicalized Motherhood: Perspectives from the Lives of African-American and Jewish Women*. New Brunswick, NJ: Rutgers University Press.

Lively, Kathryn J. 2000. "Reciprocal Emotion Management: Working Together to Maintain Stratification in Private Law Firms." *Work and Occupations* 27(1):32–63.

Loe, Meika. 2011. *Aging Our Way: Independent Elders, Interdependent Lives*. New York: Oxford.

Lois, Jennifer. 2013. *Home Is Where the School Is: The Logic of Homeschooling and the Emotional Labor of Mothering*. New York: New York University Press.

Lois, Jennifer. 2001. "Managing Emotions, Intimacy and Relationships in a Volunteer Search and Rescue Group." *Journal of Contemporary Ethnography* 30(2):131–79.

Lutfey, Karen, and Jeremy Freese. 2005. "Toward Some Fundamentals of Fundamental Causality: Socioeconomic Status and Health in the Routine Clinic Visit for Diabetes." *American Journal of Sociology* 110(5):1326–72.

Mackendrick, Norah. 2014. "More Work for Mother: Chemical Body Burdens as a Maternal Responsibility." *Gender & Society* 28(5):705–28.

Mattingly, Cheryl. 2010. *The Paradox of Hope: Journeys through a Clinical Borderland*. Berkeley: University of California Press.

McQueeney, Krista, and Kristen M. Lavelle. 2017. "Emotional Labor in Critical Ethnographic Work: In the Field and behind the Desk." *Journal of Contemporary Ethnography* 46(1):81–107.

Moller, David Wendell. 2004. *Dancing with Broken Bones: Portraits of Death and Dying among Inner-City Poor*. New York: Oxford University Press.

Nelson, Margaret K. 2010. *Parenting out of Control: Anxious Parents in Uncertain Times*. New York: New York University Press.

Ofri, Danielle. 2013. *What Doctors Feel: How Emotions Affect the Practice of Medicine*. Boston: Beacon Press.

Peräkylä, Annsi. 1991. "Hope Work in the Care of Seriously Ill Patients." *Qualitative Health Research* 1(4):407–33.

Petersen, Alan. 2015. *Hope in Health: The Socio-Politics of Optimism*. London: Palgrave Macmillan.

Petersen, Alan, and Iain Wilkinson. 2015. "The Sociology of Hope in Contexts of Health, Medicine, and Healthcare." *Health: An Interdisciplinary Journal for the Social Study of Health, Illness and Medicine* 19(2):113–18.

Pew Research Center. 2017. "Public Support for 'Single Payer' Health Coverage Grows, Driven by Democrats." June 23. http://www.pewresearch.org.

Phelan, Jo C., and Bruce G. Link. 2005. "Controlling Disease and Creating Disparities: A Fundamental Cause Perspective." *Journals of Gerontology* 60B (special issue 2):27–33.

Phelan, Jo C., Bruce G. Link, and Parisa Tehranifar. 2010. "Social Conditions as Fundamental Causes of Health Inequalities." *Journal of Health and Social Behavior* 51(S):S28–40.

Prior, Lindsay. 2003. "Belief, Knowledge and Expertise: The Emergence of the Lay Expert in Medical Sociology." *Sociology of Health & Illness* 25(3):41–57.

Pugh, Allison J. 2015. *The Tumbleweed Society: Working and Caring in an Age of Insecurity*. New York: Oxford University Press.

Pugh, Allison J. 2009. *Longing and Belonging: Parents, Children, and Consumer Culture*. Berkeley: University of California Press.Reed, Kate. 2012. *Gender and Genetics: Sociology of the Prenatal*. New York: Routledge.

Register, Cheri. 1999. *The Chronic Illness Experience: Embracing the Imperfect Life*. Center City, MN: Hazeldon.

Reich, Jennifer A. 2016. *Calling the Shots: Why Parents Reject Vaccines*. New York: New York University Press.

Reich, Jennifer A. 2005. *Fixing Families: Parents, Power, and the Child Welfare System*. New York: Routledge.Reinharz, Shulamit. 2011. *Observing the Observer: Understanding Our Selves in Field Research*. New York: Oxford University Press.

Reinharz, Shulamit. 1992. *Feminist Methods in Social Research*. New York: Oxford University Press.Rios, Victor M. 2011. *Punished: Policing the Lives of Black and Latino Boys*. New York: New York University Press.

Robinson, Carole A. 1993. "Managing Life with a Chronic Condition: The Story of Normalization." *Qualitative Health Research* 3(6):6–28.

Saha, Somnath, Jose J. Arbelaez, and Lisa A. Cooper. 2003. "Patient-Physician Relationships and Racial Disparities in the Quality of Health Care." *American Journal of Public Health* 93(10):1713–19.

Sauder, Michael. 2005. "Symbols and Contexts: An Interactionist Approach to the Study of Social Status." *Sociological Quarterly* 46(2):279–98.

Scheper-Hughes, Nancy. 1992. *Death without Weeping: The Violence of Everyday Life in Brazil*. Berkeley: University of California Press.

Schwalbe, Michael. 1996. *Unlocking the Iron Cage: The Men's Movement, Gender Politics, and American Culture*. New York: Oxford University Press.

Schwalbe, Michael L., and Douglas Mason-Schrock. 1996. "Identity Work as Group Process." *Advances in Group Processes* 13:13–47.

Sharp, Shane. 2010. "How Does Prayer Help Manage Emotions?" *Social Psychology Quarterly* 73(4):417–37.

Sharp, Shane, Deborah Carr, and Kathryn Panger. 2016. "Gender, Race, and the Use of Prayer to Manage Anger." *Sociological Spectrum* 36(5):271–85.

Shim, Janet K. 2010. "Cultural Health Capital: A Theoretical Approach to Understanding Health Care Interactions and the Dynamics of Unequal Treatment." *Journal of Health and Social Behavior* 51(1):1–15.

Small, Mario Luis. 2009. "'How Many Cases Do I Need?' On Science and the Logic of Case Selection in Field-Based Research." *Ethnography* 10(1):5–38.

Snow, David A., and Leon Anderson. 1987. "Identity Work among the Homeless: The Verbal Construction and Avowal of Personal Identities." *American Journal of Sociology* 92(6):1336–71.

Stack, Carol B. 1974. *All Our Kin: Strategies for Survival in a Black Community*. New York: Harper and Row.

Stevenson, Lisa. 2014. *Life beside Itself: Imagining Care in the Canadian Arctic*. Berkeley: University of California Press.

Sulik, Gayle. 2011. *Pink Ribbon Blues: How Breast Cancer Culture Undermines Women's Health*. New York: Oxford University Press.

Thorne, Barrie. 1993. *Gender Play: Girls and Boys in School*. New Brunswick, NJ: Rutgers University Press.

Timmermans, Stefan, and Alison Angell. 2001. "Evidence-Based Medicine, Clinical Uncertainty, and Learning to Doctor." *Journal of Health and Social Behavior* 42(4):342–59.

Timmermans, Stefan, and Mara Buchbinder. 2012. *Saving Babies?: The Consequences of Newborn Genetic Screening*. Chicago: University of Chicago Press.

van Ryn, Michelle, and Jane Burke. 2000. "The Effect of Patient Race and Socio-Economic Status on Physicians' Perceptions of Patients." *Social Science & Medicine* 50(6):813–28.

van Ryn, Michelle, Diana J. Burgess, John F. Dovidio, Sean M. Phelan, Somnath Saha, Jennifer Malat, Joan M. Griffin, Steven S. Fu, and Sylvia Perry. 2011. "The Impact of Racism on Clinical Cognition, Behavior, and Clinical Decision Making." *Du Bois Review: Social Science Research on Race* 8(1):199–218.

Vanderstaay, Steven L. 2005. "One Hundred Dollars and a Dead Man: Ethical Decision Making in Ethnographic Fieldwork." *Journal of Contemporary Ethnography* 34(4):371–409.

Villalobos, Ana. 2014. *Motherload: Making It All Better in Insecure Times*. Berkeley: University of California Press.

Wolf, Joan B. 2007. "Is Breast Really Best? Risk and Total Motherhood in the National Breastfeeding Awareness Campaign." *Journal of Health Politics Policy and Law* 32(4):595–636.

Wolkomir, Michele. 2004. "'Giving It Up to God': Negotiating Femininity in Support Groups for Wives of Ex-Gay Christian Men." *Gender & Society* 18(6):735–55.

Yamin, Alicia Ely. 2005. "The Right to Health under International Law and Its Relevance to the United States." *American Journal of Public Health* 95(7):1156–61.Zelizer, Viviana A. Rotman. 1985. *Pricing the Priceless Child: The Changing Social Value of Children.* Princeton, NJ: Princeton University Press.

INDEX

Note: Pseudonyms of study participants are denoted by *italicized* names.

164–65; and care-captaining strategy, 47, 49, 177; and care-entrusting strategy, 81, 83; "compassionate use" exception, 161–62, 220n4; and demographics of study participants, 209; immunotherapy trials, 4; and physician's awareness of current research, 220n2; and unequal access to medical resources, 12

"closure," 73, 154, 181, 191

Coleman, Dr.: and care-captaining strategy, 72; and care-entrusting strategy, 95, 98–101; and cord blood transplants, 69; and demographics of study participants, 211; and facilitating peaceful deaths, 142–43, 147–48; and hospice care shortcomings, 219n8; and role of hope in care strategies, 136, 137

Collins, Patricia Hill, 215n13

comas, medically-induced, 130

communication with medical staff: and care-entrusting strategy, 77, 84–85, 96; and declining conditions, 132–33; and preparing for death, 146; and role of hope in care strategies, 176–79. *See also* negotiating with care providers

compassion, 138–39, 146

"compassionate use" exception, 161–62, 220n4

compliance with medical instructions, 100, 217n8

computed tomography (CT) scans, 5–6

"concerted cultivation" parenting strategy, 17–18

confidence in healthcare providers, 56, 84–85, 153. *See also* care-captaining strategy; care-entrusting strategy

conflicts between parents and providers: and awareness of current research, 158, 220n2; and blended care strategies, 107–8; and care-captaining strategy, 55–56; and care-entrusting strategy, 104; and conflicting prognoses, 204–5; and coping with setbacks and declining conditions, 145; and inadequate cultural health capital, 117–21; and parental participation in medical care, 69–70; and parenting styles, 93–94

congenital diaphragmatic hernia, 117–18

Cooper, Marianne, 18

Copp, Martha, 36, 37, 206

cord blood transplants: and care-captaining strategy, 47; and care-entrusting strategy, 78, 81; and commodification of hope in private banking, 181; and coping with child's declining health, 148; and demographics of study participants, 209–10; and graft versus host disease, 50, 216n2; for mucopolysaccharidosis, 66–69; risks of, 29

Cruz, Juliana: and care-captaining strategy, 66–69, 157; and coping with setbacks, 129–31, 132–34, 149, 152–53; and emotional issues of fieldwork in fraught settings, 202, 204–5, 207; and emotion management within families, 133, 219n3

cultural health capital: and access to quality care, 213n15; adjusting medical information to parent's comprehension level, 99; and blended care strategies, 21–22, 105–6, 108, 111, 116–17, 117–21, 125; and care-captaining strategy, 20, 45, 49, 52, 57, 67, 72, 176; and care-entrusting strategy, 77–78, 98, 103–4; and demographics of study participants, 34; described 10–11; and elite cultural competence, 213n11; and emotion work of managing illness, 16; and "loving care" provision, 87; and preparing for death, 154; and religious faith, 125; and role of hope in care strategies, 179; and terminal patients, 149; and unequal access to medical resources, 9–12, 174, 184–88

cystic fibrosis, 180, 214n1

death and terminal patients: and author's experience with father's illness, 22, 25, 169–72; and care-captaining strategy 132–134; and care-entrusting strategy, 95–96; and conflicting care strategies, 148–52; and coping with setbacks and declining conditions, 129–31, 131–32; and demographics of study participants, 35; and emotional challenges of research in healthcare settings, 39;

95, 100; and demographics of study participants, 211; and facilitating peaceful deaths, 141–42, 145–46; and role of hope in care strategies, 138–39

referrals: and care-captaining strategy, 4, 7, 11, 46, 60, 111, 177; and care-entrusting strategy, 78, 83–84, 87, 92–93, 95, 102–3; and unequal access to medical resources, 186

refusing treatment, 50–51, 119–20, 151–52, 153–54, 204–5

Reich, Jennifer, 50, 75

religious faith, 7, 121–25, 137, 142, 147–48, 202–3, 205

researching illnesses and treatments: and author's experience with father's illness, 157–58, 160, 166–68; and blended care strategies, 107, 118–20; and care-captaining strategy, 46–47, 48, 68–69, 73, 103–4; and care-entrusting strategy, 84, 103–4; and discovery of Kelly-Reed programs, 216n11; emotional benefits of, 58–66, 69; and emotion in ethnographic research, 36–39; and inadequate cultural health capital, 118–21; physicians' perspective on, 99–100; and sibling-donor bone marrow transplants, 177–78; as source of reassurance, 7

respite care, 185–86

Rios, Victor, 11

Rivera, Edward: and care-entrusting strategy, 68; and community at Ronald McDonald House, 66; and coping with child's declining health, 129–31, 132–34, 149, 152–53; and demographics of study participants, 210; and emotional issues of fieldwork in fraught settings, 202, 204, 207

Rivera-Cruz, Noah: declining condition, 129–31, 132–34, 150, 152; and demographics of study participants, 210; diagnosis and treatment course, 66–69; and emotional issues of fieldwork in fraught settings, 200, 201–2, 204, 205, 207

Rivera-Cruz, Sophie: and demographics of study participants, 210; diag-

nosis and treatment course, 66–69; and emotional issues of fieldwork in fraught settings, 201–2, 204, 207; and extended-family support, 132; and fundraising events, 152; and role of hope in care strategies, 183; success of transplant, 69, 133–34

Ronald McDonald House: culture of hope and positivity at, 12, 13, 66; described, 3–4; and emotion work of managing illness, 15; and extended-family support, 132; and families' coping strategy during difficult medical moments, 102, 148, 150; funding for, 183, 214n2; and fundraising for patient expenses, 92; and housing of patient families, 79; participant interviews at, 6, 152, 173, 204, 215n8; purpose of, 25–26; as setting for study, 27–28, 31–32; solidarity among families at, 217n11; and tensions over child-rearing philosophies, 94; and unequal access to medical resources, 186–87; and US healthcare priorities, 186–87

Rowland, Anaya: 102–3, 210
Rowland, Chanice: 102, 210
Russell, Kassidy: 118–21, 210

Santos, Isabelle, 85–90, 209, 217n5, 218n5
Scheper-Hughes, Nancy, 35
Schwalbe, Michael, 220n14
second opinions, 59, 93, 157
seizures, 58–59, 61, 91
Sharp, Shane, 219n11
Shaw, Aaron, 82–83, 95, 183, 211
Shaw, Mary, 82–83, 178, 211
Shim, Janet, 10, 11
siblings of ill children: housing at Ronald McDonald House for, 79; and impact of long hospital stays, xii; and increasing life-expectancies, 180; sibling-donor bone marrow transplants, 84, 106, 177–78, 209–10
sickle-cell disease, 78–82, 123, 148, 152, 183, 200, 217n1
Small, Mario, 28–29
social capital, 157–58. See also cultural health capital

ABOUT THE AUTHOR

AMANDA M. GENGLER is Assistant Professor of Sociology at Wake Forest University.